A-Z GOVERNMENT AND POLITICS

A-Z GOVERNMENT AND POLITICS

Dr. Samayal Varadarajan

CENTRUM PRESS
NEW DELHI-110002 (INDIA)

CENTRUM PRESS
H.O.: 4360/4, Ansari Road, Daryaganj,
New Delhi-110 002 (India)
Ph.: 23278000, 23261597

B.O.: No. 1015, Ist Main Road, BSK IIIrd Stage
IIIrd Phase, IIIrd Block,
Bangalore - 560 085 (India)
Tel.: 080-41723429
Visit us at: www.centrumpress.com

A-Z Government and Politics

First Edition, 2009
ISBN 978-93-80106-43-4

PRINTED IN INDIA

Printed at Salasar Imaging Systems, Delhi-110035 (India)

Preface

This book introduces to some of the central concepts in political analysis and the evolution of political research over the centuries, Politics focuses on political ideas (political philosophy, ideologies, and political culture), institutions (constitutions, legislatures, and executives; their relationships in parliamentary and presidential systems; electoral and party systems; the bureaucracy; and the judiciary), and the international setting. One of the book's central themes is the relationship of contemporary political debates to more enduring traditions of political thought. Philosophical traditions are linked to the emergence and institutional functioning of liberal democracy, and, by virtue of the comparative approach, appreciation of the immense variety of democratic political arrangements in different countries of the world is offered.

"Politics is extremely thorough and well-researched; it covers the basics in exemplary detail. The inclusion of a discussion of political science as well as of political philosophy is particularly welcome, as it helps ground the discussion of modern institutions and processes in the history of political thought." The need of a book which would expound, within a convenient compass, and in as systematic a form as the subject-matter might admit, the chief general considerations that enter into the rational discussion of political questions in modern states. Though there were many valuable treatises dealing with particular portions of this subject.

Author

Chapter 1

Political Science

Political science is a branch of social sciences that deals with the theory and practice of politics and the description and analysis of political systems and political behaviour. Political science is often described as the study of politics defined as "who gets what, when and how ". Political science has several subfields, including: political theory, public policy, public administration, national politics, and comparative politics.

Political science is methodologically diverse. Approaches to the discipline include classical political philosophy, interpretivism, structuralism, and behavioralism, realism, pluralism, and institutionalism. Political science, as one of the social sciences, uses methods and techniques that relate to the kinds of inquiries sought: primary sources such as historical documents and official records, secondary sources such as scholarly journal articles, survey research, statistical analysis, case studies, and model building.

TERMINOLOGY AND DISTINCTIONS

There is as yet no commonly accepted term by which the science of government may be designated. The term "politics ", employed by many writers, is open to the objection that it possesses several meanings and, when used without qualification or discrimination, leads to confusion if not misunderstanding.

According to popular usage it is a term of both a science and an art, that is, it is employed to denote both the systematic study of the phenomena of the state and the totality of activities which have to do with the administration of the affairs of state. As a science it furnishes us with a mass of theoretical knowledge concerning the state; as an art it seeks solutions of concrete problems and is concerned with the processes and means by which government is actually carried on and the ends of the state are realized. In a narrow and somewhat partisan sense the term is applied to electioneering methods by which public officials are chosen and political policies promoted.

"Theoretical "politics is sometimes distinguished from "practical "or "applied "politics, the former being concerned with the fundamental characteristics of the state without reference to its activities or the means by which its ends are attained; the latter, with the state in action, that is, as a dynamic institution. Thus everything that relates to the origin, nature, attributes, and ends of the state, including the principles of political organization and administration, falls within the domain of "theoretical "politics, while that which is concerned with the actual administration of the affairs of government belongs to the sphere of "applied "or "practical "politics.

The majority of writers to-day, however, prefer the term "political science "instead of "theoretical "polities; and the simple term "politics, "instead of "applied "or "practical "politics. Some writers employ the term "science of politics, "others, the "theory of the state, "the *Staatslehre* of the Germans, because, as one author remarks, "it gives a clearer idea of the wide nature of the field of inquiry "and at the same time "avoids the necessity of a delicate and intricate discussion as to whether the study of politics is a science or a philosophy.

"In spite of all objections, however, the term "political science "has come to be more generally employed by the best writers and thinkers to describe the mass of knowledge derived from the systematic study of the state, while the meaning of the term "politics "is confined to that of the business or activity which has to do with the actual conduct of affairs of state.

Against the term "political science "the objection has been urged that it does not correspond with the facts, since there is no single science dealing with the state, but rather a group of related sciences, each concerned with particular aspects of it. Thus, it is said, the modern state presents itself under divers aspects and is capable of being studied from many different points of view. The mass of knowledge relating to each phase or aspect of the state has developed a history and a dogma of its own quite distinct from the rest.

The phenomena of each have become so numerous and complex as to create a necessity for special treatment by the investigator. Thus the tendency has been to group them into separate categories and treat them as distinct sciences, The plural form, the "political sciences, "therefore seems to correspond more nearly with the facts and is preferred by many writers, especially the French, who commonly speak of the *sciences*.

According to the latter view a political science is one which is concerned, not necessarily with the state in all of its aspects or relations, but with any particular phenomenon of the state or any class of phenomena either as a whole or incidentally, directly or indirectly. Thus there may be as many political sciences as there are conceivable aspects or forms of manifestation of the state. In this sense sociology, political economy, public finance, public law, diplomacy, constitutional history, may be denominated political sciences, since they all deal either primarily or incidentally with some class of phenomena belonging to the state.

Those who maintain that the singular form accords more nearly with the facts argue that in reality the above-mentioned sciences are rather coordinate social sciences than independent political sciences. Thus, says one writer, in support of this view, "The various relations in which the state may be conceived may be subdivided and treated separately, but their connection is too intimate and their purpose too similar to justify their erection into different sciences.

"Without attempting to pass judgment upon the respective merits of the two views, we believe that either form may be justified by distinguishing between political science in its widest and most general sense, and the auxiliaries or disciplines of that science, employing the singular to designate the former and the plural the latter. The former is the general science of the state, the state in the aggregate, the state considered from all points of view; the latter are the special or disciplinary sciences which deal with particular aspects or activities of the state. Such are the sciences of jurisprudence, political economy, public law, sociology, political and constitutional history, etc.

DEFINITION AND SCOPE

It was a saying of a great Roman jurist that all definitions are dangerous because they never go far enough and are nearly always contradicted by the facts. The truth of this observation applies as well to general propositions in political science as to those of the civil law. Nevertheless, it is equally true, as has been well said by a noted political writer, that "to obtain clear and precise definitions of the leading terms is an important achievement in all departments of scientific inquiry.

"The renowned German scholar Bluntschli defined political science as "the science which is concerned with the state, which endeavors to understand and comprehend the state in its fundamental conditions, in its essential nature, its various forms of manifestation, its development. "Gareis, another German writer, says "Political science considers the state, as an institution of power, in the totality of its relations, its origin, its setting (land and people), its object, its ethical signification, its economic problems, its life conditions, its financial side, its end, etc.

"Jellinek, one of the ablest of living European publicists, distinguishes between theoretical political science and applied political science. Theoretical political science is again subdivided by Jellinek into the general theory of the state and special or particular theory of the state. The former has for its purpose the study of fundamental principles. It considers the state in itself and the elements which constitute it; not the phenomena of a particular state, but the totality of all the historico-social aspects in which the state manifests itself.

Furthermore, the dual nature of the state, that is, its

character both as a social phenomenon and a legal or juridical institution, furnishes the basis for still another distinction, to wit, that between the social doctrine of the state and constitutional political theory. The former deals with the state primarily as a social organization, that is, as a society of individuals organized for common ends; the latter, with the state as a concept of public law, a juristic entity or legal phenomenon.

A succinct definition is that of Paul Janet, a distinguished French writer, who conceives political science to be "that part of social science which treats of the foundations of the state and the principles of government. "According to Seeley, "political science investigates the phenomena of government as political economy deals with wealth, biology with life, algebra with numbers, and geometry with space and magnitude.

"Seeley points out that as most of the commonwealths of antiquity were city states, ancient political science was little more than the science of municipal government, a truth which finds illustration in Aristotle's treatise on "Politics, "a work practically limited in its scope to the consideration of such polities only as were city states.

Modern political science on the other hand is, as has been well said, the science of the national country state and is tending to become the science of the world state. Furthermore, says a well known writer, the modern requirements of territorial expansion, representative government, and national unity have made political science not only the science of liberty but also the science of sovereignty.

All of the opinions quoted above are in substantial agreement on the essential point, namely, that the phenomena of the state in its varied aspects and relationships, as distinct from the family, the tribe, the nation, and from all private associations, though not unconnected with them, constitute the subject of political science. In short, political science begins and ends with the state.

In a general way its fundamental problems include, first, an investigation of the nature of the state as the highest political agency for the realization of the common ends of society and the formulation of fundamental principles of state life; second, an inquiry into the nature, history, and forms of political institutions; and third, a deduction there from, so far as possible, of the laws of political growth and development. In the process of evolution the appearance of new political conditions may give rise to new problems, but upon close analysis they will be seen to be problems of practical politics rather than fundamental problems of political science.

The distinction between political science and political theory or political philosophy is generally observed by the more systematic writers on the state, though a precise demarcation of the boundary lines which separate them is difficult, if not impossible.

Political philosophy is said to be concerned with a theoretical or speculative consideration of the fundamental principles and essential characteristics of the materials and phenomena with which political science has to deal. It investigates the development of political thought, and inquires into the foundations of political authority; it analyzes, classifies, and forms judgments upon the essential attributes of the state and thereby prepares the way for a true political science. It is concerned rather with generalizations than with particulars, and predicates essential qualities rather than accidental or unessential characteristics.

Again, it is said that while political science furnishes us with the results of logical thinking upon the nature and forms of concrete political institutions, political philosophy inquires into the foundations of the first principles which underlie them. A few writers make the distinction one mainly of teleology, political science being concerned with what the state ought to be, while political philosophy considers the state as it actually is. But this distinction is not generally observed.

IS THERE A SCIENCE OF GOVERNMENT

Thus far it has been assumed that the study of the phenomena of the state may under proper conditions be treated as a science. To this assumption, however, objections have been raised. Thus, it has been asserted that, on account of the magnitude and complexity of the subject-matter relating to the state, — a body of material, says an acute thinker, so rich and varied that, from the beginning, political science has been embarrassed by the weight of its wealth, — it is impossible to apply to it rigorous scientific methods of investigation.

Political phenomena, we are told, are characterized by uncertainty, variableness, and a lack of order and continuity. Much of this objection is, however, without weight. If, says Sir Frederick Pollock, those who deny the existence of a political science mean that there is no body of rules from which a prime minister may infallibly learn how to command a majority, they would be right as to the fact, but would betray a rather inadequate notion of what a science is. "There is, "he rightly concludes, "a political science in the same sense that there is a science of morals. "

For our purposes a science may be described as a fairly unified mass of knowledge relating to a single subject, acquired by systematic observation, experience, or reason, the facts of which have been coordinated, systematized, and classified. The scientific method of examining facts is not peculiar to one class of phenomena nor to one class of investigators; it is applicable to social as well as to physical phenomena, and we may safely reject the claim that the scientific frame of mind belongs exclusively to the physicist or the naturalist.

Authorities are now generally agreed that the phenomena of the state present a certain connection or sequence which is the result of fixed laws, though less immutable, to be sure, than those of the physical world; that these phenomena form proper subjects of scientific investigation; and that the laws and principles deducible there from are susceptible of application to the solution of concrete problems of the state.

All that is required to give a scientific character to the study of political phenomena is that the inquiry shall be conducted in accordance with a definite plan or system, with due regard to the relations of cause and effect, so far as they are ascertainable, and in conformity with certain well-recognized rules of scientific investigation. The consensus of scientific opinion is in favor of this proposition. Aristotle described "politics "as the master science in the highest senseand in practice he applied scientific methods to his study of Greek polities. The Germans have done more than any other group of scholars, by their profound researches and discriminating analytical methods, to give to it the character of a science.

Holtzendorff, one of the most systematic of the German writers, ably defended the claim of politics to be ranked as a science. "With the enormous growth of knowledge, "he said, "it is impossible to deny that the sum total of all the experiences, phenomena, and knowledge respecting the state may be brought together under the collective title of political science".

We must conclude, therefore, that both reason and the weight of authority justify the claim of politics to the rank of a true science. It renders practical service by deducing sound principles as a basis for wise political action and by exposing the teachings of a false political philosophy. As a science it falls short, of course, of the degree of perfection attained by the physical sciences, for the reason that the facts with which it deals are more complex and the causes which influence social phenomena are more difficult of control and are perpetually undergoing change.

On account of the impossibility of forecasting results with the same exactness and precision possible in the physical sciences, a fully developed science of the state must of necessity remain always an ideal. As yet it is still probably the most incomplete and undeveloped of all the social sciences.

POLITICAL SCIENCE TODAY

The present period of world transformation could with equal justice be called the age of science or that of astropolitics. No one imagines that political science alone among the arts and sciences will remain unaffected by the changes through which the world is moving. The distinctive concern of political science is with the political process itself, and it is impossible to believe that government and law will lie outside the accelerating tempo of history. In this inquiry, directed mainly to those who are seriously concerned with the study of government, we shall consider the future of political science from the viewpoints of scope, method, and impact.

Any problem-solving approach to human affairs poses five intellectual tasks, which we designate by five terms familiar to political scientists — goal, trend, condition, projection, and alternative. The first question, relating to goal, raises the traditional problem of clarifying the legitimate aims of a body politic.

After goals are provisionally clarified, the historical question arises. In the broadest context, the principal issue is whether the trend of events in America or throughout the world community has been toward or away from the realization of preferred events. The next question goes beyond simple inventories of change and asks which factors condition one another and determine history. When trend and factor knowledge is at hand, it is possible to project the course of future developments on the preliminary assumption that we do not ourselves influence the future. Finally, what policy alternatives promise to bring all preferred goals to optimal fulfillment?

PAST CONTRIBUTIONS

The problem-solving frame of reference is no novelty to political scientists. It is and has been, for example, common for members of the profession to concentrate on one or another of the intellectual tasks involved. A few reminders will establish the point.

Among the enduring contributions to the study of politics we number treatises that have undertaken to clarify the goals appropriate to political activity. The principal writing of this kind falls roughly into two categories, the first directed toward the specification of goal, the second toward justification.

The most successful method of specifying a positive vision is an imaginative essay in the manner of Plato *Republic* or More's *Utopia*. There are also the counterutopias, full of hell-fire and damnation, to which Orwell's 1984 belongs. The treatises that seek to justify more than to specify desirable goals rely on many modes of argument. Perhaps the principal tool is rhetoric properly keyed to the receptivities of a waiting audience.

This was true of Rousseau *Social Contract*. It is also possible for a writer to dispense with eloquence almost entirely and to depend on the cumulative impact of evidence and analysis. Such was the method of Marx in *Capital*, which sets forth a theory of power in the language and framework of economic history. Many famous works of justification dispense with rhetoric, empirical detail, or historical analysis and trust the razor of logic and the weight of authoritative citation. This mode of expression is particularly congenial to theologians and jurists.

The great bulk of writing on politics is more devoted to history than to any other dimension of the subject. It would, however, be a mistake to assume that history is written for its own sake. Even the most dreary account of changes in the structure of government is typically inspired by the hope of making available a body of data that will eventually help discharge the obligation shared by all political scientists to explain the rise and fall of political institutions. The immediate technique, however, is historical, bound to the collection and criticism of sources and to the establishing of sequences of events in time and place.

In the United States, political scientists have been captivated by the task of tracing the roots of government, law, and politics in this country to the soil of England or elsewhere and distinguishing between the original design and subsequent adaptations to American experience. Woodrow Wilson's treatise on Congressional Government is a classic work of the kind.

Systematizers deal directly with the problem of explanation by putting forward propositions that are confirmed, or open to confirmation, by empirical data. One irony of history is that writers have sometimes been identified with a single factor, a set of factors, or a single generalization that does scant justice to the scope and subtlety of their approach. Michels, for example, is known almost exclusively for his formulation of the oligarchical tendencies of mass political parties. Even Aristotle is more commonly referred to in connection with the role of the middle classes in politics than for his discussion of other subjects.

It is not inappropriate that Hobbes is immortalized as the exponent of psychological motives for political action or even that the fecund Bentham is identified with a calculus of felicity. But it does little justice to Montesquieu to narrow his originality to comments on climate, geography, and politics or to condense Spencer to axioms on centralization and external threat.

Grand theories of the probable course of future development only occasionally rise to enduring influence. In this select company, Marx and Engels take the prime position. On a far more modest scale, political scientists are continually engaged in estimating the probable strength of trends in the immediate and remote future.

For example, students of American government have been substantially of one voice in predicting such developments as the further centralization of the federal system, the rise of metropolitan regions and the decline of states, the concentration of executive power, the liquidation of ethnic discrimination, the continuation of the two-party system, the increase of litigation over civil and political rights, the continuation of controversy over civil-military relations, and the extension of social insurance coverage.

Contributions of this kind are often made jointly with proposals in the realm of public policy. No historian of the American Constitution is unaware of the attention paid by the most active drafters and defenders of the document to classical and contemporary treatises on government and law. Several of the founding fathers attained a command of the theory of government that is impressive to this day. It is necessary to go no further than to name James Madison, Thomas Jefferson, and Alexander Hamilton.

Among political scientists of the present century, we think

of the role of Woodrow Wilson, A. Lawrence Lowell, and others in founding or promoting the League of Nations. Whatever the problem, political scientists frequently appear as innovators or critics of policy. This is in fact the intellectual task that many professional students of government find most congenial.

FUTURE PROBLEMS

Political scientists, we have said, possess a tradition of distinguished achievement in many areas of problem-solving importance. As we face the future, it is safe to say that the challenges are of far reaching and unprecedented variety and importance. It is perhaps useful to glance here, however briefly, at the scope of these developments.

Will questions of value goal, of overriding objective, become more or less acute as science and technology continue their explosive course? In all probability, these issues will not recede from sight. On the contrary, the chances are that the immediate future contains a unique challenge to man's conception of himself and to the values to which he is presently committed.

We do not intend to emphasize the potentialities of modern knowledge for the destruction of man and his works, formidable as these implications are; I refer to another dimension of the problem. Among all faiths, "man "is traditionally assumed to be an identifiable and usually a cherished form of "life. "In Europe-centered civilizations -and America unquestionably belongs in this company — prevailing images of man were shaped by classical philosophy and the Judaeo Christian religion. Asia-centered civilizations have a more varied religious inheritance, mainly Buddhist, Taoist, Hindu, and Muslim.

In whatever doctrinal terms the affirmation is grounded, the articulate leaders of the world community presently employ the language of deference to human dignity. Although many differences of specification exist, it is generally understood that human dignity implies an opportunity for mobility on the basis of merit; human indignity, on the contrary, assumes the blind immobility of caste. The most obvious forms of "man "and "life "are easy to locate on the cosmic map of science. There are also marginal forms, and sooner or later the question of identity will be posed by these marginal phenomena.

Computing machines perform many intellectual tasks more quickly than men do. Even today it is no longer out of the question to design machines that repair themselves or reproduce their kind. More to the point, machines can be made with built-in criteria of "enjoyment "and with the capability of learning through experience. The original criteria, if not specified in fine detail, permit novel responses.

As it becomes more widely recognized that the differences between man or life and machines have reached a vanishing point, the question becomes: Shall we treat machines with the same deference that we give ourselves as advanced forms of life?

The same question will be posed somewhat less starkly in connection with products from laboratories of experimental embryology and related sciences. It is not easy to overcome the original image of "thingness "where a machine is involved. Induced mutants have at least the advantage of belonging to the traditional realm of "life. "We must be prepared, of course, to meet living systems whose central integrative plan is organized quite differently from the brain and nervous system of man.

The central issue will hinge on how the overriding goal of human dignity is to be interpreted. Shall the idea of "human "be redefined to bring within its field of reference many phenomena that we now tend to exclude? Shall we retain the current identification of the "human "with the biological envelope called Homo sapiens and merge the "higher "characteristics of man with a larger category — "advanced forms of life "— in which the human species may some day play a subordinate role? More specifically: When shall we extend the protection of the Universal Declaration of Human Rights to machines and mutants?

In whatever terms we eventually define the commonwealth of life or delimit the forms to be called advanced, it is plausible to believe that we will feel some residual loyalty to the symbols of what we today identify as human. Looking back from a future vantage point, the story of man will continue to seem, in some intimate sense, "our "history.

When we consider the trends that have carried the species toward or away from a conception of human dignity, it is apparent that the decisive steps toward a positive self-image were taken during the tens of thousands of years that elapsed before written records were invented. Living in migratory and occasionally settled bands, early man was in contact with protohuman forms, forms that were not always easy to distinguish from Homo sapiens. As protohuman types dropped out, the biological environment grew more stable. As "reality "was more sharply defined, man was able to achieve a clear, affirmative self-image.

The conception of the dignity of man includes an ordering principle *among* men as well as *between* men and other forms of life. It is not farfetched to conjecture that, in early generations, human survival depended on the cultivation of discipline within bands. Entirely egocentric conduct could bring disaster to everyone. When we take into account the propensity of individual members of the species to act egocentrically, it is possible to perceive the evolutionary significance of what may be called the syndrome of parochialism.

Included in the syndrome are demands by the self on the ego (and on all group members) to sacrifice for the power of common defense and for other shareable outcomes. Among the added outcomes were physical safety, comfort, convenience; those related to intimacy and respect; and those of cultivation or transmission of know-how and of physical facilities.

There are indications of the presence of common themes of fantasy and ritual and of common conceptions of cosmic order. We can summarize by saying that it was the experience of interdependency that enabled man to survive and to develop his peculiar cultures.

All this lies in the shadow before records were written. The appearance of written records is a manifestation of the greatest invention of man — urban civilization. Cities are the launching pads of mankind's meteoric rise. Urban civilization dates from about 3000 B.C., when the first cities emerged in the valleys of the Nile, the TigrisEuphrates, and the Indus.

During the preceding tens of thousands of years, man had been divided into small, independent folk societies, bound by ties of family identification, mutual sacrifice, and self-preoccupation.

It was in urban communities that traditional bonds of kinship were attenuated for the benefit of territorial units; hence, the simultaneous rise of law, legislation, and the techniques of impersonal administration. Cities most perfectly developed man is the social, not the natural man, for it is now generally admitted that the individual owes much of his character to the society of which he is a part.

The chief fault of the individualists is that they exaggerate the evils of state regulation and minimize the advantages; they misunderstand the true nature and limits of liberty and have a mistaken idea of the relation of the individual to the society of which he is a part. In short, they overemphasize the importance of the man at the expense of the group; they treat him as if he were paramount and as if he determined the character of society when in fact it is society, as has been said, that determines in a large degree the character of the individual.

Their doctrine rests on the assumption that the individual is largely a thing apart from the group of which he is a member, that he can be separated from society and treated as though his interests were entirely distinct from the interests of his fellow men. In reality, however, the individual is more than a mere fraction of society; he is the epitome of it; he is the "concise formula for the total of actions and attributes;... out of relation to other things, he is literally nothing."

"Apart from his surroundings and relationships, "says Professor Ritchie, "the individual is a mere abstraction, a logical ghost, a metaphorical specter, a mere negation. "The much-admired individual, self centered and self-contained, is, indeed, not very far from the strong and solitary wild beast.

THE METHODS OF POLITICAL SCIEINCE.

Having endeavored to show that the study of political phenomena may under certain conditions acquire the character of a science, we come now to inquire into the processes and methods by which this may be done. First of all, however, we must note the limitations and difficulties under which scientific investigation of political phenomena must of necessity be conducted.

The material with which the political scientist has to deal is very different from that with which the investigator in the physical sciences is concerned, being of such a character as not to permit of the use of artificial contrivances or apparatus for increasing or guiding our powers of observation or for registering results.

Not only must the investigator work without the assistance of mechanical aids, but he is handicapped by the fact that the phenomena with which political science deals do not follow one another according to invariable laws of sequence, but rather at indeterminate intervals, constituting, as a noted writer observes, an "interminable and perpetually varying series.

"There is an essential difference between physical and social phenomena. The facts of history and social life cannot be reproduced at our volition and made the subject of experiment with a view to determining what is best under a given set of circumstances.

Social facts never recur at regular intervals as the manifestations of general forces, but rather as the actions of certain individuals. The facts of natural science are susceptible of evaluation; they are governed by uniform and invariable laws. Each particle of matter is identical with every other of its own kind. An atom of carbon or a molecule of carbonic acid is not different from any other atom or molecule, but the units of the social organism may differ infinitely from one another.

There are no general and invariable laws governing social

phenomena. Those which have been postulated by the ancient philosophers and some modern sociologists are but vague and glittering generalities.

Not until the eighteenth and nineteenth centuries did the phenomena of the state come to be generally regarded as a proper field for scientific investigation, since which time the literature of the subject has been enriched by the investigations of many scholars, among whom may be mentioned Von Haller, Von Mohl, Waitz, Zacharia, Holtzendorff, and Bluntschli in Germany; Rousseau, Montesquieu, De Tocqueville, and Laboulaye in France;

Locke, Bentham, Paley, Lewis, Brougham, Austin, Mill, Seeley, and Sidgwick in England; and Hamilton, Madison, Woolsey, and Lieber in America. Among those who have made special contributions to the methodology of political science Auguste Comte, John Stuart Mill, Alexander Bain, and Sir George Cornewall Lewis deserve particular mention. Comte conceived the principal methods for the scientific study of social phenomena to be three in number, namely, observation, experiment, and comparison.

Mill recognized four methods: the chemical or experimental, the geometrical or abstract, the physical or concrete deductive, and the historical method, the first two of which he considered to be false methods, the last two, the true ones. Bluntschli considered the true methods of political investigation to be the philosophical and the historical. A recent French writer who has devoted a volume to the subject of methodology in political science recognizes six possible lines of investigation: first, the sociological; second, the comparative; third, the dogmatic; fourth, the juridical; fifth, the method of good sense; and, sixth, the historical.

Other writers dwell upon what they are pleased to call the biological and psychological methods. Without considering each of these in turn we may observe that some of them are hardly applicable to the study of political phenomena, while others are nothing more than particular forms of the comparative method — a method so broad as to comprehend the processes of accumulation, arrangement, classification, coordination, elimination, and deduction. We may well question the claim of the experimental method to a rightful place in the methodology of political science because, as has already been stated, the nature of society is such that it cannot very well be made an object of artificial experimentation. "We cannot, "says Sir George C.

Lewis, "treat the body politic as a *corpus vile* and vary its circumstances at our pleasure for the sake only of ascertaining abstract truth. We cannot do in politics what the experimenter does in chemistry. We cannot try how the substance is affected by change of temperature, by burning, by dissolution in liquids, by combination with other chemical agents, and the like. We cannot take a portion of the community in our hands as the king of Brobdignag took Gulliver, view it in different aspects and place it in different positions in order to solve social problems and satisfy our speculative curiosity.

"If the chemist wishes to study the effect of a combination of certain substances, he can create by artificial processes conditions favorable to the investigation and exclude disturbing agencies. He may isolate the phenomenon with which he deals and expose it to certain selected influences, leaving the surrounding medium unchanged. But if the political scientist wishes to experiment with democracy, for instance, he cannot select a state at will, introduce his democracy and wait for determinate results.

He will find himself powerless' to exclude extraneous influences, such, for example, as famines, commercial crises, insurrections, or other happenings which might destroy the results of the experiment.

But while scientific experimentation, as the term is employed in the physical sciences, is inapplicable to the study of politics, practical experiments, the *experimenta fructifera* of Bacon, are being constantly made, consciously or unconsciously. It is true, as Comte points out, that political experimentation really takes place whenever the regular course of state life undergoes conscious or unconscious change. Government, of necessity, is constantly trying experiments on the community.

Indeed the whole life of the state is a succession of activities which, in a sense, are experimental in character. The enactment of every new law, the establishment of every new institution, the inauguration of every new policy, is experimental in the sense that it is regarded merely as provisional and tentative until experience has proved its fitness to become permanent.

By observing the operation of a new law or a new policy and then enlarging or diminishing its scope as experience suggests modification, the legislature is able to adapt its provisions to the needs and desires of the community. The process is in the nature of an experiment whose purpose is not the ascertainment of a general truth but experiments for the purpose of testing and improving the institution.

The so-called sociological method considers the state primarily as a social organism, whose component parts are individuals, and seeks to deduce its qualities and attributes from the qualities and attributes of the men composing it. It seeks to interpret the life of the state by applying to it the theory of evolution in the same way that the growth of the individual is explained by evolution.

Closely akin to the sociological method is the biological, which attributes to the state the attributes of a living organism and which attempts to define and classify its separate parts, to describe its structure in the nomenclature of anatomy, and to differentiate and analyze its functions and trace its life processes according to the methods and terminology of the biological sciences.

Among those who have made notable contributions to the study of organized society from the sociological and biological points of view may be mentioned Auguste Comte, Herbert Spencer, the Austrian scholars Gumplowicz and Schäffle, and the French writers Durkheim, De Greef, Fouillee, and Letourneau, and the Russian Lilienfeld. Comte in this study of society dwells at length upon what he calls "social physics "and "social physiology.

"Spencer, who was deeply infatuated with the biological analogy, drew a striking parallel between the social and animal organisms, pointing out that each possessed a "sustaining system, "a "distributing system "and a "regulating and expending system. "

The first criticism to be made of the sociological and biological theories is that they are not so much methods of investigation as points of view from which the state may be considered. The biological method rests mainly upon analogy instead of upon real similarity in essentials. It requires but little reflection to see that the resemblance between the body politic and the human organism is at best only superficial, that the laws of growth and change which govern the one are inapplicable to the growth and development of the other, and that little or nothing is to be gained by dwelling upon the analogy.

Essentially the same judgment may be passed upon the so-called psychologicalmethod, which in recent years has been overexploited by a certain class of writers, mostly French, who have attempted to explain social phenomena and interpret social institutions through psychological laws.

A method of treatment which enjoys great favor among German political writers and to a less degree among the French is the juristic or juridical method. It is the aim of this method, according to Jellinek, to "determine the content of the rules of public law and to deduce therefrom the conclusions to which they lead.

"It regards political science as a science of legal norms having nothing in common with the science of the state as a social organism. It conceives the relations of the state always as "offentliche Verhältnisse, "political concepts as "Rechtsbegriffe "and describes the constitution and activities of the state only in terms of their "rechtliche Natur.

"In short, it treats society, not as a social phenomenon, but as a purely juridical regime, an *ensemble* of public law, rights, and obligations, founded on a system of pure logic and reason. The state as an organism of growth and development, however, cannot be understood without a consideration of those extra-legal and special forces which lie back of the constitution and which are responsible for many of its actions and reciprocal reactions. Any view. therefore, which conceives the state merely as an institution of public law is as narrow and fruitless as the Hegelian doctrine which goes to the opposite extreme and considers it merely as a moral entity.

The comparative method, first employed by Aristotle, later by Montesquieu and still more recently by De Tocqueville, Laboulaye, Bryce, and others, aims through the study of existing polities or those which have existed in the past to assemble a definite body of material from which the investigator by selection, comparison, and elimination may discover the ideal types and progressive forces of political history.

Only those states which are contemporaneous in point of time, as Jellinek remarks, and which have a common historical basis (*Boden*) and common historical political and social institutions may be compared with advantage. The comparative method, observes M. Saleilles, a noted French publicist, discovers the "general current "which runs through the whole body of constitutions and upon which experience has set the stamp of approval

"The danger of the comparative method lies in the liability to error to which it is susceptible in practice, since, in the effort to discover general principles, the diversity of conditions, due to different circumstances, such as the temperament and genius of the people, economic and social conditions, moral and legal standards, political training and experience, are apt to be ignored or overlooked.

J. S. Mill has undertaken to show that the comparative method may assume several forms, the "most perfect "of which is the process of *difference* by which two politics identical in every particular except one are compared with a view to discovering the effect of the differing factor. Thus two states are compared which are similar as regards their natural wealth, legal systems, racial conditions, etc., but one of which maintains a restrictive trade system.

If, therefore, one is found to be prosperous and the other not, a general conclusion is postulated with regard to the effect of restrictive commercial policies upon the national prosperity.

The method of *indirect difference* compares two classes of "instances "which agree in nothing but the presence of a factor on the one side and its absence oil the other.

Thus one state which maintains a protective system may be compared with two or more states which have nothing in common but a free trade policy. By the method of *agreement* two polities wholly different with the exception of two common factors may be compared. Thus two states agreeing in no particular except in having a restrictive trade system and in being prosperous are compared with a view to establishing a connection between the restrictive policy and the prosperity. Like the method of difference, it is inadequate because its results are likely to be affected by extraneous circumstances, or, as Bain says, by a "plurality of causes with an intermixture of effects. "

What is really a particular form of the comparative method is the historical method, for the facts relating to past politics have little value for political science until they have been subjected to the several processes of treatment which, as stated above, may be comprehended under the general term "comparison. "It is almost a commonplace to-day to affirm the necessity of historical study as a basis for the scientific investigation of political institutions which have historical backgrounds. They can be fully comprehended only through a knowledge of their past; how they have developed, how they have become what they are and to what extent they have responded to the purposes for which they were originally destined.

The maxim that constitutions grow instead of being made would have no meaning apart from this truth. The historical method, says Sir Frederick Pollock, "seeks an explanation of what institutions are and are tending to be, more in the knowledge of what they have been and how they came to be what they are, than in the analysis of them as they stand. "It brings in review the great political movements of the past, traces the organic development of the national life, inquires into the growth of political ideas from their inception to their realization in objective institutions, discovers the moral idea as revealed in history and thereby points out the way of progress. What Professor Seeley calls the "irresistible temptation to mix up what ought to be with what is "finds an illustration in the ideas of Sidgwick and Pollock (which were also the ideas of Plato and Aristotle), according to which the main object of political science is the discovery of the perfect or ideal state.

To realize this purpose, political science must first proceed to inquire what is the end of the state, and having satisfactorily answered this question, must ascertain what institutions and laws are best adapted for the attainment of this end. Seeley criticises this method as unnatural and fruitless. Instead of beginning with an inquiry into the purpose of the state and the characteristics of the best state, he would proceed, first, with classifying the states which he wished to study; second, with analyzing the structure of a particular state and distinguishing the functions of its several organs; third, with tracing its growth and development, noting any abnormal conditions in its life history; and, fourth, with philosophizing upon the nature of the state in general.

The vast mass of facts collected by different observers must be subjected to rigid scientific tests. "We must, "he says, "think, reason, generalize, define, and distinguish; we must also collect, authenticate, and investigate. If we neglect the first process, we shall accumulate facts to little purpose, because we shall have no test by which to distinguish facts which are important from those which are unimportant; and, of course, if we neglect the second Process, our reasonings will be baseless and we shall but weave scholastic cobwebs. "

RELATION OF POLITICAL SCIENCE TO OTHER SCIENCES

Political science is not the only science which deals with men in organized society, for, as we have seen, the state manifests itself under the forms of a social as well as a political organism and indeed is not without a psychical and a physical element. Although an autonomous science in the sense that it is not a mere discipline of some other science, it does not stand entirely unrelated to other sciences any more than the state stands isolated in the universe of phenomena.

We can no more understand political science, as the science of the totality of state phenomena, without a knowledge of the allied sciences or disciplines, than we can comprehend biology without chemistry, or mechanics without mathematics. Paul Janet, a noted French writer, has well said that political science is "closely connected with political economy or the science of wealth; with law, either natural or positive, which occupies itself principally with the relations of citizens one to another; with history, which furnishes the facts of which it has need; with philosophy, and especially with morals, which gives to it a part of its principles.

"Other writers, like Jellinek, have treated geography, physical anthropology, ethnology, psychology, and ethics as among the studies auxiliary to political science, Formerly there was a disposition to exaggerate and emphasize to their common detriment the independence of each branch of knowledge, but the tendency of modern thought is to accentuate the relations instead of the differences. In this connection Sidgwick has aptly remarked that it is for the good of any department of knowledge or inquiry to understand as thoroughly as possible its relation to other sciences and to see clearly what elements of its reasonings it has to take from them and what in its turn it may claim to give them.

First of all, political science touches at many points sociology, which may be described as the fundamental social science. As has been well said, the political is embedded in the social, and if political science remains distinct from sociology, it will be because the breadth of the field calls for the specialist, and not because there are any well-defined boundaries marking it off from sociology,

While, however, the two sciences touch at many points, so that there are no natural boundaries between them, their spheres have been pretty definitely differentiated for purposes of scientific investigation. It is well, therefore, to recognize that the domains and the problems of the two sciences are by no means the same.

In general, we may say that sociology is concerned with the scientific study of society viewed as an aggregate of individuals (the social aggregate) or, as has been said, it is the "science of men in their associated processes "; while political science deals with the political aspects of a particular portion of society viewed as an organized unit. Political science is concerned with one form only of human association, namely, the political; it has, therefore, a narrower and more restricted field, and begins much later with the life of the race than does sociology.

In sociology the unit of investigation is the *socius,* that is, the individual viewed not merely as an animal and a conscious being, but also as a neighbour, a citizen, a coworker, in short, a social creature, In political science the unit of study is the state as distinct from the nation, the tribe, the clan, the family, or the individual, though not unconnected with them; that is, its primary subject is a definite portion of society which manifests, in a comparatively high degree, a political self-consciousness and which has become organized politically.

In the second place, political science is closely related to history. It is, as Jellinek remarks, almost a commonplace today to affirm the necessity of historical study as a basis for a proper understanding of institutions, whether they be political, legal, or social. The political scientist should study, not only the nature of political institutions, but how they have developed and to what extent they have fulfilled the purposes of their existence, History furnishes us in a great measure the materials for comparison and induction.

This is especially true of political history, which concerns itself with the formation of states, their growth, and their decline. The relationship was tersely expressed by the late Professor Seeley, who said "political science without history is hollow and baseless; or to put it in rhyme: history without political science has no fruit; and political science without history has no root. "

While history furnishes much of the data for political science it is not true, as Freeman once declared, that history is past politics or that politics is present history. Not all of history is "past politics. "Much of it like the history of art, of science, of inventions, discoveries, military campaigns, language, customs, dress, industries, religious controversies—has little, if any, relation to politics and affords no material for political investigation. On the other hand, not all political science is history. Much of it is of a purely philosophical and speculative character, and cannot therefore be assigned to the category of history.

The function of history is to narrate and interpret a succession of events; to discover how institutions have persisted and changed from generation to generation; to trace tendencies and laws of growth. It is not restricted in its sphere to those parts of society which manifest political consciousness and which have received political organization, but deals with the record of man prior to as well as subsequent to the organization of the state.

The function of political science, historically considered, is to explain political institutions, and it is concerned only with that part of history which is capable of throwing light upon their present character. According to certain writers, its principal problem is the teleological one of determining what ought to be, so far as the constitution and functions of government are concerned, while history is concerned with what has been.

Thus, although their problems are distinct, they have a common subject in the phenomena of the state, and therefore their spheres touch at many points and overlap at others. To fully comprehend political science in its fundamental relations we must study it historically, and to interpret history in its true significance we must study that politically. As studies they are therefore mutually contributory and supplementary. "Politics are vulgar, "said Professor Seeley, "when not liberalized by history, and history fades into mere literature when it loses sight of its relation to politics. "Separate them, says Burgess, and the one becomes a cripple, if not a corpse, the other a will-of-the-wisp.

Seeley conceived history to be the name of the residuum which is left when one group of facts after another has been taken possession of by some science. Ultimately, he says, a science will take possession of the residuum, and this science will be political science. Many of the facts of history, he points out, are no longer recorded in historical treatises, but have been appropriated by other sciences.

Thus the facts of the past relating to meteorology, biology, hygiene, surgery, anti various other sciences and arts are not recorded in historical, but in scientific treatises. Physiology has taken possession of a definite group of historical facts; pathology, of another; political economy is appropriating the facts of industry; jurisprudence, of law; etc. If this process of appropriation continues, all the facts of history in the end will be swallowed up. Already historians deal meagerly with the facts regarding the phenomena of the sciences and arts, contenting themselves with referring the reader to some special treatise for information.

With political economy, —or economics, to use the more modern term, —political science is closely related; indeed, it is classed as a branch of political science by at least one noted economist. It was first called "political "economy by the Greeks, and was defined by them as the art of providing revenue for the state.

Senior remarks that as late as the eighteenth century political economy was regarded as a branch of statesmanship particularly by the physiocrats, and that those who assumed the name of political economists avowedly treated, not of wealth, but of government. His own conception of the scope of political economy was affected by this view, and he laid it down as a principle that this science involved a "consideration of the whole theory of morals, of government, and of civil and criminal legislation.

The first systematic English writer on the subject, Sir James Stewart, in his "Inquiry into the Principles of Political Economy ", enunciated this view when he said: "What economy is in the family, political economy is in the state.... The great art, therefore, of political economy is first to adapt the different operations of it to the spirit, manners, habits, and customs of the people, and afterward to model these circumstances so as to be able to introduce a set of new and more useful institutions. "Nine years later, Adam Smith published his "Inquiry into the Nature and Causes of the Wealth of Nations, "in which he stated the objects of political economy, "considered as a branch of the science of a statesman, "to be two: first, to provide adequate "revenue or substance for the people or, more properly, to enable them to provide it for themselves "; and, second, to supply the state or commonwealth "with a revenue sufficient for the public service. ""It proposes, "he said, "to enrich both the people and the sovereign. "

Without quoting further from the earlier writers, it is clear that they conceived economics to be a branch of the general science of the state. Writers of the present day no longer hold to the earlier conception, yet there is no difference of opinion among them concerning the existence of a close relationship of economics and polities as ancillary social sciences. Political and social life is obviously intermixed with, and the activities and even the forms of government are profoundly influenced by, economic conditions.

Conversely, there is a distinct interaction of politics upon economics. The production and distribution of wealth are to some extent determined by the existing forms of government. The solution of many economic problems must come through political channels, while, on the other hand, some of the fundamental problems of the state have their origin in economic considerations.

Thus tariff laws and trade restrictive acts, generally, are favored or opposed largely on economic grounds and to a great extent the whole question of the relation between government and liberty is at bottom an economic problem. The burning questions of present-day politics: government control of public utilities, the relation of the state to corporate enterprise, and its attitude toward the whole question of capital and labour, are at the same time fundamentally questions of economics; indeed, the whole theory of government administration is largely economic.

Chapter 2

The Nature of the State

DEFINITIONS AND DISTINCTIONS

Definitions of the state, as the German writer Schulze has remarked, are innumerable, almost every author having his own, and scarcely any two being alike.

The English writer Holland defines a state as a "numerous assemblage of human beings, generally occupying a certain territory, among whom the will of the majority or of an ascertainable class of persons is by the strength of such a majority or class made to prevail against any of their number who oppose it.

"Hall, viewing the state primarily as a concept of international law, says, "The marks of an independent state are that the community constituting it is permanently established for a political end, that it possesses a defined territory and that it is independent of external control.

"The German writer Seydel says, "A state comes into existence whenever a number of men who have taken possession of a part of the earth's surface unite themselves together under a higher will. "Grotius defined the state as a "perfect society of free men united for the sake of enjoying the advantages of right and the common utility. "Vattel, in almost the same language, defined it as a "body politic or society of men who seek their wellbeing and common advantage in the combination of their forces.

"Burgess defines the state as a "particular portion of mankind viewed as an organized unit, "which is substantially the same as the definition given by Bluntschli, who says, "The state is the politically organized people of a definite territory. "The United States Supreme Court in an early case defined a state as "a body of free persons united together for the common benefit, to enjoy peaceably what is their own and to do justice to others. "

Phillimore says a state for all purposes of international law is "a people permanently occupying a fixed territory, bound together by common laws, habits, and customs into one body politic, exercising through the medium of an organized government independent sovereignty and control over all persons and things within its boundaries, capable of making war and peace and of entering into all international relations with the communities of the globe.

"Other writers have emphasized the spiritual and moral nature of the state to the neglect of its other aspects. Thus Hegel defined it as "the incorporation of the objective spirit "; while Pufendorf conceived it to be simply "a moral person endowed with a collective will. "Such definitions are manifestly based on a one-sided view of the state and consequently bring out but one of its many characteristics.

If one more definition may be added to the long list already given, I would offer the following: The state, as a concept of political science and constitutional law, is a community of persons more or less numerous, permanently occupying a definite portion of territory, independent of external control and possessing an organized government to which the great body of inhabitants render habitual obedience. The essential constituent elements, political, physical, and spiritual, of the modern state are all brought out in this definition.

They are: first, a group of persons acting together for common purposes; second, the occupation of a determinate portion of the earth's surface which constitutes the home of the population; third, independence of foreign control; and fourth, a common supreme authority or agency through which the collective will is expressed and enforced.

The term by which the ancient Greeks designated the state was *polis*, the modern English equivalent of which is "city.

"They never grasped the idea of the territorial or country state. Their political science was, as has been said in the preceding chapter, the science of city states, for it was with the city that their state life was identified. To the Romans likewise the state was the civitas or respublica.

To them the Roman state was identical with the city of Rome, Italy and the provinces being only dependencies of the mother city. The conception of the state as embracing non-urban land or country territory made its appearance slowly during the Middle Ages.

The word "state "(stato) first appeared in Italian political literature and presently came to be applied, not to the city community alone, but also to the country territory embraced within the jurisdiction of the governing city. In the course of the sixteenth and seventeenth centuries the words state, appeared in English, French, and German literature, though in France Bodin as late as 1576 preferred the term "republic "as the subject of his famous treatise.

Regarding the meaning of the term "state, "we may observe that it has a popular signification and a meaning technical to political science. In the popular sense the term is often used synonymously with "nation, ""society, ""country, ""power, ""government, "etc.

Technically it has a more precise and exact meaning which is not indicated by any of the above terms. It is very commonly employed to express the idea of the collective action of society as contradistinguished from individual action, as when we speak of "state "aid to education, "state "intervention in industrial affairs, etc. In states having the federal system of government the term possesses a double signification, being employed to designate the federation as a whole and also the autonomous political communities composing it.

A still narrower and obviously incorrect use of the term is its employment to designate non-autonomous provinces of monarchical states as is done in Prussia and Austria. The effect of this somewhat loose dualistic employment of the term to designate both the real state and its subdivisions is to introduce confusion into the terminology of political science, and misconceptions into political thinking. It is unfortunate that neither the English, the German, nor the French language contains a suitable term by which the component members of federal unions may be designated and a different one for describing the larger commonwealth of which they are the constituent parts. Finally, the fact that the state is both a concept of constitutional law and of international law has led to additional ambiguity of usage.

In the next place, we must distinguish between the terms "state "and "government "often employed by political writers as if they were identical in meaning. In reality they represent widely different concepts and upon the recognition of the distinction between them depends the true understanding of some of the most fundamental questions of political science. As has already been remarked, the state is a sovereign community, politically organized for the promotion of common ends and the satisfaction of common needs, while the government is the collective name for the agency, magistracy, or organization, through which the will of the state is formulated, expressed, and realized.

The government is an essential element or mark of the state, but it is no more the state itself than the brain of an animal is itself the animal, or the board of directors of a corporation is itself the corporation. In earlier times, it was not uncommon to identify the ruling sovereign with the state and the famous saying attributed to Louis XIV has often been quoted as an example of such identification. If the government and state were identical, the death of the reigning sovereign or the overthrow of the government would necessarily interrupt, if not destroy, the continuity of the state life. But as a matter of fact changes of governmental organization do not affect the existence of the state.

States possess the quality of permanence. Governments, on the contrary, are not immortal; they are constantly undergoing change as a result of revolution, of the extinction of dynasties, or through legal processes, yet the state continues unimpaired and unaffected. Governments are mere "contrivances, "to use the language of Professor Seeley, through which the state manifests itself. They possess no sovereignty, no original unlimited authority, but only derivative power delegated by the state through its constitution. To understand clearly, therefore, the nature of each and the relation of one to the other we must avoid identifying them either in thought or treatment.

STATE AND NATION;

THE PRINCIPLE OF NATIONALITY IN THE ORGANIZATION OF STATES

In the next place, the state must be distinguished from the nation. Primarily the state, as has been said, is a legal or political concept, while the nation, if the natural meaning suggested by the etymological derivation of the word be regarded, is a racial or ethnical concept. There is no necessary connection between the two, and the best writers never employ the terms synonymously and without discrimination.

In reality a nation is not a portion of society politically organized; that is, it is not a state, but in its perfect form it is a portion of society definitely separated from the rest of the world by natural geographical boundaries, the inhabitants of which have a common racial origin, speak the same language, have a common civilization, common customs and traits of character, and a common literature and traditions.

This is, as has been said, the perfect nation, not the actual nation as it exists in the world to-day and which popular usage conceives it to be. Some authorities, however, do not consider all the elements mentioned above as absolutely essential to the existence of a nation.

Thus Burgess defines a nation as a population having a common language and literature, a common tradition and history, common customs and a common consciousness of rights and wrongs, inhabiting a territory of a geographic unity. He does not seem to consider common descent or identity of race as an essential element but regards community of speech and geographic unity as the principal distinguishing marks.

The French publicist, Pradier-Fodere, defines a nation as

"the union of a society of inhabitants of the same country, speaking the same language, governed by the same laws, connected by identity of origin, physical characteristics, and moral dispositions, by community of interests and sentiments and by a fusion of existences acquired by the lapse of centuries. "Again he says, "Affinity of race, community of language, of habits, of customs and religion, are the elements which constitute the nation. "Calvo, in his work on "*International Law,* "holds substantially the same opinion, emphasizing the fact that the idea of the nation is associated with origin or birth, community of race, community of language, etc.

Community of race and language are undoubtedly the most usual and satisfactory tests for determining the existence of a nation. Identity of race implies kinship, while community of language supplies the medium through which the people understand one another and become friends rather than strangers. Community of language is also a powerful instrument of intellectual and social intercourse and opens the way for the development of a common political consciousness.

Gumplowicz, a noted European publicist, however, considers the test of a nation to be simply "community of civilization "which expresses itself in a common language. Identity of speech and similarity of civilization, he declares, are the outgrowth of a common historic past rather than the result of a common ethnic origin. The ethnic origins of many modern nations, as he shows, are diverse and unknown and hence cannot be an infallible test.

Thus the German, Italian, Spanish, and French "nationalities "were developed, not from a common stem, but from heterogeneous race elements. Yet each ultimately developed a common language and a common civilization, and these, rather than identity of race origin, are really the distinguishing marks of the nation in each case. Community of religion was once considered an essential mark of the existence of a nation, but with the rise of religious freedom the influence of religion as a bond of national unity has largely disappeared.

As has been stated above, the state and the nation are

rarely identical; in earlier times they were less frequently so than now. A single state may in fact embrace within its limits several nations or nationalities.

The English state embraces within its geographical boundaries at least one nation and various nationalities, notably the Celts of Ireland, the French of lower Canada, the Dutch of South Africa, and others. The kingdom of Hungary includes Slav, Roumanian, Teutonic, and other nationalities. The Belgian state embraces in addition to its dominant French population a considerable Flemish element. Russia contains within its vast boundaries many diverse race elements: Slavs, Lithuanians, Finns, Tartars, Roumans, and others.

Switzerland embraces parts of three nations: French, Germans, and Italians. The United States contains in addition to its Teutonic and African populations other important race elements such as the Germans, Scandinavians, Italians, and Irish, though none of these are sufficiently numerous, compact, or isolated, geographically, to constitute distinct ethnic unities.

On the other hand, the limits of the state may be narrower than those of the nation, and hence several states or parts of states may be embraced within the same ethnic unity. Thus the French republic and the greater part of the kingdom of Belgium are embraced within the limits of the same nation. The greater part of the German Empire and parts of the Austrian and Swiss states are embraced within the Germanic nation, while the population of Central and South America is largely the same in ethnic origin and language, yet is spread over many states.

It is evident, therefore, that not every state is a nation nor every nation a state; one is sometimes broader, sometimes narrower, in area, than the other, and hence there is frequent overlapping. The tendency of the last century has been in the direction of identification, that is, toward the organization of states with boundary lines coincident in a general way with those of nations.

This tendency rests on the great principle of nationality, which seeks to bring those populations having the same ethnic origin and language under the same political organization so as to constitute a single body politic. The principle does not, however, mean that every nation, however small, has an inherent right and a duty to organize itself into a state, for obviously not every nation possesses the requisite population or the political capacity for creating and maintaining a state organization.

It is generally agreed, for example, that the Celtic peoples of western Europe, as well as various nationalities in southeastern Europe, together with certain peoples of Asia, have not given evidence of sufficient political capacity to organize and maintain states. Politically weak and incapable peoples everywhere must submit to the guidance and tutelage of the stronger and more highly endowed nations, politically speaking; and some writers go to the length of maintaining that it is the duty of the latter, in the interest of the civilization of the world, to force state organization upon backward races by such means as in their judgment may be necessary to accomplish the result, even to the extent of clearing their territories of their presence and of making it the abode of civilized man.

Considerations of national unity and political stability require that, so far as possible, the principle of nationality should be respected in the organization or reorganization of states; and the experience of the last century teaches that wherever it has been disregarded, as it was, for example, by the Congress of Vienna in 1815, when territories and peoples were divided among the victorious powers without regard to race, nationality, religion, or antecedents, the results have been disastrous and readjustments have become inevitable in the course of time.

Wherever geographic and ethnic lines coincide, there is a strong impulse to political organization within these limits — at is, the nation tends to organize itself into a state. During the Middle Ages the principle of nationality played little part in the organization of states, and indeed it did not come to be fully accepted until comparatively recent times. During the nineteenth century it exerted a powerful influence upon the political readjustments which took place in Europe. It contributed to the political enfranchisement of Greece, Roumania, Servia, and Bulgaria, and ultimately to the independence of some of them; it brought about the unification of the German and Italian states; it led to the disruption of the unnatural union between Belgium and Holland, and to the rounding out along national lines of the boundaries of various other European states. It is to-day at the basis of some of the largest questions of European politics.

It overtops all other questions in the politics of Austria-Hungary where the population is a conglomeration of different races, speaking different languages, having little common sympathy, and each animated by national aspirations of its own. In Austria, Bohemia demands national autonomy, the German element is struggling for supremacy of control, the Czechs are fighting for recognition of their language by the state, etc. In Hungary, the struggle between the various nationalities is intense, almost to the point of disruption.

The Magyars demand official use of their language in the army and in the civil service; the Slovaks, Poles, Ruthenians, Serbs, Slowenians, Croatians, and other nationalities represent so many different ideals, temperaments, and elements of dissension. The principle of nationality is at the bottom of the Pan-Germanistic movement, which seeks to unite under a single state organization all the German-speaking populations of western Europe: the German Empire, Alsace, part of Lorraine, most of Switzerland, part of Holland and Schleswig, and part of Austria.

It is at the foundation of the Pan-Slav movement, which would unite all the Slavs of eastern Europe under a common scepter: Poles, Slowenians, Moravians, Serbs, Czechs, and Croatians, now found in Prussia, Russia, Austria, Saxony, and Turkey. The same principle would bring together the Scandinavian races: Norwegians, Swedes, and Danes; establish the independence of Finland; secure the autonomy of the Flemish population in Belgium; give home rule to Ireland; and lead to a readjustment of the boundaries between France and Germany and between Italy and Austria.

Nationality, which is but another name for national

kinship, has been a powerful force in bringing into relation petty states and holding them together against the disintegrating forces of sectionalism and particularism, while lack of it has been a potent cause of disruption in many states. Ethnic homogeneity coupled with geographic unity are undoubtedly among the most powerful factors in maintaining political solidarity, and it should be the ambition of every state to organize itself so as to secure these elements of national strength and stability.

Struggling nationalities, according to some writers, should be encouraged to separate themselves from unnatural unions and establish independent existences, rather than be suppressed as they were in Europe during the early nineteenth century. Whenever there are within the limits of a state several more or less populous nationalities, with widely different customs and degrees of civilization and especially when they constitute distinct geographic unities, the danger of dissension and of disintegration makes it worth while to consider whether the welfare of the peoples directly concerned and the civilization of the world would not be promoted by a voluntary division of the state and its reorganization along national lines.

This has happened as a result of revolt and successful war many times in the history of the past, and is likely to happen again in the future. In any case the state should strive by all proper means to render its population ethnically homogeneous and thereby remove one of the most potent sources of national discord. Some writers maintain that where the outlying provinces of a state exposed to the attacks of a dangerous neighbour are inhabited by an alien and disaffected nationality, the state is justified in adopting extreme measures to bring about their assimilation with the rest of the population, and may in case of necessity remove them bodily from the exposed district and deport them to other parts or distribute them throughout the state in such a way as to destroy their national aspirations.

This has been justified on the ground that with states, as with individuals, self-preservation is the first law of nature. It was upon considerations of this character that the Emperor

Napoleon forced the use of the French language upon the German inhabitants of Alsace and that Prussia is to-day demanding the use of the German language in the schools of the province of Posen. Not widely different in principle is the present policy of the Emperor Francis Joseph in insisting upon the use of a common language in the army of Austria-Hungary, and of the United States in attempting to protect by restrictive legislation its population against the deleterious effects of an undesirable foreign immigration. Some writers go to the length of holding that the wishes of the local inhabit. ants are entitled to no respect whatever when considerations of national unity require their annexation to another country.

Thus the German argument for the annexation of Alsace was based, not on the theory that the Alsatian population desired annexation to Germany, for as a matter of fact they preferred union with France, but on the ground that they were German in origin and spoke the German language.

The French, on the contrary, have defended their designs on the Rhine on the ground that the Rhine is the natural geographical frontier of France, and that the annexation of the territory in question would mean a rounding out and a completion of her national unity. Similarly Italian writers have demanded the annexation or absorption of the Italian-speaking communities in Austria and Switzerland because they are Italian in race and language.

What has been said above in regard to the right of the state within reasonable limits to take extreme measures to preserve itself against the dangers of ethnic heterogeneity in its population must not be understood as an argument in favor of the reckless disregard of the rights of nationalities. Considerations both of humanity and of public policy require that their peculiar customs and institutions should within the limits of national security be respected.

Except in extraordinary circumstances, they should be allowed to retain their own language, their local law, and such of their institutions as are peculiar to them and suited to their local conditions. But it is no injustice to small nationalities within the state not to be allowed the use of their language in the national parliament, or in the army, though considerations of convenience, regardless of any question of moral right, usually make it advisable to permit to each nationality the use of its own language in the local governments.

On the other hand, the principle of nationality in its strictest form, in cases where several states are organized within the limits of a single nation, especially if it constitutes at the same time a geographic unity, would require the union of the several states under a common sovereignty, either through voluntary federation or through the absorption of the smaller states by the larger.

It was through the latter process that the German Empire and the kingdom of Italy were welded into national states. In each case the more powerful and progressive state within the nation took the initiative and gathered about it such of its neighbors as voluntarily consented to become members of the union, and by compulsion forced the rest to merge their existences into the larger organization; and thus the political boundaries of the new states were brought into approximate harmony with their geographic and ethnic lines.

There is no difference of opinion now that the welfare of the peoples directly concerned, the peace of Europe, and the civilization of the world were promoted by the organization of these great national states in the place of the petty commonwealths which formerly existed; and none but the political doctrinaire troubles himself to-day about the means by which this great work was accomplished. Professor Burgess, speaking on this subject, well says: "And who does not see that the further rounding out of the European states to accord still more nearly with the boundaries which nature has indicated would be in the interest of the advancement of Europe's political civilization and of the preservation of the general peace?

It would expel the Turk from Europe; it would put an end to the Russian intrigue in the valley of the Danube; it would give Greece the vigor and power to become a real state; and it would bring the petty states of Switzerland, Denmark, Holland, Luxembourg, Belgium, and Portugal to contribute, in far greater degree, to the political civilization of the world, and receive, in far greater degree, the benefits of that civilization, than their present conditions permit. Even then there would be weak places enough in the boundaries of each national state, but their number would be greatly decreased, and the temptation to invasion which they offer greatly lessened.

The political history of Europe during the past century goes far toward justifying the conclusion that the states of the future are to be national states, not necessarily states whose political, geographical, and ethnic boundaries are identical, but those in which there is a fair approximation to this ideal. Some writers, notably Dahlmann and Von Mohl in Germany, Mancini, Maniani, and Pierantoni in Italy, and Burgess in America, come pretty near to the point of contending for the principle that the boundaries of states and nations should coincide; that is, that there should be a state for every nation and a nation for every state.

A strong criticism of this position has been made by Gumplowicz, who asserts that there is no historical or sociological justification for the view that "mono-national "states possess elements of advantage over those composed of a number of nationalities.

He asserts, on the contrary, that there is more popular freedom in "poly-national "states than in those whose populations are ethnically homogeneous, and he cites Switzerland, "the freest state in Europe, "as an exampleEven Bluntschli, who is an extreme advocate of the principle of nationality in the organization of states, admits that ethnic heterogeneity is not an unmixed evil, since the presence of foreign elements in the state may be a means of "keeping open connection with the civilization of other states "and may "serve as an alloy to give strength and currency to the nobler metal.

"De Parieu quotes the Emperor Francis II of Austria as once saying to the French ambassador: "My people are strangers to one another and yet it is for the better. They never have the same ills at the same time. In France, when there is an epidemic of fever, you all have it the same day. I have

Hungarians in Italy and Italians in Hungary. Each suspects his neighbour; they never understand one another and in fact detest one another. Their antipathies, however, conduce to order and their mutual hate to the general peace. "

THE ORGANIC THEORY OF THE STATE

One of the qualities usually attributed to the state is that of organic unity. A mere mass of human beings unconnected by some sort of unifying bond does not constitute a state or even a society Concerning the nature and degree of this unifying element a number of theories have been advanced by sociological and political writers.

One of these is the so-called *monistic* theory, which conceives organized society to be an association in which the individuals composing it have no really independent existence of their own but are swallowed up, as it were, like atoms in the whole mass, owing all that they are and all that they have to the society of which they are a part. Then there is what has been called the *monadnistic* theory, which goes to the other extreme and considers society as a mere aggregation of individuals or groups, in which there is no real unity, each individual being largely independent of the rest, owing nothing to society, and, except for a sort of accidental juxtaposition, standing in isolation from his neighbors.

In the third place, there is the dualistic conception, which represents a compromise view. It considers the relation of the individual to society to be one of partial dependence only. His existence is neither merged in that of the whole as though he existed solely for society, nor is he entirely isolated from, and independent of, his social surroundings. Finally, there is the organic view, which considers society as analogous in structure to a biological organism, the relation of the individual to the whole mass being similar to that which exists between the cell and the organism of a living being.

The organic theory, says Jellinek, is one of the oldest and most popular theories concerning the nature of the state. Plato compared the republic to a great man and insisted that the best-ordered commonwealth was one whose structural organization resembled most nearly in principle that of the individual. As the whole body feels the pain and sympathizes with an injured member, so, he declared, the whole society is affected by injury to each individual of which it is composed. Cicero likewise drew an analogy between the state and the individual, likening the head of the state to the spirit which rules the human body.

The state was personified by medieval writers like John of Salisbury and Marsiglio of Padua; Althusius was fascinated with the biological analogy; and many of the writers of the eighteenth century attached an importance to it out of all proportion to its value. The French Revolution, with its accompanying doctrine that the state was merely an artificial creation, tended to check the spread of the organic theory; but toward the middle of the nineteenth century a reaction against the French philosophy set in, and the conception of the state as an organism came to have numerous advocates.

Indeed, the fascination for the organic theory, with its analogies and parallelisms, became so widespread that political science seemed in danger of being appropriated by natural science. One of the most extreme advocates of the organic theory was the noted German scholar Bluntschli, in his "Theory of the State "and in his "Psychological Studies concerning State and Church

The state, he declares, is the very "image of the human organism. "Each has its member parts, its organs, its functions, its life processes, and between those of the state and human organisms there exists a deep and striking resemblance. He pushes the biological analogy so far indeed as to impute sexual qualities to the state, it being personified as masculine in character as contradistinguished from the church, to which he attributes the attribute of femininity.

His comparison of the structure and life processes of the state to those of the human body is at times almost amusing. p. v. The state, to him, is "no mere artificial lifeless machine, "but a "living spiritual organic being. "As an oil painting, he says, is something more than a mere aggregation of drops of oil, as a statue is something more than a combination of marble particles, as a man is something more than a mere quantity of cells and blood corpuscles, so the nation is something more than a mere aggregation of citizens and the state something more than a mere collection of external regulations.

As the animal organism is made up of living members or germ cells, interdependent one upon the other and, upon the whole, each performing its peculiar functions in the life economy of the organism, so the state organism is composed of individuals, not isolated and disconnected like the atoms of an inorganic body, but closely related and dependent upon one another and upon the whole society, somewhat as a limb of the human body or the branch of a tree is dependent upon the main trunk.

In origin, structure, and function, say the advocates of the organic theory, there is a striking resemblance between the social body and the animal organism. Each comes into existence through natural rather than artificial processes, each possesses organs whose functions are similar in many respects, and each changes and grows according to laws instead of by mere chance.

Rousseau, who saw a close resemblance between the body politic and the human body, compared the sovereign power of the state to the head of an individual; the laws and customs to the brain; the judges and the magistrates to the organs of will and sense; commerce, agriculture, and industry generally to the mouth and stomach which prepare and digest the food; and the public finances to the blood, which a wise economy, through the medium of the heart, distributes throughout the entire organism.

Herbert Spencer, in his "Principles of Sociology, "worked out a most elaborate analogy between organized society and the biological organism. Both the animal and social bodies, he affirms, begin as germs, undergo a process of continuous growth, the parts, as they develop, becoming more and more unlike, and exhibiting greater complexity of structure. As the lowest type of animal is all stomach, respiratory surface, or limb, so primitive society is all warrior, all hunter, all hut builder, or all tool maker.

As society grows in complexity, division of labour follows, i. e. new organs with different functions appear, corresponding to the differentiation of functions in the animal, in which "fundamental trait "they become "entirely alike. "In each case there is a mutual dependence of parts, the full performance of the functions of each member being essential to the health and preservation of the rest.

If the iron worker in the social organism stops work, or the miner, or the food producer, or the distributor fails to discharge his natural functions in the economy of society, the whole suffers injury just as the animal organism suffers from the failure of its members to perform their functions. Thus the "parallelism between social and animal life "is maintained.

The slow but constant replacement of cell tissue and blood corpuscle in the animal organism, by which it is destroyed and reproduced again, we are told, is paralleled by the processes in society, by which it is permanently maintained, notwithstanding the deaths of the component members. Spencer attributes to both the animal organism and the social body a "sustaining system "consisting of alimentation in the former, and production in the latter; a "distributing system "consisting of the circulatory apparatus in the human body, and the transportation system in society; and a "regulatory system, "the nervous system in the animal, governments and armies in the state.

In spite of all these elements of resemblance Spencer admits, however, that there is one "extreme unlikeness "in the structure of the body politic and the animal organism. The latter, he says, is concrete in structure, that is, its units are bound together in close contact; while the social body is discrete, its units being free and "more or less widely dispersed. "He readily admits that the difference is "fundamental, "though, he says, "upon close examination it will not put comparison out of the question, "for it can be shown that "the social aggregate, though discrete, is still a living whole.

"There is still another difference between the two organisms, he says, which "greatly affects our notion of the ends to be achieved by social organization, "namely, the lack of a "nerve sensorium "in the social body. In the animal, consciousness is concentrated in a small part of the aggregate; in the social organism, it is diffused throughout the aggregate.

The conclusion of practical politics which Spencer draws from the failure of the analogy at this point is that the welfare of the aggregate in society, considered apart from that of the units, is not an end to be sought; that, in short, society exists for the benefit of its members, not its members for the benefit of society. Upon the dissimilarity which he finds between society and the biological organism, or rather upon the discrete nature of the social organism, he builds up his individualistic political philosophy, which has seemed to some to be wholly inconsistent with his organic theory of the state.

The Austrian publicist Albert Schäflle is another writer who has greatly overworked the biological analogy. In four large volumes entitled "The Structure and Life of the Social Body "he examines at great length the anatomical, physiological, biological, and psychological resemblances between society and the animal body and asserts that society is an organism whose protoplasm or unit is man, the state or government in the one corresponding to the brain in the other. His work as a whole exhibits evidence of enormous learning and wide research, and the theory of the organic nature of society is supported with ability and ingenuity.

Of a similar character and magnitude is the work of Paul Lilienfeld, a Russian sociologist, whose "Thoughts concerning the Social Science of the Future ", published in five volumes between 1873 and 1881, constitutes an elaborate exposition of the organic theory, including the laws of social psychology and social physiology.

He goes even beyond Spencer and Schäffle in the emphasis which he places on the organic character of society, and in his advocacy of the biological analogy. Among others who have explained and defended the organic theory may be mentioned the French writers: Auguste Comte, Tarde, Letourneau, De Greef, Fouillee, and Rene Worms; the Polish writer Gumplowicz; and the Germans Ahrensand Waitz. Of these the French sociologist Worms is to-day probably the most eminent advocate of the organic theory. In his "*Organism and Society* "he expounds and defends the biological analogy, maintaining that the anatomy, physiology, and pathology of society possess striking similarities to the structure, function, and pathology of living beings.

If the organic theory meant simply that the state is something more than an aggregation of individuals crowded or massed together without any unifying bond, in other words, that it is a society in which the members individually are in a peculiar sense dependent upon the whole and the whole in turn is conditioned upon the parts, no well grounded objection to it could be sustained.

Even the biological analogy up to a certain point, though sub serving little or no practical purpose, is harmless and scientifically unobjectionable, for manifestly there are certain elements of resemblance between the structure and functions of the state on the one hand and those of living beings on the other. But at many points the comparison utterly fails and the resemblance becomes pure fancy. Thus the resemblance between the cells of a biological organism and the human beings who constitute the body politic will be seen upon close examination to be exceedingly superficial.

The former are mechanical pieces of matter, with no independent life of their own, each being fixed in its place, having no power of thought or will, and existing solely to support and perpetuate the life of the whole; the latter are intellectual and moral beings, each having a will of its own, possessing the power of foresight, movement, and selfcontrol, and a physical life independent of the whole of which they are a part. Each individual has to a large extent the shaping of his own life; and his place in the organism is not determined for him nor are his activities regulated by central organs.

This lack of consciousness and will on the part of the cells of the animal organism and its presence in the state organism is one of the instances where the analogy fails. With the animal organism the dependence of the parts on the whole is essential, and the relation intrinsic; if they are severed from their connection, as a branch from a tree or a limb from an animal, they perish and cease to be living matter. With the state, on the contrary, the separation of a member does not result in destruction, physically speaking; the individual separated from the whole is still an individual.

Moreover, the laws of growth, development, decay, and death which govern the life of the human organism are scarcely analogous in any sense to those which reign in the world of politics. An organism grows and develops from within by internal adaptation, not by the addition from without of new parts; while the state changes rather than grows, and does this, for the most part, by the process of formal alteration as a result of volitional power and conscious effort of the members. Its growth, if such it may be called, is largely the result of the conscious action of its individual members and is to a great extent self-directed.

The elements of volition and of conscious effort do not enter into the growth of an organism; it changes in obedience to the operation of blind mechanical forces of nature, the parts having no power to alter the direction of its growth or to add to its stature. Indeed, as Jellinek remarks, growth, decline, and death are not necessary processes of state life though they are inseparable from the life of the organism.

The state does not originate or renew itself as a plant or an animal does. In fact, to quote Jellinek again, many modern states like the German Empire, Italy, and some of the Balkan commonwealths owe their existences to the sword rather than to any cause that may be compared to the procreative or generative processes through which plants and animals come into existence.

Our conclusion must be that the biological analogy, in the form in which it is usually stated, is not only fanciful and absurd, but even mischievous, and would not merit notice were it not relied upon by some respectable writers as the justification of an important theory concerning the relation of the state to the individual members composing it — a subject which will be discussed in a later chapter of this book.

Some of these biological comparisons are ingenious and

well stated; to many writers they have proved fascinating and seductive; to others they have constituted the basis of an argument for a theory of the state which would sacrifice the individual to society.

The organic theory, in the sense in which it is understood by many writers, rests on mere analogy, and we would do well to heed Lord Acton's warning about analogies and parallelisms lest we come to grief.

For this reason Jellinek suggests that we had better reject the theory in toto lest the danger from the large amount of falsity in the analogy should outweigh the good in the little truth which it contains. It is difficult to see what is to be gained by the attempt to identify or compare the state with an organism.

At this stage of the world's political development neither the identification nor the resemblance is necessary to establish the supremacy of the state over the individuals who compose it.

Chapter 3

Essential Elements of the State

PEOPLE

THE first element which enters into the physical make-up of the state is the population which constitutes its membership. To each inhabitant may be attributed the quality of *citizen* when be is viewed as an active participator in the common will, and of *subject* when he is thought of as a passive member with no share in the public power.

Legally all persons within the jurisdiction of the state are, of course, subjects of the state, and in most monarchical countries the term "subject "is commonly employed to designate all who owe obedience, regardless of whether they enjoy full civil and political rights or not. Citizenship is not necessary to membership in the state for certain purposes, and as a matter of fact there is a more or less numerous body of aliens in every state, who are at the same time members, so far as the right of protection and the duty of obedience are concerned.

Citizenship, however, is the normal relation, and the state may insist upon it as a condition to the enjoyment of civil rights as well as political privileges.

There is no rule or political practice governing the number of persons necessary to entitle a community to recognition as a state; as a matter of fact the populations of the existing states of the world vary quite as widely as the areas of their territories. Some writers in the past have, however, undertaken to lay down within broad lines certain principles which should determine the amount of population necessary to the existence of a state, and some have even assumed to fix exactly the minimum and maximum number of inhabitants; but manifestly any such rules must be arbitrary and worthless. Aristotle was certain that there ought to be a limit. The number, he said, should neither be too small nor too large, but large enough to be self-sufficing and small enough to be well governed. Rousseau, without attempting to fix upon any particular number, laid down the rule that there should be a certain proportion between the population of the state and the extent of its territory.

A political body, he declared, may be measured in two ways, viz. by the extent of its territory and by the number of its people, and there is between these measurements a relation which should give to the state its true dimensions. The extent of land should be sufficient to nourish the inhabitants, and there should be as many inhabitants as the land can sustain. In another place he argued that the larger the population of the state, the less the liberty of the individual, because his share in determining the sovereign will must be correspondingly less.

About the nearest approach to a safe rule is to say that the population must be sufficient to provide both a governing body and a number of persons to be governed, and of course sufficient to support a state organization. If the other elements are fully present, this number need not be considerable. Changes in the population of the state, of course, have no more effect upon its corporate existence than do changes in the territorial area. Populations are continually augmented by natural increase and by immigration and decreased by emigration and other causes, but unless the loss is so great as to render the maintenance of a state organization impossible the existence of the state remains unaffected.

TERRITORY

Another physical constituent in the make-up of the state is the land or territory which serves as the abiding place of those who constitute its membership. In a peculiar sense territory is the physical basis of the state. "As the state has its personal basis in the people, "says Bluntschli, "it has its natural basis in the land; a people does not become a permanent state till it has acquired a territory.

"A population unattached to a definite portion of the earth's surface is nothing more than a wandering horde or migratory band. History abounds in examples of nomadic peoples like the Jews after their dispersion and before their settlement in Palestine, the German tribes during their wanderings after the break-up of the Roman Empire, the "trekking "Boers of South Africa after the abandonment of their original lands for a new home to the north, but until they ceased wandering and settled themselves upon a definite portion of territory they never became states, though they may have been states in the making. There can be no such thing as a migratory state. The state, as its etymological meaning suggests, is associated with a fixed abode. Sovereignty is no longer considered personal but territorial.

The territory of the state consists not only of a definite portion of land, but also of the rivers, lakes, and canals within its limits, and if the state touches upon an open sea it includes in addition a maritime belt generally recognized to be three miles in width measured from low-water mark. Whether this maritime belt is to be considered actually as part of the territorial domain of the state or merely a part of the open sea over which the state is permitted by the law of nations to exercise jurisdiction for certain purposes, there is a difference of opinion among publicists.

The territorial domain of the state is not the property of the state or of any ruler; the patrimonial state, in which the monarch was considered the ultimate owner of the land, is a thing of the past. Rulers can no longer, as they often did in medieval times, sell, pawn, give away, or partition their d mains as though they were private property. The modern state exercises imperium, not dominium, over the land embraced within its limits; that is, the ownership of the land belongs to private individuals, subject always, of course, to the right of expropriation by the state for public purposes.

The right of private ownership has become so completely

dissociated from the old patrimonial idea that cessions of territory to foreign states, according to the public law of the civilized world, are no longer considered as affecting in the least the private ownership of the lands so alienated.

The territory of the state may be "integrate "and contiguous, like that of Switzerland; or it may be dismembered and a part of it non-contiguous, like that of Great Britain; or it may be an enclave, that is, entirely inclosed within the territory of another state, like the Republic of San Marino, for example, which is an inclosure of Italy.

State boundaries may be natural or artificial, that is, they may be bodies of water, mountain ranges, deserts, forests, and the like, or mere surveyors' lines marked by posts, monuments, stones, trenches, walls, etc. If the boundary is a navigable stream, the line ordinarily runs through the middle of the most navigable channel, the filum aquae or Thalweg; if non-navigable, it follows an imaginary line midway between the two banks.

Where mountain ranges constitute the boundary, the dividing line, in the absence of special treaty stipulations, follows the crest of the watershed. Disputes concerning boundaries between states have been common in the past and are not infrequent even to-day among the newer states of the world. During the nineteenth century the boundaries of various European states, notably those of Turkey, Bulgaria, Servia, Montenegro, and Roumania, were adjusted by international commissions created by general treaty arrangements.

The extent of a state's territory has an important bearing not only on the question of its capacity for self-defense, its power and influence in the family of nations, but to some extent upon the form of its governmental organization and its activities. There is some difference of opinion among practical statesmen as well as political theorists as to whether vastness of territorial domain is a source of strength or weakness, especially when part of the territory to noncontiguous, remotely situated, and inhabited by alien races.

On the whole, however, the advantage seems to be on the

side of empire, and it is the ambition of most modern states to increase the extent of their territories. In recent years we have seen something of a scramble among European states for additional land in Africa, and even the United States, which until lately was satisfied to pursue its destiny on the continent of North America, has acquired extensive dominions beyond the seas.

There is no rule or practice concerning the extent of territory necessary to constitute the home of a state, any more than there is regarding the amount of population. As a matter of fact, states have varied in size all the way from the city states of antiquity to the vast empires of to-day. At the present time they vary from the petty republics of Monaco and San Marino, embracing only a few hundred square miles of territory, to the British and Russian empires and the United States, containing millions of square miles. There have always been small states, both monarchies and republics, and they have maintained themselves by the side of their more powerful neighbors until this day. It is, therefore, absurd, as Bluntschli remarks, to try to fix a limit to their size.

During the medieval age the states of Europe were small and numerous. The present states of France, Italy, Germany, and Spain were all divided into a number of petty monarchies and republics. Almost every lordship, says Bluntschli, many towns and even villages maintained independent existences with their own constitutions.

But, on the whole, the territorial area of states has increased since the seventeenth century. The modern tendency is toward a consolidation of those whose territories lie within the same geographic unity and whose populations belong to the same nationality; and hence the states of the future in all probability are likely to be more extensive in area than those of the present.

The increasing need of the European states for more territory in which to develop their national energy, for the support of their surplus population, and for their expanding commerce has in late years led to an organized movement among them to take possession of such uninhabited portions of the globe as remain unclaimed. Within a very few years the greater part of Africa has, as has been said, been partitioned out among the powers of Europe. So rapid has been the movement that it has been impossible to take effective possession of these vast territories except at a few accessible points, and the consequence has been the invention of a curious political institution, known as the "sphere of influence, "as a means of delimiting the share of each claimant. The practice of leasing territories from other states for commercial, military, and naval purposes, where they cannot be purchased or otherwise acquired, has also recently been adopted by a number of governments.

About all that can be said in regard to the extent of territory is that it ought to be large enough to sustain the population. Rousseau, in his "*Le Contrat social,* "discussed the subject at some length and attempted to lay down certain general principles regarding the size of the state as he did in regard to the amount of population. Nature, he declared, has fixed a limit to the territory of the state as to the stature of a well-proportioned man.

It ought not to be too vast in extent to be well governed nor too small to maintain itself. Administration, he asserted, becomes difficult at great distances, as a weight becomes heavier at the end of a long lever. It becomes more onerous in proportion as degrees are multiplied, and it enforces the laws in remote communities with less vigor and celerity, while the people feel less affection for a government with which they rarely come in contact.

Some writers, in discussing the subject, distinguish between democracies and monarchies. The natural limit of a democracy, said Madison, is that distance from the central point which will just permit the most remote citizens to assemble as often as their public functions demand, and will include no greater number than can join in those functions; so that the natural limit of a republic is that distance from the centre which will barely allow the representatives to meet as often as may be necessary for the administration of public affairs.

Alexander Hamilton pointed out that vast extent of territory contributes to the natural strength of the people, while smallness of territory encourages usurpers to make attempts upon their liberties. The smaller the territory, he said, the more difficult for the people "to form a regular or systematic plan of opposition, "while the larger the territory, the more "competent the people to a struggle with the attempts of the government to establish a tyranny. "

Nevertheless, as Bluntschli remarks, the power of a state is not always to be measured by its mere extent. Thus France and Germany, with nearly one tenth the territory, are more powerful states than Russia. The European territory of Great Britain comprises only about half the superficial area of either Germany or France, yet without its dependencies it would compare favorably in power and influence with either. The Greek city states were petty indeed in point of territory, yet Athens took her place by the side of Rome in the history of the world.

A state with vast extent of territory, especially when a part of it is noncontiguous and remote, is difficult to defend in war, and vigilance as well as power may be necessary to protect the outlying dependencies.

A city state or a country state of small area is obviously better suited to certain forms of government and methods of administration than a state of vast area where some of the parts are remotely situated from the seat of government. A pure democracy might be successful in the former when it would be unworkable in the latter.

The republican form of government, Jellinek observes, is well adapted to small states, while monarchy, as a rule, is better suited to large ones, though he admits that recently the success of certain great democratic republics has thrown doubt on the rule. "There is, "says John Stuart Mill, "a limit to the extent of country which can be advantageously governed or even whose government can be conveniently superintended from a single centre.

There are, "he said, "vast countries so governed; but they, or at least their distant provinces, are in general deplorably ill administered, and it is only when the inhabitants are almost savages that they could not manage their affairs better separately. "

The enlargement or reduction of the territorial area of the state does not ordinarily affect its international capacity or interrupt the continuity of its life. Sardinia, for example, was enlarged to nearly four times its original area and its name changed, yet its identity was never considered destroyed nor its treaty obligations impaired.

Prussia, after the peace of Tilsit in 1807, lost nearly one third of its territory; Saxony by the treaty of Vienna in 1815 was reduced to one half its former size; France in 1815 and 1871, Turkey in 1829 and 1878, Austria in 1859 and 1866, Mexico in 1848, — all lost more or less considerable portions of their territory but in no case was the corporate existence of the state affected. As an international entity the state, however, may cease to exist by being annexed to another state, by voluntarily merging itself into another state, by being absorbed, or by partition of its territory among neighboring states.

Geographical situation and the shape and conformation of the territory, as well as extent of domain, have an important bearing upon the institutions and national life of the state. These factors determine the occupations and industries of the people, the extent and variety of the natural resources, and to some extent the national character and even the laws, institutions, and activities of government. Many of the great political writers of the past, like Plato, Aristotle, Machiavelli, Bodin, Montesquieu, Comte, and Hume, dwelt upon the influence of natural phenomena upon the character and institutions of nations.

Buckle, in his "History of Civilization, "emphasized to the point of exaggeration, as has been said, the influence of climate, soil, and food upon the industrial, intellectual, and political development of certain states. Montesquieu, in his *"Esprit des Lois "*, undertook to establish a connection between climatic influences and the laws of the state and between the fertility of the soil and forms of government. His conclusions, however, abound in paradoxes, and his estimate of the effect of climatic influences was greatly exaggerated.

That the course of history — economic, social, and political — has, however, been determined at many points by geographical factors is incontestable. The existence of the petty states of ancient Greece, and the virtual failure of all attempts to unite them, separated as they were by intersecting mountain ranges and arms of the sea, afford one of the earliest and most striking illustrations of this truth.

Nothing is clearer than that geographic isolation is unfavorable to political unity. It not only retards, in the beginning, the unification of neighboring races, but also the union of different communities of the same race; it promotes prejudices and want of sympathy, and, when political union has once been established, particularism and disunion. Moreover, lack of geographic homogeneity determines to a certain extent the activities, if not the form, of government. People occupying the different parts of a state which are separated from each other by high mountain barriers, impenetrable deserts, or large bodies of water develop local peculiarities and have local needs which require special legislation.

An insular state like England is not only economically dependent upon distant parts of the world, but by reason of its exposure to attack from the outside must give constant attention to questions of national defense. The fact that Switzerland has maintained its local life comparatively undisturbed by the powerful states about it for more than a thousand years is due largely to the geographical conditions which environ its folk. It might also be shown that the distinctive political ideas and institutions of the Dutch have been determined to some extent by the geographical situation of that country and the heroic struggle with nature which it has entailed.

GOVERNMENT AND SOVEREIGNTY

A third essential mark of the state is the existence of an agency through which the collective will may be ascertained and expressed and the ends of the state realized. This agency, magistracy, contrivance, or organization we call government. A mere mass of people occupying a particular portion of territory do not constitute a state until they have organized themselves politically and established a civil government.

They must, in short, possess a juristic personality and have a common will. The governmental organization may be simple and its functions few and restricted in their sphere of operation, but there must be a political agency of some kind; there must be governors and governed — some who command and others who obey. If there are none who possess authority and none who obey, remarks Bluntschli, there is no state but only a condition of anarchy.

In the great states of to-day the governmental organization is vast in extent and complex in structure, but, as in the case of territory and population, quantity and extent are not the tests of statehood. The simple rudimentary government of an African prince, if capable of commanding and enforcing obedience, fulfills the requirements of political organization.

A final constituent political principle of the state is sovereignty, in some respects the most important and distinctive of all the marks of state organization. In popular usage, sovereignty means the original, supreme, and unlimited power of the state to impose its will upon all persons, associations, and things within its jurisdiction; in short, it is that quality of the state by virtue of which it may command and enforce obedience to the exclusion of all other wills. In popular usage the term also has reference to the independence of the state from foreign control, that is, its right to live its life and pursue its ends independently of the will of other states.

The former attribute is sometimes described as internal sovereignty, the latter as external sovereignty. Sovereignty is thus a concept both of municipal law and of international law. Whatever may be the differences of opinion regarding its nature and abiding place, the majority of writers are agreed that there can be no state without sovereignty. There must be some supreme power which in the last analysis is entitled to lay down commands and able to compel obedience. It is this which distinguishes the state from all other associations and organizations. Take it away and the state becomes a mere voluntary pact or association.

Nevertheless, a few writers of high standing do not consider sovereignty to be an essential element of state existence. There are many communities, they maintain, which have their own constitutions and systems of internal administration, and hence may be rightfully described as states, though they may be under the control, wholly or in part, of other states, so far as their foreign relations are concerned. Such are the so-called protectorates and suzerain communities which abound in Africa and the orient.

Some of them are free from outside control so far as their internal polity is concerned, and sometimes to a large extent as regards their foreign relations. Some of them send and receive diplomatic representatives or at least consuls, and sometimes they conclude commercial conventions or treaties. Such communities are classified as dependent or part-sovereign states, but according to the strict tests of political science they are not states, but parts of other states. They may become states by shaking off their real or nominal dependence, but until then they are in legal contemplation mere dependencies of other states.

OTHER ATTRIBUTES AND ASPECTS OF THE STATE

Land and people, government and sovereign power, are thus the indispensable, eternal marks of the state. But states possess other qualities and characteristics in addition to these. Most writers, for example, attribute to the state the qualities of permanence and continuity. It is not meant by the quality of permanence, however, that a particular state once established endures as such forever, for as a matter of fact history abounds in examples of states whose existences have been terminated through absorption by other states or through a voluntary merging of their existences into that of other states.

Indeed, it would be quite possible for the existence of a state to be terminated by the voluntary withdrawal of the inhabitants from its territory or their compulsory removal, or by the perishing of the entire population in a common disaster. What is meant by saying that the state is a continuous and permanent establishment — *eine dauernde Einrichtung*, as the Germans describe it — is, that since the state is essential to the happiness, if not the very existence, of mankind, the world must continue under state organization for all time. No other organization or association can fulfill its purposes, and whenever a particular form of state disappears, another will succeed to its place, and thus the continuity of its life will be preserved.

It is not to be understood, of course, that changes in the governmental organization or internal polity of the state necessarily destroy or interrupt its continuity. The governmental organization of the state, in fact, is not infrequently changed by revolution, or through legal alteration, yet the corporate existence of the state itself continues unimpaired and unaffected.

Governments are not immortal; they are merely the agents or instrumentalities through which the state for the time being acts, and they may be changed or superseded at the will of the sovereign. Monarchies may be transformed into republics and republics into monarchies, the rank and titles of rulers may be changed, absolute principles may be superseded by constitutional principles, without legal effect upon the identity of the state, its corporate personality, its rights or its obligations.

Only when the internal changes in its structure result in prolonged anarchy is the existence of the state itself involved. France, for example, set aside its dynasty, transformed its government from a monarchy to a republic, then to an empire, again to a monarchy, then became a republic again, again an empire, and is now a republic for the third time, but the continuity of the state as such has remained unchanged through all the political transformations through which it has passed.

The state manifests itself also under other forms and reveals other qualities and attributes, depending upon the multifarious points of view from which it is considered.

Viewed objectively, it reveals itself to us as a concrete working organization, not a mere mental abstraction or collectivity of individual will relations. Considered subjectively, it appears to us, as the etymological derivation of the word implies, as a condition or status rather than a dynamic organization.

Looked at from still another viewpoint, the state is primarily a social phenomenon; an association for the realization of the common social interests of mankind. Some writers, looking at it from another viewpoint, lay great stress on the state as a legal concept, — *ein Rechtsbegriff,* as the Germans say.

They dwell upon its character as a juristic person, a corporation of public law, the bearer of public rights and obligations. The juristic personification of the state has always been a favorite theme of a certain class of German and French writers. Some of them, following the theories of the Roman law, have attributed to it only a limited juristic personality, while others have emphasized its character as a real juristic person in the strictest sense of the word.

Continental European writers generally dwell upon the distinction between the state as a public govern mental power — a *Korperschaft des offentlichen Rechts* -which legislates, commands, and exacts obedience, on the one hand, and its character as a fiscal personality or ordinary corporation of private law, on the other hand. As *fiscus* the state is a concept of private law, capable of entering into all or almost all the relations of private law.

As such it enters into contractual engagements very much as a private individual or corporation does; acquires, owns, and administers property; employs agents; brings suits in the courts and sometimes allows itself to be made a party to suits at the instance of private persons. Thus the state possesses both a public and a private character, exercises *imperium* and *dominium,* governs and transacts business, etc.

On the continent of Europe the distinction between the state as a public power and as *fiscus* possesses great practical importance owing to the rule generally prevailing there that the government is responsible to the individual in damages for violations of contracts to which it is a party as well as for torts committed by its officers and agents. This liability of the state as *fiscus* is enforced by suits brought by the injured individual either in the ordinary judicial courts, as in Germany, or in special administrative tribunals, as in France.

In England and the United States, where the idea of the state as a corporation has had less development and where the legal responsibility of the state to the individual through suits for damages is hardly recognized by the public law of either country, the distinction between the state as a public corporation and as fiscus is of less importance.

Finally, some writers, especially Germans, distinguish between the *concept* of the state (*Staatsbegriff*) and the *idea* of the state (*Staatsidee*). The *concept* of the state, says Bluntschli, presents us a picture of actual states from the standpoint of their nature and essential characteristics; the *idea* of the state is that of the state in the splendor of imaginary perfection, the state not yet realized in fact, but toward which mankind should strive.

The distinction is not entirely fanciful, though the accuracy of the terminology may be open to question. What is intended, is to distinguish between a concrete state as it actually is or as it has existed in history and the state in the abstract, no particular state but the state in general. The one is the result of concrete thinking, of inductive logic; the other of philosophical speculation and abstract reasoning. "The *idea* of the state, "says Burgess, "is the state perfect and complete; the *concept* of the state is the state developing and approaching perfection. From the standpoint of the *idea* the state is the world viewed as an organized unit.

From the standpoint of the *concept* the state is a particular portion of mankind politically organized. The former is the real state of the perfect future; the latter the real state of the past and the present and the imperfect future. With the progress of mankind and the development of the world the two will tend to become identical. "

Chapter 4

The Origin of the State

PRELIMINARY OBSERVATIONS

Inquiry into the circumstances surrounding the origin of the state belongs largely to the realm of theory and speculation. History records the principal facts regarding the establishment of particular commonwealths by men already accustomed to political life; it tells us how and under what circumstances state organization has spread to new lands hitherto unoccupied or inhabited by people politically unorganized, and how new forms of state organization have superseded other forms. But the circumstances and conditions under which primitive men first saw the light of political consciousness and came to associate themselves together under some form of political organization are facts veiled largely, if not wholly, in the mists of obscurity.

Authentic history throws little light on the subject, and we must look for the most part to the new sciences of sociology, ethnology, and anthropology to help us in fathoming the mystery. Aristotle tells us that the state was the highest and last of the associations formed by man, as it was the only selfsufficing one — that is, the only one capable of satisfying all the needs of man.

We are therefore probably safe in saying that it has existed in some form, rudimentary or otherwise, wherever civilized men have lived together in any considerable numbers. But our knowledge concerning the nature of this early authority and of the procedure by which it was established rests largely on inference and generalization rather than upon historical proof.

Various theories concerning the original institution of political authority have been advanced by historical and political writers, but as yet it can hardly be said that there is any common agreement among them as to the true origin. The oldest of these theories, as Jellinek remarks, is that which attributes the establishment of the state, mediately or immediately, to God or some superhuman power.

The theory assumes that the will of God was made known by revelation mediately or immediately to certain persons who were his earthly vicegerents, and by them communicated to the people by whom obedience was a religious as well as a civil duty.

The divine theory, as an explanation of both the historical origin of the state and its justification, was widely defended in earlier times, when many of the chief political writers were at the same time churchmen and theologians. Biblical support for it is found in such passages as Paul's admonition to the Romans: "Let every soul be in subjection to the higher powers; for there is no power but of God; and the powers that be are ordained of God. "

During the Middle Ages this doctrine became a sort of Christian dogma and was at the bottom of the teaching that rulers of states were the anointed representatives of God. The celebrated Augsburg Confession of 1530 placed the stamp of approval on it when it declared that "all authority, government, law and order in the world have been created and established by God Himself.

"The idea that in some form the state is an institution of God and that rulers govern by divine right, that there is "a divinity that doth hedge a king, "lasted until the end of the eighteenth century and in some countries even later. The theory was especially strong in France, where the claim that the "king of France holds his kingdom and his sword only from God "was frequently asserted in the controversies between the French kings and the Papacy.

We find the same claim put forth in the famous treaty of the Holy Alliance concluded in 1815 between the sovereigns of Austria, Russia, and Prussia, where it was solemnly asserted by their Majesties that they looked upon themselves as being delegated by Providence to govern their peoples, that the Christian nations of which they and their subjects were a part acknowledged no sovereign but God, to Whom belonged all power, and that their duties as rulers were pointed out to them by the same divine authority. The idea in less extreme form is still maintained by some of the rulers of Europe to-day, notably by the present German emperor, who has frequently asserted the claim to rule by divine right.

The belief of the masses of the common people in the divinity of kings still persists in parts of eastern Europe, but as a doctrine of political philosophy it received its death blow at the hands of Grotius, Hobbes, and Locke. The doctrine of divine right has had its advocates among political writers, no less than among kings.

Bossuet, a noted writer of the seventeenth century, in his "*Politics as derived from the Scriptures,* "boldly asserted that God established kings as His ministers through whom He ruled over His people, like a father over his children, and who were accountable only to Him for their acts. The Protestant monarchomachs of the sixteenth century, the Spanish Jesuits, and the noted Filmer in his "*Patriarcha,* "written in the middle of the seventeenth century, taught essentially the same doctrine.

James I of England, before his accession to the throne, in a short treatise entitled "*The True Law of a Free Monarchy,* "laid down the dogma that kings rule by divine right and that subjects have no recourse against them, and he supported his claims by arguments drawn both from the Scriptures and the law of nature. Upon these high authorities he affirmed the doctrine of the sacrosanctness of the royal office and declared that as it is blasphemy to dispute what God can do, so it is presumption and high contempt to dispute what a king can do.

Of the merits of the theocratic theory as an account of the historical origin of the state, there is now little difference of opinion among political philosophers. The doctrine that the state was established by an ordinance of God, that its magistrates are divinely appointed, that they are accountable to no authority but God, the ruler and lawgiver of the state, now has few supporters. The fact is, the state is no more the direct and immediate creation of a supernatural power than any of the multifarious associations into which mankind has entered. The authority which the state exercises, whatever its origin, must be exercised through human agencies and must be humanly interpreted, that is, in the last analysis, it is only what the state chooses to make it.

We may accordingly dismiss the doctrine of divine right with the statement that it never was anything more than an invention of men, designed to bolster up the claims of certain rulers to hold their crowns independently of the will of the people and to govern absolutely and without accountability to any authority except such as they might choose to render to God. If the theory meant simply that the Creator implanted in the breast of man the instinct for order and the impulse which manifests itself in political organization, we could accept it.

The idea that rulers are directed and supported by a supernatural power is very strong among primitive peoples. They are accustomed to call religion to their aid and to seek a religious sanction for their important acts. Obedience to the state is inculcated by them as a religious duty, and religious worship is usually supported by their governments.

Thus Rome had its national religion and its own national gods, and the whole of the *jus sacrum* was regarded as a part of the Roman public law. In the early stages of the life of the state the ministers of religion are the dominating class, the lawgivers, the statesmen, and the judges. The names of Numa Pompilius in Rome, Lanfranc, Anselm, and Wolsey in England, Mather, Hooker, Cotton, Edwards, and Davenport in North America, belong almost as much to political as to ecclesiastical history. The pillars of the early state, says Burgess, are usually churchmen; the priestly class are exalted above the rest of society, and the unfaithful are denied membership in the state.

THE COMPACT THEORY

A theory of state origins which has profoundly influenced

the political thought of Europe and America for two centuries is that which is popularly described as the "social compact "or the "social contract. "This theory ascribes the institution of political authority to contract or convention, that is, to the deliberate and voluntary agreement of the members of the community who, through the instrumentality of a covenant, organize themselves into a body politic.

This explanation of how the state originated, as well as of its right to be, has had many advocates since the seventeenth century and has furnished the pretext, if not the justification, for numerous revolutions and the institution of new governments in the place of old ones. Most of its advocates assume, to start with, the existence of a pre-social or a pre-civil condition of mankind, antecedent to the establishment of the state, in which men were unrestrained by the prescriptions of positive human law, but were subject only to those of the moral law, the law of nature or the instincts of reason.

This hypothetical condition or status, says the philosopher Thomas Hill Green, is "a state in which every individual is free to do as he likes, and from which individuals escape by contracting themselves out. "This condition of society is described by the writers on the compact theory as the state of nature, the *status naturalis*.

Before proceeding farther with a consideration of the doctrine of the social compact it will be well to distinguish between the two applications which have been given to the theory. In the first place, the "compact "theory may be, and has been, employed to describe an association or agreement among the members of a community, still in a state of nature, by which civil authority is established. In the second place, it may refer to an agreement or a relation between the people of a community already politically organized, on the one hand, and a particular magistrate or ruler, on the other.

In the first case, the parties to the compact are the individuals of the community, each with one another and with all; in the second place, the parties are the whole society in its corporate capacity, on the one hand, and an agent or ruler, on the other. By some writers the former is described as the social compact, the latter as the *political or governmental* compact. The one represents the act by which men in a state of nature establish a political or civil society; the other the act by which a political society already established institutes a particular government. One represents a theory of the origin of the state, the other a theory of the institution of a particular government. The first transaction, therefore, necessarily precedes the latter in point of time and is an essential preliminary condition to the establishment of the latter.

Thus the people of a given community may organize themselves by covenant into a political society without making a compact with a particular ruler or governing body, but they cannot contract with a ruler until they have become a political society and hence have acquired that corporate capacity without which contracts cannot be entered into by bodies of men.

The idea that the authority of rulers rests on compact or contract between them and the people is as old as Plato, and its supporters have been able to cite in support of the theory numerous historical examples from the Old Testament. Such, for instance, were the covenants between the elders of Israel and David by which the latter was anointed king, between God and His people relative to the installation of Saul as king, between Josiah and the people on the one hand and the Lord on the other, the covenant which God made with Noah after the flood, and many others.

The principles of the Roman law of contract also gave support to the idea, and the great Roman jurist Ulpian seems to have considered the relation between the Roman emperor and the people as being in the nature of a compact. Throughout the Middle Ages and the early modern period the theory of the contractual basis of political authority exerted great influence upon the political thought of the time, but it should be remembered that it was not the theory of the origin of civil society — not the original social compact but the theory of the relation between the people and their magistrates, between the state and its governing authority.

In this form it had such advocates as Hooker, Milton, Buchanan, Johannes Althusius, Languet, Filmer, Grotius, Pufendorf, and others. Instances of actual contracts between people and kings are, however, few, and those which have been relied upon are hardly such as to establish the claims of the theory as a historical fact.

Nevertheless it is sometimes maintained that if the theory cannot be successfully defended as descriptive of an actual historical transaction, it can at least be accepted as a rational interpretation of the relationship which exists or should exist between the people and their rulers.

In the sixteenth and seventeenth centuries, when the struggle against absolutism was well under way, the theory came to be relied on as a justification of the right of the people to depose their rulers when they were guilty of violating the terms of the compact made or supposed to have been made between them and their subjects.

It was, for example, appealed to in justification of the deposition of Queen Mary by the Scots, who asserted that "royal power was nothing else but a mutual covenant or stipulation between king and people, "— an idea which had been enunciated and defended by one of their countrymen, George Buchanan, in his "*Rights of Kings among the Scots,* "published in 1579. The doctrine of contract was not defended by political writers alone; it was sometimes admitted by kings themselves as expressing the proper relation between them and their subjects.

James I of England confessing in an address to Parliament in 1609 that "the king binds himself by a double oath to the observation of the fundamental laws of his kingdom, tacitly as by being a king and so bound to protect as well the people as the laws of his kingdom; and expressly, by his oath at his coronation, so as every just king in a settled kingdom is bound to observe that paction made to his people by his laws, in framing his government agreeable thereunto according to that paction which God made with Noah after the Deluge.

"Eighty years after this royal deliverance the English people appealed to the "paction "theory as a justification for the deposition of James II and the election of a new sovereign to succeed him. The Convention of 1689, which declared the throne vacant and which fixed the crown on William and Mary, asserted that James had "endeavored to subvert the constitution of the kingdom by breaking the original contract between king and people "and with having "violated the fundamental laws. "

Turning now from the theory of the political or governmental compact which seeks to explain or interpret the relation between society and its rulers, if not the actual transaction by which particular magistracies are instituted, we come to consider in the next place the theory of the social compact, the primary original association, through which the state of nature is transformed into the civil state and the natural man into a citizen with legal rights and duties.

As already stated in an earlier part of this chapter, the writers who have supported the theory of the social compact have predicated as a theoretical starting point the existence of a pre-civil or pre-political condition of mankind which they describe as the "state of nature, "though they differ in important particulars concerning its real character. Hobbes, who was the first writer to attempt to describe in detail the state of nature, considered it to be a state of perpetual strife among the members of the society; a war, potential if not actual, of all against all; a state of constant struggle, of fierce and brutal competition, and of distrust and suspicion, the hand of each being against all.

This condition, Hobbes argued, was the inevitable result of the inherent egoism of man, who by nature is a self seeking creature, with a "perpetual and restless desire of power, "a desire for the gratification of his appetites, a craving for glory which ends only with his death. Men in the natural state, he said, were like famished wolves, seeking to devour one another. Natural right, which to him was simply natural might, Hobbes defined as nothing more than "the liberty that each man hath to use his own power for the preservation of his own nature.

"In such a state of society there could, of course, be no

distinction between legal right and wrong, or of justice or injustice, for there is no law, and in the absence of law there can be no such things as justice or injustice, right or wrong. Might alone under such circumstances determines right, and to every one belongs whatever he has the physical power of appropriating and keeping.

To Locke, on the other hand, the state of nature appeared to be not necessarily a state of brutal strife among wild men, but rather one in which peace and reason prevail, for man is not, as Hobbes maintained, inherently vicious, but is animated generally by the instincts of reason and justice. He defined the state of nature as a "state of perfect freedom to order their actions and dispose of their persons as they think fit, within the bounds of the law of nature, without asking leave or depending upon the will of any other man.

"But though this be a state of liberty, he continues, yet it is not a state of license. "The state of nature has a law of nature to govern it, which obliges every one; and also a law of reason, which is that law which teaches all mankind who will but consult it. No one ought to harm another in his life, health, liberty, or possessions, for all are the workmanship of one omnipotent and infinitely wise Creator.

"There being no common authority empowered to enforce the law of nature, Locke observed that "every man hath a right to punish the offender and be executioner of the law of nature, even to the taking of life. thereby freeing society of a criminal who having renounced reason and the laws of God hath declared war against all mankind, and may be destroyed as a lion or a tiger.

And this in accordance with the great law of nature, 'whoso sheddeth man's blood, by man shall his blood be shed. ' "Locke's conception of the state of nature thus differs from that of Hobbes in that while, according to him, the liberty of the individual is not limited by human law, yet it is limited by the law of nature and the dictates of reason; and hence the "natural "man has a right, not to everything he is physically capable of appropriating, but only to such things as he can use without depriving others of a similar advantage. In short, with Locke natural liberty is not the same as physical power; it is rather might limited by the natural right of others.

Concerning the existence of a law of nature, Locke says "it is certain that there is such a law, and that, too, as intelligible and plain to a rational creature and a studier of that law as the positive laws of commonwealths, nay, possibly plainer. "Nevertheless, he did not regard the state of nature as an ideal condition. He admitted that there were "many things wanting "in such a state.

Although man in the state of nature, he said, is the "absolute lord of his own person and possessions, equal to the greatest and subject to nobody, "yet the enjoyment of his wide freedom is "very uncertain and constantly exposed to the invasions of others, "while the enjoyment of his property is "very unsafe and very insecure. "First of all, there is the want of an established known law received and allowed by common consent to be the standard of right and wrong and the common measure to decide all controversies between them.

"For though the law of nature is plain and intelligible to all rational creatures, yet men, being biased by their interest as well as ignorant for want of study of it, are not apt to allow of it as a law binding to them in their application of it to their particular cases. "There being no common judge or authority to interpret the law of nature and settle disputes in accordance with that law, each individual must be both judge and executioner and the "inconveniences "are very great where men are judges in their own cases.

In short, in the state of nature, "every man must be his own law court, and every man his own policeman. "Locke's view that the state of nature was not a condition of warfare and struggle but rather one of peace and order, though somewhat wretched and inconvenient, was in substance the view of Milton in his "Tenure of Kings and Magistrates ", and of the German jurist Pufendorf in his "De Jure Naturse et Gentium, "published in 1672.

They conceived the state of nature rather as a prepolitical than a pre-social state, that is, a condition of society in which men were united by social bonds, but yet without political organization, whereas Hobbes identified the state of nature with a condition of society still in a virtual state of savagery.

The French writer Rousseau, the third of the great triumvirate of political philosophers to expound and popularize the social compact theory, conceived the prepolitical state of mankind to be one approaching the ideal rather than an actual primitive historical condition. In his "Discourse on Inequality, "published in 1754, he declared it to be in some respects the happiest period of human existence. In "*Le Contrat social* ", where he elaborates his views more at length, he describes the state of nature as one "where all is common "and where

"I owe nothing to those to whom I have promised nothing. I recognize as belonging to others only what is not useful to me. This is not the case in the civil state where all rights are fixed by law. "Again he says, "Man is born free and he is everywhere in chains. "From a condition of primitive simplicity in which man was unfettered by the shackles of authority, where he was free to live his life without being bound by the artificial bonds of human laws, he has been driven by his own inherent sinfulness into the civil state, where he is more or less a slave to the whims of authority.

Poetic imaginations have often pictured the state of nature as an earthly paradise, in which happiness, innocence, and the joys of unrestricted freedom abound without limit, where equality reigns, where the yoke of law and the burdens of state press upon the shoulders of no man and where none are subjects and none sovereigns.

But we are safe in saying that no such condition of society ever had any existence except in the imagination of the poet or the philosopher. If any considerable numbers of the human race ever lived in a state of nature, so called, the conditions could not have been very different from what Hobbes conceived them to be.

Escape from this intolerable condition took place, we are told, through the process of compact or covenant; that is, the men of the community "contracted "themselves out of the natural state into a civil state. The advocates of the compact theory all agree that in general this was the manner of escape, though they differ as to the exact nature of the procedure. Thus, observes Hooker, there is no relief for mankind from the "grievous injuries and wrongs "of the pre-civil state but by "growing into composition and agreement amongst themselves by ordering some kind of public government, by yielding themselves subject thereunto.

"According to his view, the social and political compact were successive parts of the same process, the one being a preliminary stage of the other. That is, the people first covenanted among themselves to submit to a common superior, and then in their organized capacity they chose a particular ruler and entered into a compact with him by which they promised obedience in return for protection.

It was, said Hobbes, as if each individual should say, I authorize and give up my right of governing myself to this man or this assembly on this condition, that thou give up thy right to him and authorize all his actions in like manner. "Thus there is a mutual surrender of natural rights and a bestowal of all "power and strength "upon a common superior in return for better secured legal rights and the substitution of a single will in the place of a multitude of conflicting wills.

Each individual surrenders for the common benefit his natural right to do what he will and receives in return the assurance of protection and security in that which he has or may rightfully possess. Thus, according to Hobbes, there is, in addition to the fundamental original pact by which the state is created, a subsidiary pact, by which each man agrees to obey the person or assembly who is the choice of the majority. "This done, the multitude so united in one person is called commonwealth or in Latin a *civitas*, and the person or persons upon whom this power is bestowed is called the sovereign and all others are subjects. "The covenant thus made is irrevocable without the consent of both parties to the contract.

"I readily grant, "says Locke, "that civil government is the proper remedy for the inconveniences of the state of nature which must certainly be great where men may be judges in their own case. "Nevertheless, he asserts that certain kinds of civil government (or misgovernment) are worse than the state of nature (or anarchy), the "inconvenience being all as great and as near, but the remedy farther off and more difficult. "The answer therefore to the question whether civil government is preferable to the state of nature depends on the character of the government.

On the whole, the "inconveniences "and "uncertainties "of the natural state outweigh the advantages, and men are soon "driven into society, "where they "take sanctuary under the established laws of government and therein seek the preservation of their property. "Accord-` ing to Locke, the transformation occurs through the action of the people in "incorporating "themselves into a body politic "wherein the majority have a right to act and conclude the rest. "They "covenant "with each other to establish a government, — a covenant they are bound by the law of nature to observe, — and out of this covenant the obligation of obedience and submission arises.

"There and there only, "he said, "is political society where every one of the members hath quitted the natural power, resigned it up into the hands of the community in all cases that exclude him not from appealing for protection to the law established by it. "This is the original social compact by which civil society is established in the place of the natural state, not the governmental compact between an already organized society and a particular sovereign.

According to Locke, the covenant is between people and king; according to Hobbes, the king was not a party, but only the people each with all. Hobbes considered that the authority bestowed on the sovereign was not through agreement but rather through the surrender of certain rights to him. Not being bound himself as a party to the agreement, he could not be deprived by deposition of the authority bestowed upon him, and hence to resist him was to return to the state of nature. In other words, the right of the sovereign to rule is irrevocable and indefeasible.

Locke, on the other hand, regarding the king as a party to the covenant, held that he might forfeit his office through a violation of the terms upon which he was vested with authority. Hobbes was in fact the apologist and defender of the Stuart pretensions to rule by divine right; Locke was the exponent and advocate of the principles of the English Revolution against the absolutism of the Stuart kings.

Rousseau's idea of the social compact was, as has been said, that of the "original association "by which the state of nature was transformed into the civil state, not the act by which a particular government was instituted. There is, he said, but one contract and that is the agreement to form a civil society. That done, a government is established by a legislative act authorizing the government and an executive act appointing the magistrates, but there is no contractual element in the process.

He thus agreed with Hobbes in holding that the king was no party to the compact, but, unlike Hobbes, he maintained that the surrender of rights was not to a monarch, but to the whole society. "Each of us, "he said, "puts his person and faculties into a common stock under the direction of the general will, and we receive each member as an indivisible part of the whole. This "act of association produces a moral and collective body "or a "public personage, "which formerly took the name of "city, "but is now called a "republic "or "body politic. "It is called the *state* when passive, the *sovereign* when active, and a *power* when compared with its equals. Rousseau, unlike Hobbes, upheld the sovereignty of the people rather than the absolutism of the king.

According to Hobbes, the passage from the state of nature to the civil state is through a surrender of rights to a sovereign; according to Locke, through the institution of a common superior, to secure rights which already existed in the natural state; according to Rousseau, through the surrender of rights, not to a sovereign king, but to the sovereign people.

Regarding the nature of the original association by which the "passage "from the precivil state was effected, he said, "each man giving himself to all gives himself to none; and there is not an associate over whom he does not acquire the same right as is ceded, an equivalent is gained for all that is lost, and man is free to keep what he has. "Again he remarks, "What man loses by the social contract is his natural liberty and an unlimited right to anything that tempts him which he can obtain; what he gains is civil liberty and the ownership of all that he possesses.

"The passage from the state of nature to the civil state, continued Rousseau, produces in man a very remarkable change, by substituting in his conduct justice for interest and giving to his actions a moral force which they lacked before. True, he loses "several advantages "by the change, but the others gained are so very great in comparison that he ought to "bless without ceasing, the happy moment which took him forever from it [the state of nature] and made of a dull stupid animal an intelligent being — a man. "

The idea that man in passing from the state of nature to the civil state exchanges his natural liberty for civil liberty was supported by many writers of Rousseau's time and thereafter. Blackstone stated the nature of the transaction and the advantages of the change as follows: "Every man when he enters society gives up a part of his natural liberty, as the price of so valuable a purchase; and, in consideration of receiving the advantages of mutual commerce, obliges himself to conform to those laws which the community has thought proper to establish.

And this species of legal obedience and conformity is infinitely more desirable than that wild and savage liberty which is sacrificed to obtain it. For no man that considers a moment would wish to retain the absolute and controlled power of doing whatever he pleases, the consequence of which is, that every other man would also have the same power, and then there would be no security to individuals in any of the enjoyments of life. Political, therefore, or civil liberty, which is that of a member of society, is no other than natural liberty, so far restrained by human laws and no farther as is necessary and expedient for the general advantage of the public.

CRITICISM OF THE COMPACT THEORY

The doctrine that the state originated in compact or

contract enjoyed a wide popularity during the seventeenth and eighteenth centuries, but during the nineteenth it underwent a searching criticism, if it did not receive its death blow, from the hands of such scholars as Ludwig von Haller, Jeremy Bentham, Sir Henry Maine, Thomas Hill Green, Edmund Burke, Professor Bluntschli, Sir Frederick Pollock, Professor Ritchie and many others.

Indeed, before the publication of Rousseau's celebrated "Contrat social, "the English philosopher Hume had demolished the theory by showing the inconsistency of contract as the relation between the governed and the governors. Bentham did not consider the theory worthy of extended consideration, and after referring approvingly to Hume's "demolition "of the theory, dismissed it with the following remark, "I bid adieu to the original contract; and I left it to those to amuse themselves with this rattle, who could think they needed it.

"Sir Henry Maine asserts that nothing could be "more worthless "than such an account of the origin of society and government as that given by Hobbes, while Sir Frederick Pollock characterizes it altogether too harshly as one of the "most successful and fatal of political impostures. "

In the first place the theory is unhistorical. As we have already said, history does not afford a single well-authenticated instance of a state which came into existence through deliberate and voluntary agreement among men who were not already accustomed to political authority. Historically, observes T. H.

Green, the theory is a fiction. The classical example usually cited by the advocates of the theory is that of the famous Mayflower compact, by which a body of emigrants to America in 1620 entered into an agreement whereby they "solemnly and mutually, in the presence of God and of one another, covenanted and combined themselves together into a civil body politic for their better ordering and preservation.

"When Carlyle objects that Jean Jacques could not fix the date of the social contruct, "says Professor Ritchie, "it would at least be a possible retort to say that the date was the 11th of

November, 1620. "But upon examination this as well as the other instances relied upon by the advocates of the theory will be seen to be not examples of the founding of new commonwealths by men in a state of nature, but merely the transplanting to new lands of political institutions by men already subject to political authority.

Indeed, in the case cited above, the transaction was nothing more than the extension of an already existing state to a country not yet inhabited by civilized races. The Mayflower covenanters, in fact, expressly acknowledged that they were "loyal subjects "of an existing sovereign, instead of men trying to escape from the state of nature. If the compact theory

meant nothing more than that the extension of the state to new territories, by men already subject to state organization or the creation of a new state form in the place of one already existing, is sometimes the result of convention, historical examples in abundance could be cited.

In the second place, the theory must be rejected upon grounds of philosophy and reason. It is impossible to believe that men in a state of nature could have "contracted "themselves into the civil state by a deliberate and conscious act of convention. The theory assumes the existence of what is manifestly not present in the minds of men still in the natural state, namely, an already highly developed political consciousness.

"It presupposes, "observes Burgess, "that the idea of the state with all its attributes is consciously present in the minds of the individuals proposing to constitute the state, and that the disposition to obey the law is already universally established. Now we know that these conditions never exist in the beginning of the political state of a people, but are attained only after the state has made several periods of its history. "Civil society never began by a contract between individuals or between an unorganized mass of individuals and a magistrate.

The conventional element belongs to a later stage of social development. The idea of contract may, as has been said, play an important part in changing the form of an already existing state, in creating new forms of government, or in extending the state to new territories by persons already subject to political authority; but that does not explain the circumstances of the original creation of the state.

The form of convention, however, which we have described as the *political* or *governmental* compact is not impossible, and, indeed, there are some historical examples of such transactions; but the theory even in this form necessarily assumes the existence of a people already organized and capable of entering into contractual relations. Men in a state of nature cannot enter into compacts with rulers; they must first become organized, and when they have done this, they already constitute a state.

The theory of the *governmental* compact, therefore, does not explain the origin of the state any more than does the theory of the *social* compact; it only explains a particular transaction in the later development of the state life or defines the nature of the relationship between the people in their politically organized capacity and their governing authorities. The theory of the social contract, says Green, implies a false notion of rights. Since those who contract must have rights, the theory implies that individuals have certain rights independently of society, which they bring with them to the transaction.

The notion of covenant as the origin of political authority rests also on a false basis. It would be just as logical, says Ludwig von Haller, to speak of a contract between an individual and the sun that he would allow himself to be warmed by it, or between him and the frost that he would clothe himself better.

It is sometimes argued, however, that although the contract theory cannot be accepted as an explanation of a historical fact, that is, as an account of the origin of some actual state in the past, it may nevertheless be received as descriptive of the proper relationship between the state and its citizens. But even in this form the theory is sound only within very narrow limits, if at all, for modern political science does not regard the relationship between the individual and the state as contractual in character.

If it were, then it would follow logically that any individual would be free to become a party to the contract and hence a member of the state, or to refuse at will and thus remain in a condition of outlawry. Such a view tends to make the state a matter of individual caprice, and if the doctrine is followed out to its logical conclusion, is subversive of authority and leads to anarchy and dissolution.

The obligations of the citizen manifestly do not rest on a contractual basis. If so, what shall we say of the binding force of a covenant when the original contracting parties have disappeared? Does the state expire with the death of the partners, and must it be renewed by their successors, or is the original contract binding forever upon future generations who have never consented to the agreement?

The state, declared Edmund Burke, in his "Reflections on the French Revolution, ""ought not to be considered as nothing better than a partnership in a trade of pepper and coffee, calico, or tobacco, or some other such low concern, to be taken up for a little temporary interest and to be dissolved by the fancy of the parties. ""It is, "he continues, "a partnership in a higher and more permanent sense -a partnership in all science; a partnership in all art; a partnership in every virtue and in all perfection.

As the ends of such a partnership cannot be obtained in many generations it becomes a partnership not only between those who are living, but between those who are dead and those who are to be born. "The individual thus becomes a member of the state, not by admission as to a business partnership, not through voluntary adhesion to a contractual agreement; but he is born a member and becomes entitled to the rights and subject to the obligations which it creates, just as he is born into the world of nature and becomes subject to the laws of nature and to the restraints imposed upon him through the necessities of his very existence.

The obligations of allegiance and obedience do not rest upon covenant or consent, but rather upon the general interests or necessities of society, or upon grounds of utility. We can no more account for them on the basis of consent than we can account for the obedience of the child to the parent on the theory of compact. These relations are independent of our consent, and we enter into them so naturally that we do not stop to inquire into their origin or causes any more than we do about the principle of gravity or the operation of the laws of nature in general.

The theory of the social compact, as the basis of political authority, like the theory of divine right, was invented for a specific purpose, namely, to establish the right of resistance upon the part of subjects to sovereigns whenever the latter violated their obligations to the former. During the period of the Tudor and Stuart absolutism in England, when the rights of the people were recklessly violated by tyrannical kings, the theory was developed that as the subject owed the sovereign obedience, the sovereign in turn was bound to protect the subject and govern him justly.

From this the idea gradually spread that kings owed their authority to the people and could be deposed by them for abuse of that authority. In short, the relation between rulers and subjects came to be regarded as contractual in character.

If the contract theory meant no more than that the relation between rulers and subjects is one of reciprocal rights and obligations, of protection and obedience, we should be under the necessity of accepting it in its entirety.

To maintain, says McKechnie, that "all men ought to have a share in molding the form of the constitution of a state is a logical and intelligible position; but to hold that the individual atoms vote the state itself into existence as the result of a unanimous plebiscite is absurd. It is to ignore the great truth established for all time by Aristotle, that man is by nature a political and social animal and therefore necessarily the member of some state, however crude.

THE PATRIARCHAL AND MATRIARCHAL THEORIES

"The patriarchal theory of the origin of political society, "says J. F. McLennan, one of the most learned students of primitive social organization, "stated in its simplest form, represents society as the enlargement of the family, and the family as a group composed at first of a man and his wife and children. "With the expansion of the original family through the marriage of the children new families are founded, but the authority of the father of the first family, as chief or patriarch, is acknowledged, so long as he lives, by the whole body of descendants, however numerous.

In the course of time all the families descended from the original father, if they hold together, form a very large group which we may call a tribe. Withdrawals from the tribe and removal to new territories constitute the nuclei of new tribes, and so in the course of time many new tribes come into existence. Being united by ties of blood, the tribes naturally act together for common purposes, particularly in the prosecution of foreign war.

In time they establish some common form of authority and thus become a state, at first necessarily simple and rudimentary. Such an example was afforded by the ancient Jewish nation, founded by the union of the twelve tribes made up of the descendants of Jacob, the original first father. In the patriarchal family the element of paternity is of course the chief fact. Blood relationship is traced only through males, and from the same ancestor; that is, kinship is purely agnatic. Furthermore, the *patria potestas* of the Roman law is the basis of all authority, that is, the father of the family controls all business, religious, and other relations of all descendants, no matter how numerous.

The patriarchal theory, observes McLennan, "so simple and natural, used to be generally accepted as palpably true, like the fact of the sun moving daily round the earth. No one thought of proving it and but few of seriously doubting it. "Its most notable exponent and advocate in the nineteenth century was the learned Sir Henry Maine in his "*Ancient Law* "and in his "*Early History of Institutions.*

"In the former work Maine asserts that "the effect of the evidence derived from comparative jurisprudence is to establish that view of the primeval condition of the human race which is known as the patriarchal theory, which is defined as the theory of the origin of society in separate families, held together by the authority and protection of the eldest male descendant. "Regarding the genesis of society, he says: "The elementary group is the family connected by common subjection to the highest male descendant. The aggregation of families forms the *gens* or house. The aggregation of houses makes the tribe. The aggregation of tribes constitutes the commonwealth. "

More recent supporters of the patriarchal theory are the English writer Donisthorpe and the French writer Duguit. The very first state that ever existed, says Donisthorpe, was a human family, consisting of a mother and her offspring. The family, he asserts, is the earliest form of state. In course of time families are drawn together in little groups and loosely compounded under a single head, constituting the patriarchal state, in which the unit consists of the descendants of a living male who exercises power over them.

The federation of patriarchal groups leads to the clan, or house, having a common name and held together by common interests. These *gentes* tend to coalesce until we have the tribe and eventually the nation, which organizes itself into a state. With most people of Aryan or Semitic origin, says Duguit, the patriarchal family has been at some time the general form of social group.

The male parent, by virtue of his age, sex, and ancestry, is recognized in primitive society as being invested with a particular prestige. He is the natural chief, the governor of the little state of which the members of the family are the governed. The ancient city was merely a union of families in which political power belonged to the father.

In recent years historical and sociological investigation has thrown considerable doubt on the soundness of the patriarchal theory. The theory lacks historical proof to substantiate it. Among its more notable critics are McLennan, in the work already cited, Morgan, in his "Ancient Society, "and Edward Jenks, in his "History of Politics. "These writers reject the proposition that the family, related only through males, and ruled over by a patriarch, was universal in ancient society, or even general. There are many examples of rude societies now existing, says McLennan, in which the family differs radically from the patriarchal family, and there is much evidence to show that such families existed in early times before the patriarchal family. In other words, according to their theory the matriarchal family, founded on kinship through females, was the primary social fact.

The only direct historical evidence produced in support of the former theory, they assert, is that the patriarchal family existed in early Rome; while there is evidence on the contrary to show that neither the elements of *patria potestas* nor agnation existed in the primitive Hebrew family, nor in Greece, nor among the early Germans. McLennan's theory is that the genesis of civil society goes back of the patriarchal family to the stage of polyandry and to the matriarchal family, the former of which subsequently developed into the monogamous family and the latter into the patriarchal state. The same view is held by Edward Jenks, who declares that the theory that the "beginnings of society are to be found in the single household or group of descendants of a living man "has been "exploded.

"Recent discoveries, he asserts, have proved that "the earliest social group, so far from being a small household of a single man and his wives, is a large and loosely connected group called a pack or horde, organized for matrimonial purposes on a very artificial plan, which altogether precludes the existence of a single family. In such a condition of society promiscuity of sexual relations prevails, and kinship is traced, not through the father, but through females. Likewise, Jenks asserts that the process by which families expand into clans and clans into tribes according to Maine's conception is, in fact, the reverse.

The tribe is the oldest as it is the primary group; in time it breaks up into clans; these in turn break up into households and ultimately these are dissolved, leaving the individual members to constitute the units of society. Examples of such societies are found among the primitive races of Australia, the

Malay Archipelago, and to some extent among the early Celtic races of England and Scotland.

Concerning the merits of the matriarchal theory, we may say, as has been said of the patriarchal theory, that the historical proof of the universality of the matriarchal family among primitive peoples is lacking. Doubtless both theories account for the genesis of particular state organizations, though even then we must take into consideration other forces and elements which enter into the process of political organization.

Our knowledge of the social institutions of primitive peoples in historic times makes it impossible to believe that either type of family prevailed universally in ancient times, or indeed that the state should have developed through the enlargement and expansion of either. The family and the state are totally different in essence, organization, functions, and purpose, and there is little reason to suppose that one should have developed out of the other or that there should have been any connection between them.

THE FORCE THEORY

A theory advocated by some writers is that which attributes the institution of the state to compulsion, as where a powerful individual, through sheer physical strength or preeminence of leadership, brings under his subjection people hitherto unorganized politically and imposes upon them his authority. Thus Hume, in his "Original Contract, "holds that the state came into existence when a tribal chieftain or other leader who had acquired great influence over his followers during war maintained his control over them after the restoration of peace.

At first he may have ruled by persuasion rather than by command, until he could employ force to reduce to subjection the refractory and disobedient. Manifest necessity, the theory holds, would prompt those who fought on the same side to array themselves under one leader. Having led his followers to victory, he naturally enjoyed a prestige and wielded an influence that enabled him to establish and perpetuate his control over them in civil affairs.

As an explanation of how the state originated, the force theory has few advocates to-day among political writers; yet as an explanation of the basis of state authority it is, of course, largely correct. If it meant nothing more than that force and power are the most distinctive characteristics of the state, in short, that the state, unlike all other associations of mankind, possesses the power to compel obedience from its members, no objection could be made to it. It undoubtedly possesses, as Bluntschli remarks, a "residuum of truth "in the prominence which it gives to an indispensable element in the constitution of the state (*Macht*), and he might have added it tends to correct the false impression often created by the contract theory, that political authority always rests upon the voluntary consent of those who are subject to it.

Force and compulsion have played an important part in the consolidation of states and in the erection of new state forms. Some of the greatest empires of to-day have been established through "blood and iron, "and it is not altogether improbable that we shall see more of blood and iron methods in the future. In this sense, as McKechnie remarks, all constitutions and governments founded on the idea of authority are really modifications of the theory of force..

THE HISTORICAL OR EVOLUTION THEORY

We are therefore led to the conclusion that the state is neither the handiwork of God, nor the result of superior physical force, nor the creation of resolution or convention, nor a mere expansion of the family. Unlike the contrivance or agency through which it manifests itself and which we call government, the state is not a mere artificial mechanical creation, but an institution of natural growth, of historical evolution.

The idea is well stated by a high authority as follows: "The proposition that the state is the product of history means that it is the gradual and continuous development of human society, out of a grossly imperfect beginning, through crude but improving forms of manifestation, towards a perfect and universal organization of mankind.

It means, to go a little deeper into the psychology of the subject, that it is the gradual realization, in legal institutions, of the universal principles of human nature, and the gradual subordination of the individual side of that nature to the universal side. "As Burgess aptly remarks, the light of political consciousness did not dawn upon men in a state of nature all at once, and hence the decision to establish the state could not have been sudden and deliberate, as the contract theory presupposes.

The idea of the state must have required a long period for its development among a people unaccustomed to political authority and unacquainted with the nature and forms of political organization. Political self-consciousness, wholly lacking at first, in time appeared in the minds of a few of the natural leaders, then it spread by degrees throughout the mass of the population and finally became general. At first the state came into existence merely as an idea, that is, it appeared in a subjective form, without being a physical fact. Before its manifestations could be felt and its ends realized it must have an objective existence in institutions and laws.

In short, a constitution expressing the collective will must be created and then a magistracy must be established in accordance with the constitution. Historically, this marks the starting point for the state, but for political philosophy it is but an episode, a stage of development, in the transition from natural to civil society. "The solemn adoption by a people, "says an able writer, "of such a fundamental instrument is but the act through which that which has formerly existed in a more or less undefined and vague state is brought into a definite and positive state.

"The state exists in subjective form as soon as the common consciousness reaches that stage of development from which we may date the beginning of the movement which culminates in the formal institution of political authority. This point may in fact be reached long before the state is known and understood. The clothing of the state with the external forms of organization is not the final stage in the process, for the simple and rudimentary character which it takes in the beginning must go on developing and expanding as the political consciousness spreads among the masses of the people. With advancing civilization it tends to become more complex in form, more universal in its range of activities, more indispensable to the needs of mankind. But it never attains its final and complete development.

Rightly understood, all of the best elements in the several theories discussed above enter into the historical the. ory. The divine element appears in the fact that the Creator has implanted in the human breast the impulse which leads to association, and in the part played by religion in bringing primitive man out of barbarism and accustoming him to law and authority.

The element of compulsion exercised by those who possess natural superiority is a powerful ally of both religion and evolution in bringing the natural man into political and social relationship with his fellows.

Finally, the elements of contract and consent which lie at the basis of all association play an important part in the process of establishing and reorganizing particular governments.

No one of these elements alone accounts for the existence of the state, but all working together, some more prominently than others; and all, aided by the forces of history and the natural tendencies of mankind, enter into the process by which uncivilized peoples are brought out of anarchy and subjected to the authority of the state.

Chapter 5

Forms of State and Associations of States

PRINCIPLES OF CLASSIFICATION

So far as their legal nature and their fundamental purposes are concerned, all states are essentially alike and permit of little or no differentiation. In other respects, however, they possess elements of difference, like objects of nature, and may be classified from various points of view.

Thus, as regards the form of their constitutions, their governmental organizations, their territorial area, the extent of their resources, the degree of influence which they exert in the political affairs of the world, etc., they present a multitudinous variety of types. From the viewpoint of territorial area the types range all the way from petty principalities to vast empires embracing as much as one eighth of the earth's surface.

From the standpoint of their military and naval strength and of their influence in international relations they may be classified as the "great powers "and the "lesser powers, "though legally they all stand on a footing of equality.

In a treatise on political science, however, classifications based on territorial area, population, resources, and similar characteristics have little value. Such classifications, for example, as agricultural, commercial, and industrial states have no more interest for the political scientist than a classification of animals on the basis of size, strength, or colour has for the natural scientist. For our purpose, the basis of classification must be some scientific principle, some juristic or political characteristic, which will serve to distinguish states in their essence and fundamental constitution.

Two such principles or bases of classification have commended themselves to writers on political science. They are: first, the form of governmental organization through which the state manifests itself; and second, the number of persons in whom the sovereign power of the state rests. Classification on the basis of forms of government has been a favorite, if not the accepted, principle among political writers; but it is open to the objection of being unscientific and, to some extent, illogical.

To classify states on the basis of the nature and forms of their governments is very much like classifying railroads, for example, with respect to the organization of their boards of directors. Such a classification in its last analysis is nothing more than a classification of governments, not a classification of states.

Strict logic, therefore, would seem to require an observance of the distinction between states and their governments, and a classification of each on the basis of some distinctive characteristic of its own. Much confusion and misconception have resulted from the failure to observe this important distinction. In this work, we shall, as far as possible, observe the distinction and shall consider first the forms of state.

MONARCHIES, ARISTOCRACIES, AND DEMOCRACIES

On the basis of the number of persons in whom the sovereign power is vested states may be classified as monarchies, aristocracies, and democracies. A monarchy is a state directed by a single supreme will; an aristocracy is one in which the exercise of sovereignty resides in a comparatively small number of persons; while a democracy is one in which the exercise of sovereignty rests with the mass of the population. This was the famous classification of Aristotle and in substance it was adopted by Cicero, Polybius, and other ancient political writers. In his "*Politics* "Aristotle, apparently without distinguishing between state and government, said: "We usually call a state which is governed by one person for the common good, a monarchy; one that is governed by more than one, but by a few only, an aristocracy....

When the citizens at large govern for the public good it is called a polity, which is also a common name for all other governments. "Aristotle further subdivided each of the above forms on the basis of the manner or motive according to which the sovereignty was exercised. Thus, according to him, there were three pure or normal forms and three corrupt or abnormal types.

In a pure monarchy the power of the state is completely identified with the person of the individual who is the bearer of the sovereignty; he is not sovereign one moment and subject the next; he is always the state. The old Roman maxim, Quod principi placuit legis habet vigorem, and the more modern French proverb, Qui veut le roi, si veul la loi, fully describe the attributes of a real monarch.

In strictness there can be no such thing as a limited monarchical state, for all states are legally absolute and unlimited. There may, however, be limited monarchical governments. The so-called limited monarchical state is in fact a democratic or aristocratic state having a constitutional government in which the executive power is vested in a monarch.

The Aristotelian classification has been criticised on several grounds. In the first place, the classification, it is said, does not rest on any organic fundamental principle, but upon mere numbers and hence is mechanical rather than spiritual, quantitative rather than qualitative in character. The answer which has been made to this criticism is that the number of ruling persons may indicate the degree to which political self-consciousness has spread among the population and hence the capacity of the people for self-government.

Professor Seeley criticised Aristotle's classification on the ground that it was scarcely applicable to the states with which we have to deal to-day. In view of the "marvelous difference "between the "country states "of the present and the city states of Aristotle's day, said Seeley, they cannot be placed in the same class.

In essence, however, the states of antiquity were not different from those of to-day, though of course there was a wide difference in the form and character of their governments. Again, it is objected that since there are practically no civilized states to-day in which actual sovereignty, political as well as legal, is reposed in a single person or a small class, the classification of states on the basis of the location of sovereignty is practically worthless.

Furthermore, the attempt to distinguish between aristocracies and democracies must inevitably lead to hair-splitting, since there is no fixed criterion for determining where the one ends and the other begins. Moreover, a practical difficulty is encountered when we attempt to apply such a principle of classification to a state like Great Britain, where the legal sovereignty is in the legislature, and the political sovereignty is in the electorate.

On the former basis England would have to be classed as an aristocratic state; on the latter as a democratic state, though it is officially and popularly styled a monarchy. But if the Aristotelian classification be confined to its original meaning, the objections will not appear so well founded as they seem. Most of the confusion has arisen from the failure to discriminate between forms of state and forms of government, and from the practice of treating as monarchies all states that have hereditary executives, however democratic they may be otherwise.

Such usage puts into the same class states as widely different as Great Britain and Turkey, and in different classes those so nearly alike as Great Britain and the United States. If rightly applied, the Aristotelian principle will not produce any such absurd classifications.

THEOCRACIES

The so-called theocratic state is one in which the ultimate sovereignty is attributed to some superhuman or spiritual being. German writers on the state generally distinguish between two types of theocracy, the *pure* form and the *dualistic* or *limited* form. The pure theocracy is one in which the supernatural person to whom the sovereignty is attributed is alleged to rule directly and immediately without the aid of human intermediaries.

The limited or dualistic theocracy is described as one in which the immediate ruler is not God, but a human king who rules as his vicegerent and acts as the interpreter of the divine will, which is made known to him by revelation. He is guided and directed by God, to whom alone he is responsible. In the dualistic theocracy there is a separation between religious and civil affairs, each being administered by different authorities. The pure theocracy belongs to the most primitive stage of society; the dualistic type to a later, though still somewhat undeveloped, stage.

Bluntschli gives as examples of pure theocracies Ethiopia, ancient Egypt, Persia, and the kingdom of the Jews. To this list Von Mohl adds ancient Mexico and Peru. The Mohammedan states of the Middle Ages were also largely theocratic in character.

Mohammed considered himself the vicegerent of God, and the Koran contained the law and jurisprudence by which his people were governed. The caliph was both emperor and pope, and religious and temporal affairs were not clearly differentiated from one another. Other states of Europe until comparatively recent times possessed theocratic elements; and, as is well known, some of the early communities of North America were founded on a religious basis.

The so-called theocracy was one of the most common forms of primitive state organization and was well adapted to the infancy of political communities, since religion is the most powerful agency for organizing and fixing to the soil wandering, barbaric tribes, inculcating in them respect for authority and placing them in a position of receptivity for civilization.

It was religious influences that led the Teutons along the path of civilization and brought them under the yoke of law, that lay behind the political organization of western Europe by the Carolingians, that promoted the organization of the scattered tribes of Russia into a state; and it is to-day very largely the power which secures the attachment and loyalty of the masses to the Russian throne.

In the same way it was Mohammedanism that wrought the feeble states of Islam into a mighty state organization, which founded populous cities and overthrew empires. It would be easy to show that the English state had its roots in the church. For a long time the alliance between church and state was the main support of the state; indeed down to the reign of Anne, says Seeley, the English church was the English state in a certain sense.

For many centuries the church continued to exercise a wide degree of civil jurisdiction, and churchmen enjoyed equal authority with the officials of the state in the performance of the various secular functions. But as time passed the state everywhere tended to become more and more secularized, came to lean less upon the support of the church, and finally was able to support itself without religious props.

"Theocracies and despotisms, "observes an able writer, "have their place in the historical development of the state; and their work is as indispensable in the production of political civilization as is that of any other form of organization. We have not done with them yet, either.

The need of them repeats itself wherever and whenever a population is to be dragged out of barbarism up to the lowest plane of civilization. "Juridically, however, the theocracy is not a distinct form of state, but is either a form of monarchy or aristocracy. The sovereignty may be imputed to God or some other extramundane power, but the fact remains that whoever, whether priest or prophet, in the final analysis, interprets the will of this supernatural authority and enforces its commands, is, so far as political science and constitutional law are concerned, the actual legal sovereign.

Ultimately God may be the ruler and source of authority, but his power must be humanly interpreted, made known, and immediately exercised through human agencies. The so-called theocratic state must, therefore, according to the basis of classification which we have laid down as the correct one, be either a monarchy or an aristocracy.

OTHER CLASSIFICATIONS

Many attempts have been made by later writers to improve on Aristotle's classification. Thus, Machiavelli and Montesquieu classified states as monarchies and republics, and this classification has been followed by a number of recent scholars. The German scholar Waitz classified states as republics, theocracies, kingdoms, unitary states, composite or compound states, federal states, and confederations. Von Haller classified them as principalities and free communities, the latter being subdivided into patrimonial states, priestly states, and military states.

Gareis, a more recent German writer on political science, recognizes two general types of state: the unitary state and the composite state. The first is the simplest form of state, though it may be divided for convenience of administration into provinces, districts, etc., having little or no local autonomy. The composite state is one composed of communities which themselves have certain of the characteristics of states. Composite states, says Gareis, are of three kinds: real unions, federal unions, and confederations. This classification is followed by many writers, especially those on international law. Pradier-Fodere, a noted French publicist, classified states as separate or independent and as united. The first class he subdivided into

- Personal unions,
- Real unions,
- Incorporate unions.

The second group he subdivided into

- Confederate states and
- Federal states.

One of the most distinguished German writers, Robert von Mohl, in his "Encyclopedia of the Political Sciences, "written about the middle of the nineteenth century, attempted a most elaborate classification of states, though without reference to any single consistent principle or criterion. His classification was as follows: first, patriarchal states; second, theocracies, or those which have a religious purpose and which are under the guidance and direction of a supernatural power; third, patrimonial states; fourth, classic or antique states, such as those of early Greece and Rome; fifth, legal states, or those whose sphere of action is determined by law and whose activites are regulated by legal norms; and sixth, despotic states, or those which are ruled without regard to the prescriptions of law.

Von Mohl recognized also a form which he called the military vassal state, and he subdivided classic states into monarchies, aristocracies, and democracies. An examination of Von Mohl's classification will show, as has been said, that it is based upon no single logical or scientific principle. Some of the forms which he enumerates overlap one another, while others are wholly inapplicable to the states of the present day. Thus, the patriarchal state is at the same time a monarchy and so is the theocracy, the despotism, and the patrimonial state.

Moreover, all states are despotic in the purely legal sense, and all states are legal states in the sense that they are the source of law and govern according to the prescriptions of law. To classify states as "classic "or antique is about as logical and scientific as to classify them as "territorial "states, "human "states, "medieval "states, "modern "states, etc. Such terms do not belong properly to the nomenclature of political science, but to that of literature and history, and hence such classifications have little or no scientific or practical value.

Bluntschli conceived the "fundamental "forms of state to be four in number: monarchy, aristocracy, democracy, and ideocracy or theocracy, the last in its perverted form being styled by him an idolocracy. In addition, he recognized a group of "secondary "forms which he considered necessary to complete the Aristotelian classification, namely, free, half-free, and unfree states.

Theocracies, he said, tend to become unfree states; aristocracies "gravitate "toward the half-free class; while democracies naturally belong to the free 'type, although they may become despotisms. Furthermore, he added confusion by attempting to classify states as civilized monarchies, patriarchal kingships, feudal monarchies, military and judicial principalities, absolute, limited, and constitutional monarchies, compound states, mixed states, and various others.

Some writers have recognized the existence of a mixed state made up of a combination of monarchical, aristocratic, and democratic elements. Aristotle himself seems to have considered the ideal polity to be a "mixture "of oligarchy and democracy. Rome was cited by both Cicero and Polybius as an example of the mixed type, being composed of monarchic, aristocratic, and democratic elements, and Cicero considered the best state to be the mixed form.

Blackstone and Rousseau are sometimes cited as recognizing the mixed form, but it is clear froman examination of their classifications that they were thinking of forms of government rather than of forms of state. Bluntschli defined a mixed state as "one in which monarchy, aristocracy, or democracy is moderated or limited by other political factors, "as, for example, a monarchy which is limited by an aristocratic senate or by the people acting through a primary or a representative body.

But obviously such a combination is nothing more than a form of government, not a form of state. Bluntschli indeed admitted that such a "mixture does not create a new form of state, for the sovereignty is still in the monarch, the aristocracy, or the people. "The truth is, there can be no such thing as a mixed state. The state is a unity; its attributes are incapable of combination and intermixture. A monarch and an aristocratic body cannot both be sovereign at the same time, and hence the state cannot be a monarchy and an aristocracy at the same time any more than a number can be at once singular and plural.

SIMPLE AND COMPOSITE STATES; PERSONAL AND REAL UNIONS

Many writers, as has been said, classify states as simple and composite. A simple state is one which has a single supreme government and exerts a single will, whether it be that of an individual or an assembly. It may for convenience of administration be subdivided into provinces, departments, communes, counties, etc.; or it may possess non-contiguous territories, such as colonies and dependencies; or it may even include territorial divisions that were formerly independent states, like Ireland and Scotland.

But so long as the subdivisions are legally nothing but historical or administrative circumscriptions without an extensive local autonomy as of right, the state is simple in form. Such a Commonwealth is sometimes described as a unitary state because the governmental organization is a unit rather than dualistic or federal in character. The administrative districts into which such a state is divided possess neither the name, the traditions, nor the characteristics of states, and whatever powers of government they exercise or whatever rights of autonomy they possess are delegated to them by the central government, and may be modified or withdrawn at its pleasure.

The empires and kingdoms of Europe with their vast outlying possessions, to which are delegated important powers of local government, are nothing but unitary states, because the local governmental organizations are the creations of one central power, which determines their competence and to which in the last analysis they are completely subject.

Where two or more states, wholly separate and distinct in their external and internal relations, are associated together under the same reigning sovereign, we have what is called a personal union. The only bond of connection is the crown. Each of the associated states is entirely independent of the other; each has its own constitution and laws, its own distinct political organization, and its own citizenship and local institutions. The acts of their common sovereign in relation to each of the member states have no application within the territories of the other nor any binding effect upon its citizens.

Indeed the subjects or citizens of the one are foreigners to the other. Though physically the same person, the sovereign possesses two distinct legal personalities and may enjoy widely different powers and attributes in the different states composing the union.

He may be an absolute ruler in one and a constitutional ruler in the other. In international as well as internal relations each constitutes a distinct and separate personality, so much so that one might make war upon the other without affecting the union, or declare war against a third power without involving the belligerency of its associate. The distinguishing characteristic of a personal union, says Hall, is that states employ for the time being the same agent for a particular class of purposes; but they are in no way bound by or responsible for each other's acts.

Such a condition may result from treaty stipulation or, as is more commonly the case, from the operation of identical succession laws which fix the crown upon the same dynasty. In the latter case the union necessarily ceases with the extinction of the dynasty, each state then being free to choose a different sovereign. It may also happen that the reigning sovereign of one state is formally chosen by another state to rule over it, in which case the union ceases with the death of the common ruler unless it is renewed by the joint election of a successor.

Likewise, if the ruling prince is overthrown by revolution in one state, and the succession thereby changed, the union is necessarily terminated. It may also be terminated where the law of succession is different, as, for example, where a woman should come to the throne in one of the states, but would be ineligible in the other.

Examples of personal unions were the union between Spain and the old German Empire under Charles V, 1520-1556; between England and Hanover from 1714 to 1837, terminated by the accession of Victoria as Queen of England, the laws of succession in Hanover not permitting females to succeed; between Holland and Luxembourg, 1815-1890; between Schleswig-Holstein and Denmark, 1776-1863; and finally, the general act of the Berlin Conference of 1885, followed by a Belgian law of the same year, which declared that the relation between the king of the Belgians and the Congo state should be exclusively personal in character. The so-called composite state is one composed of two or more states or of communities which have a wide autonomy as of right, and which often possess the name and always some of the characteristics of states. Pradier-Fodere describes it as a union of a "certain number of states which have internally independent governments though not individually sovereign. "It differs from the simple state in that it is itself constructed out of states, or at least out of communities which were once states and which are still organized like states and retain a limited international capacity.

The degree of sovereignty or local autonomy, as the case may be, which the component members retain, as well as the character of the international person which they collectively constitute, depends upon the nature of the act by which the union has been created. Composite states are usually classified as real unions, confederations, and federal unions and, some writers add, states maintaining protectorates and suzerainties.

A "real union "results from the joining together of two or more states, not merely through the employment of a common ruler, but through the creation of common constitutional or international arrangements for the administration of certain common affairs. Such a union occurs, says Hall, when states are indissolubly combined under the same monarch, their identity being merged in that of a common state for external purposes, though each may retain distinct internal laws and institutions.

It differs from the personal union in that the associated states or component members are organically united by constitutional bonds and have common organs of government and a single international personality for most purposes. It also possesses greater elements of permanence, its existence being unaffected by the death of the common sovereign or the extinction of the reigning dynasty.

The most notable example of a real union to-day is that between Austria and Hungary. The union between the kingdoms of Norway and Sweden from 1815 to 1905 was also an example. The former rests upon constitutional compact, the act of union being embodied in a pair of identical statutes adopted by the parliaments of the two states in 1867.

They not only have the same ruling sovereign (who, it may be observed, enjoys different titles and dignities in the two states and is crowned separately in each), but a common legislative body for limited purposes, a common army organized on the same basis and commanded in a common language, a common diplomatic service, a common court of accounts, a common tariff and trade union, and common ministries of war, finance, and foreign affairs. The expense of the joint administration is borne by the two states according to a proportion agreed upon by them. In international intercourse the union represents a single personality, though for most purposes of internal administration each state retains its own sovereignty and independence.

The terms of the agreement by which Norway and Sweden were joined were embodied in a treaty of August 6, 1815. According to the agreement Norway recognized the king of Sweden as its sovereign and representative in international relations, though the constitution of Norway expressly declared that Norway should remain a "free, independent, and indivisible empire.

"The treaty of union regulated the procedure to be followed in both kingdoms for the election of the successor of their common sovereign. The two states maintained a common diplomatic and consular service, though, unlike the Austro-Hungarian arrangement, their foreign relations were not conducted through the agency of a common Norwegian-Swedish ministry, but through the Swedish foreign minister, who managed the external affairs of both states.

The two states had different commercial and naval flags and distinct systems of internal administration; and each had its own army under the command and direction of the joint king. Unlike the Austro-Hungarian union, there was nothing in the nature of a common legislative assembly, nor were there any joint ministries of state.

Matters of common interest, which could not be regulated by the joint king, were dealt with by the concurrent action of the parliaments of the two kingdoms. The joint arrangements were indeed so few and unimportant that some writers have treated the relation as simply that of a personal union, though this is incorrect, since the perpetuity of the union did not depend upon any dynasty or law of succession. The increasing dissatisfaction of Norway and its desire for a real joint ministry of foreign affairs and a separate consular system led to the disruption of the union in 1905 by the secession of Norway and the conclusion between the two states of a treaty of permanent separation.

CONFEDERATIONS

"A confederation, "says Hall, "is a union strictly of independent states which consent to forego permanently a part of their liberty of action for certain specific objects, and they are not so combined under a common government that the latter appears to their exclusion as the international entity. "It is a permanent association of states for the joint exercise of their rights of sovereignty for the common advantage.

It differs from a mere alliance in having a fixed central organ for ascertaining and giving effect to the wills of the component states, in the greater variety of its objects, and in the intent of perpetuity. But, says Austin, a system of confederated states and a number of independent states connected by an ordinary alliance cannot be distinguished precisely through general or abstract expression. The former is intended to be permanent, the latter temporary; while the ends or purposes embraced by the compact are commonly more numerous and more complicated than in the case of the temporary alliance.

Though popularly treated as a form of state, a confederation is in fact no state, but a league or a band of states rather than a "banded state ". The component members of a confederation retain their internal sovereignty, dignity, and political organizations and, to a greater or less extent, their external sovereignty. They are therefore real states, not mere administrative circumscriptions with a limited local autonomy, and their relations to one another are of an international character. There is no single sovereignty, but as many sovereignties as there are states composing the confederation. Confederations rest on compact or articles of agreement rather than upon constitutional law.

They have only a limited juristic personality and then mainly in international relations. They have as such no citizens or subjects to whom their commands can be directly addressed, or from whom obligations or duties may be required. Being composed of sovereign states, their governmental organizations rarely operate directly upon individuals, but reach them only through the medium of the state organizations.

The will of the confederation is but the sum total of the wills of the component states, and is expressed, not in statutes framed by a real legislative body, but in ordinances or resolutions framed by a quasi-diplomatic body consisting of plenipotentiaries representing the governments of the several states composing the confederation. These plenipotentiaries usually vote by states and according to the instructions of the governments which they represent.

Their resolutions have no binding effect upon individuals as such, but are addressed, as already said, to the organizations of the component states, and are usually inoperative until adopted by their governments and given the force of law within their jurisdictions.

The congress or diet of a confederation has no power to enforce its resolutions except by "federal execution, "that is, by the use of force against a recalcitrant member. Most of the confederations in the past have in fact had no executive or judicial machinery, and have therefore been compelled to rely upon the good faith of the member states to enforce their commands.

Usually the component members are free to withdraw at will and thus dissolve the confederation, and the confederate authorities have no constitutional power to restrain a disaffected member and compel it to remain in the confederation against its will.

History abounds in examples of confederations, for the

tendency of neighboring states to associate themselves together for purposes of defense and for the furthering of their common interests has proved to be almost as strong as the social impulse among individuals.

Among the ancient Greeks, confederations were numerous, the more important being the Delian, Lykian, Achaean leagues. In some cases the component members were federated together much more closely than in others. The constitution of the Achaean League, for instance, provided for a common executive magistracy, a legislative body, and even a rudimentary judiciary.

Its organization was, in fact, so highly developed that it is considered by some writers to have been essentially a federal union rather than a confederation. Leagues and confederations among the early Italian cities were not uncommon, though they never attained the perfection and degree of importance of those of Greece. During the medieval period several important federations were formed, among which may be mentioned the Rhenish Confederation, which eventually embraced some seventy members.

Then came the Hanseatic League, which was originally organized for the promotion and protection of trade, but which gradually developed into a great political power that waged war and negotiated treaties, and eventually came to exercise an important influence on the international affairs of Europe.

It had a sort of central legislative organ and a crude judicial machinery for the adjudication of disputes among the members. The Holy Roman Empire, the most extensive federation formed before the nineteenth century, eventually embraced several hundred states of varying types and importance — free cities, ecclesiastical territories, and hereditary monarchies.

It maintained a common Diet and several imperial courts. Other examples were: the Swiss confederations of 1291-1798 and 1803-1848, which grew out of the union of three small cantons, but which in the course of time came to embrace all of them; and the United Netherlands, 1576-1746, composed of the Dutch provinces.

The two best-known modern examples of confederations were the United States of America from 1781 to 1789 and the German Confederation, 1815-1866. The former turned out to be little more than what the articles of union described it to be, namely, a "firm league of friendship "among the states composing it.

It was expressly declared in the articles of agreement that each member of the confederation retained its sovereignty, freedom, and independence and every power, jurisdiction, and right not expressly delegated to the confederation. Its avowed object was to provide common protection against attack upon any or all of the states.

The collective will of the confederation was ascertained and expressed through a congress of delegates constituted without any reference to the populations of the component states. No common administrative or judicial organs were created, the enforcement of the resolutions of the congress being left to the individual states. The powers conferred upon the general congress were so meager and the means of enforcing its will so inadequate that it perished, to use the language of De Tocqueville, through the excessive weakness of its government.

The German Confederation embraced at first thirtyeight states of varying rank and importance — kingdoms, grand duchies, principalities, and free cities. It was declared to be a "perpetual league "for the purpose of preserving "the external and internal security of Germany and the independence and inviolability of the confederate states.

"The collective will of the members was expressed through a Diet of plenipotentiaries which sat at Frankfort under the presidency of Austria. They were appointed by the governments of the states which they represented, and voted according to instructions. The Diet had the power to send and receive ambassadors, to declare war and conclude peace in the name of the confederation, and, under certain conditions, to intervene in the affairs of the individual states.

Each state, however, retained the right of legation and could enter into foreign alliances, provided they were not directed against the security of the confederation or of any one of the component states. In case war was declared by the confederation, no state could conclude peace without the consent of the confederation.

No member of the confederation could make war against another member, and in case of differences between them the disputes were to be submitted to the decision of the Diet. There was an imperial court which had a limited jurisdiction, but there was no common administrative machinery, the enforcement of the resolutions of the Diet being left mainly to the individual states.

FEDERAL UNIONS

Where several states unite themselves together under a common sovereignty and establish a common central government for the administration of certain affairs of general concern, or where a number of provinces or dependencies are similarly united by their common superior, the component members still retaining a large local autonomy, but surrendering the management of the whole or nearly the whole of their external affairs to the central government, we have a federal union, or, as is often said, a federal state.

The historian Freeman, writing in 1863, said that the four most famous federal commonwealths of history were: the Achaean League in the later days of ancient Greece; the Confederation of Swiss cantons from 1291 to the present; the United Provinces of the Netherlands, 1579-1795; and the United States of America, 1789-1863, which Freeman predicted was at that time nearing its end.

The first and last mentioned, he said, represented the"most perfect development of the federal principle which the world has ever seen, "though there were several ancient confederations "whose constitutions must have realized the federal idea almost as perfectly as the more famous league of Achaea.

Strictly speaking, however, there can be no such thing as a federal state. What is popularly called a federal state is in fact a democratic or aristocratic state having a federal system of government, that is, a dual form of government under a common sovereignty. In this chapter, therefore, our discussion will be restricted mainly to a description of the legal nature of the association created by a union of states under a federal organization, and the discussion of its governmental system will be reserved for the chapter on "Forms of Government.

The historian Freeman, who employs the terms "federal government "and "federal state "without discrimination, says, "The name federal government may be applied to any union of component members where the degree of union between the members surpasses that of more alliance, however intimate, and where the degree of independence possessed by each member surpasses anything which can fairly come under the head of mere municipal freedom.

"Again, he observes that a "federal commonwealth in its perfect form is one which forms a single state in its relations to other nations, but which consists of many states with regard to its internal government.

Ordinarily the distinguishing marks of a federal union are: first, the existence of a number of political communities possessing of right their own constitutions and forms of government, and being supreme within a certain more or less extensive sphere reserved by their own action; and, second, a common constitution and government, for the direct administration of certain general concerns.

Unlike a confederation, a federal union is not a mere league of independent states associated together for purposes mainly of common defense, but it is a union resulting from the merger of a number of political communities for the regulation of various matters common to all the component members. It is a sort of composite state, a new creation of constitutional law, not a band of states connected together by international agreement.

The act by which a federal union is established is not a mere compact, but a constitution. In its external relations it resembles a "real union, "while internally it bears some resemblance to a confederation. On its international side, observes Hall, it consists of a central government to which the conduct of all external relations is confided and in the absence of any right on the part of the states to separate themselves from it. 1 It differs from a confederation in the character and degree of the relationship subsisting between the members composing the union and in the possession by the former of a central organization endowed not only with practically exclusive powers in relation to foreign affairs, but also with important powers of government as regards internal affairs of common concern. In a federal union the component parts are subject to a common sovereign, and collectively they form a single united state.

In a confederation the parts have no common sovereign, and they do not constitute a single political society, but each is itself a sovereignty. In the federal system there is but one real state, one central government and a number of local governments; in short, the state is coextensive in organization with the organization of the central government. In the confederate system, on the contrary, there are as many states as there are component members.

Some writers, like Freeman, De Tocqueville, John Stuart Mill, Wheaton, and the authors of "*The Federalist*, "distinguish between *perfect* and *imperfect* federal unions. The difference is one mainly of degree. The former is one which contains no elements of confederatism.

It is one in which the central government is fully supreme in all external affairs and in certain specified internal affairs of general concern; which acts directly and immediately upon all individuals within the federation; and which possesses the power and means of enforcing its own declared will. This is what the German writer Brie calls the "ideal federal state. "2 An imperfect federal union is one in which remnants of confederatism survive, one, in short, which is organized more like a confederation than a unitary state.

The component states possess a limited power in the management of foreign affairs; the acts of the central government are enforced by the individual state governments and "its powers consist simply in issuing requisitions to the state governments when, within the proper limits of the federal authority, it is the duty of these governments to carry it out. "The German Empire is a good example of what has been called an imperfect federal union.

The truth is, most federal unions belong to the imperfect type; that is, they represent a mixture of federalism and confederatism. Thus, in the organization of the German Empire the structure of the *Reichstag* and the judiciary is federal in character, while the *Bundesrath* is based on the confederate principle. The states composing the Empire retain a limited power of legation and of military administration, while the execution of the laws of the Empire devolves largely upon the local governments.

Certain of the states, moreover, are endowed with important special privileges of which they cannot be deprived without their own consent. These and other features give it a confederate character in a more marked degree than is found in any other existing federal system. The republic of the United States possesses also, though to a less extent, the qualities of both a federal union and a confederacy.

This was first pointed out by Madison, who showed that the constitution in its method of adoption, ratification, and amendment, as well as in the organization of the Senate, was confederate in principle, while as regards the sources of the powers of the government, the organization of the army, and the execution of the laws it was federal in character.

In its normal form the government of a federal union, as has been said, acts upon individuals rather than upon the component state organizations; its will is exerted immediately and directly upon the citizens who compose it, and does not reach them simply through the medium of the local governments. Unlike the confederation, there is a general as well as a local citizenship, and all persons within the jurisdiction of the central government owe it direct and immediate allegiance.

If war breaks out among the component states, it is civil war, not international war. The component parts of a federal union may themselves be monarchies, or republics, or both; or they may be mere provinces or colonial dependencies, possessing a wide autonomy. Thus, the German federal empire is constructed out of kingdoms, grand duchies, principalities, and free cities. Switzerland is a federation of cantons, some of which have governments organized on the representative principle, others being pure democracies.

The federal union of the United States is composed partly of republics called "states, "and partly of dependencies called "territories. "All the component members (except the territories) are on a footing of equality, none of them enjoying special privileges such as are common in the German Empire. In Canada and some of the Latin-American federations the component parts are simply provinces with more autonomy than belongs to provinces of unitary states.

The communities of which federal unions are composed are not states in the strict sense of the term, though in most federal systems popular usage designates them as such. It is true, however, that in most cases these communities were originally sovereign and independent states, and when they became federated they naturally retained the name, a good deal of the dignity, the historical traditions, and even some of the powers of sovereign states. But, in reality, by the act of federation they lost their sovereignty and with it that quality which most distinguished them as states.

By merging their separate existences into a new and larger personality they became in strict law mere political units, non-sovereign communities, yet withal retaining a degree of local autonomy and of political importance which is not enjoyed by the administrative subdivisions of a unitary state. Unlike the latter they retain, as of right, their own constitutions, their own political arrangements, and the right to participate in the collective will.

While the view here expressed is that the component parts of a federal union are not in reality states, many writers, particularly among the Germans, hold the contrary opinion. They maintain that since the members of a federal union possess all the attributes and characteristics of real states except that of full sovereignty, they may properly be treated as states, rather than as mere administrative circumscriptions. Among the German writers who take this view are Laband, Jellinek, and Seydel. Laband, in explaining the juridical nature of the German federal empire, attributes to the component members the character of real states, while at the same time denying to them the possession of sovereignty.

His doctrine is based on the view that the distinguishing characteristic of the state is not sovereignty, but rather the power to command and enforce obedience, and since the individual members of a federal union possess such power, they may be rightfully designated as states.

But it may well be observed that if the power to lay down commands and compel obedience be a correct juristic test of the state character, it is difficult to avoid the conclusion that a province or a municipality has an equal claim to be considered a state. The possession of mere local autonomy or independence of action in certain matters — mere power in a local organization to express a will and enforce its commands — is not a mark of statehood. If a non-sovereign community may be rightfully treated as

a state, the distinction between states and mere administrative districts disappears or becomes very indistinct indeed. If, however, by the power to command and compel obedience is meant only original, underived, and independent power, then that is undoubtedly sovereignty — a power which the component parts of federal unions certainly do not possess. The individual members of a federal commonwealth have no power to determine their status in the union of which they are a part, or to alter their relations with one another or with the central organization, or to determine the extent of their own jurisdiction or sphere of action.

That power in the last analysis lies outside their jurisdiction and, wherever it resides, there is the state. In international relations they are non-entities; in internal affairs they are, legally speaking, nothing but widely autonomous, largely self-governing parts of a state. Whatever the historical process by which federal unions are created, whether, as Lincoln asserted of the American federal republic, they are older than the component parts or the reverse, the parts are the creations of the will of the people as a whole, and they continue to exist subject to that will. If they existed prior to the establishment of the union, they were re-created by the act through which it came into existence and were reinvested by it with the powers which they subsequently possessed.

Many writers have attempted to explain the relation between the federal union and its parts by attributing a portion of sovereignty to each. This theory assumes that sovereignty is capable of being divided and distributed at will. According to this view the state formed by the union of the parts is sovereign in respect to those matters which by the constitution are committed to its care, while the component members are equally sovereign with respect to those matters intrusted to them. In other words, each is sovereign within its constitutional sphere.

This view has been ably defended by such scholars as Waitz, S. Meyer, Schulze, Bluntschli, Gerber, Rüttiman, Von Mohl, and Treitschke in Germany; by Freeman and Oppenheim in England; by De Tocqueville and Rivier in France; and by Kent, Story, Cooley, and others in America. It is also the view that has been uniformly maintained by the United States Supreme Court. Since a discussion of this question would involve a consideration of the theory of divided sovereignty, it will be passed over until that subject is reached in the course of this work.

Federal states, so called, have usually been created in one of two ways: first, they have been formed by a voluntary coalescing of a number of sovereign and independent states; or, the federal system has been imposed from without, as where a unitary state has established federalism among the provinces of which it is composed. An example of the latter method was furnished by the creation of a federal republic out of the provinces of the Empire of Brazil in 1889.

A somewhat similar procedure was that by which the colonial provinces of British North America and the Australian Colonies were federated in 1867 and 1900 respectively. In both cases the federation was constructed, not out of already existing independent states, as was the case in the United States and Germany, but out of a group of colonial dependencies. Two conditions, observes Dicey, must be present in the formation of a federal union: first, there must be a body of communities (states, cantons, colonies, provinces) connected by locality, history, race, or the like, capable of bearing, in the eyes of their inhabitants, an impress of common nationality; second, there must exist a "very peculiar sentiment "among the inhabitants; that is, they must desire union without unity, must be able to adjust the conflicting ideas of union and separation and to reconcile the advantages of national union with the disadvantages of a division of a power and diversity of legislation.

There must be a wish to form for many purposes a single state without surrendering the individual existences of each. A "federal state "indeed is nothing more than a "political contrivance intended to reconcile national unity and power with the maintenance of state rights "through an adjustment satisfactory to both elements. 2 The history of federal states shows that they have generally been formed under the pressure of international necessity rather than under that of internal needs.

Whatever the method of procedure by which a federal union is established, there must be a common organic act or constitution defining the relation between the federated state and the parts of which it is composed, and marking out for each its own sphere of action. This constitution must be paramount in respect to the constitutions of the component members, otherwise the maintenance of the federation intact will be impossible. It is also essential

that this constitution should be written. The foundations of a federal state, to quote Dicey again, rest on a "complicated contract, "and the arrangements which it establishes cannot safely be left to mere understanding or convention. Its articles must therefore be reduced to writing, and they ought to be clearly and fully stated on all fundamental points so as to remove the possibility of misunderstanding. The failure to do this in the constitution of the United States left open important questions which became the source of long and violent controversy and ultimately of civil war. These articles should not only be written, but they should possess a certain degree of rigidity; that is, they should be rendered incapable of alteration by either the central or local governments, but should be alterable only by the power which created both and defined their spheres.

Finally, there ought to be a common tribunal empowered to interpret the prescriptions of the federal constitution, to judge of the limits of the respective spheres of the central and local governments, and to hold in restraint the tendencies of each to encroach upon the domain assigned by the constitution to the other. This tribunal should be empowered to determine all controversies among the component states themselves as well as between them and the central government, and it ought to have also the power to set aside the provision of any local constitution or law which is inconsistent with the constitution or laws of the union.

PART-SOVEREIGN STATES

Many writers, as has been said, treat as states for limited purposes certain communities not in the possession of full sovereignty, and hence they do not consider sovereignty an essential mark of the state, at least for international purposes. Communities of this kind, while dependent to a greater or less extent upon other states, nevertheless usually possess large powers of local self-government and a limited international personality. But if we observe strictly the test laid down in an earlier chapter for determining the state character, we cannot regard such communities as states, but only as dependencies or parts of other states.

The designation of states as part-sovereign is based upon the assumption that sovereignty is capable of being divided — a theory which the best writers regard as quite inadmissible, and the fallacy of which we shall endeavor to establish in our chapter on sovereignty.

Examples of so-called part-sovereign states, *Unterstaaten* as the Germans call them, are:

- The component members of federal unions;

- Communities under the suzerainty of other states; and
- Communities under the protection of other states.

The degree of autonomy possessed by each and its status as an international entity depend upon the particular circumstances of each case, there being no general rule governing the matter.

Regarding the first class of so-called part-sovereign states — the members of federal unions — we have already pointed out that rarely do they possess even the most limited international personality. Although they are often called states and regarded as real states by some German writers of high standing, yet the weight of the best scientific opinion is adverse to such a view.

The second group of so-called part-sovereign states, namely, communities under the suzerainty of other states, are, says Hall, portions of states which during a process of gradual disruption or by the grace of the sovereign have acquired certain of the powers of an independent community, such as that of making commercial conventions or of conferring their exequaturs upon foreign consuls. 1 The paramount state is called the suzerain, and its relation to the subject state is described by the term "suzerainty. "2 The relation between the suzerain state and the vassal state depends upon the circumstances of the particular case.

In general it may be said that the vassal community has only such rights as have been expressly granted to it by the paramount state. It always has a certain international capacity, but is subject to a greater or less extent to the paramount state in the management of its foreign affairs. It is, however, generally independent of foreign control as regards its internal affairs. In the conduct of the foreign relations of the dependency the suzerain may have the full power of initiation, or partial initiation, or only the negative power of veto over the acts of the vassal state.

Examples of communities under the control of a suzerain are Egypt and, until recently, Bulgaria. Egypt is a tributary and vassal state theoretically under the suzerainty of the

Ottoman Porte, but in fact it is under the administration of England. It has a hereditary ruler of its own, but he receives his investiture from the sultan.

It sends and receives consuls, who may bear the added title of diplomatic agent, and has the power to conclude commercial and postal treaties with foreign states without the consent of the suzerain. Bulgaria, by the Treaty of Berlin, 1878, was made a "tributary and autonomous principality "under the suzerainty of Turkey. Like Egypt, it had the power to send and receive consuls and diplomatic agents, and in 1885 it waged war against Servia without the consent of Turkey, although its right to do so was denied.

Bulgaria, however, has recently declared its independence of Turkey. Moldavia and Wallachia were also formerly under the suzerainty of Turkey. The former South African Republic under the suzeraintyof Great Britain was another example of this type of part-sovereign state. By a treaty of February 27, 1884, with Great Britain, it engaged to conclude no treaty with any other power than the Orange Free State without approval by the crown of England.

The suzerain status is usually temporary and is generally terminated by the action of the vassal in throwing off its dependence, as Roumania did in 1878 and as Bulgaria did in 1908; or by conquest and annexation by the suzerain, as was the case with the South African Republic during the late Boer War. The third form of the so-called part-sovereign state is the "protected state. ""For the purposes of international law, "says a noted authority, "a protected state is one which, in consequence of its weakness, has placed itself under the protection of another power on defined conditions or has been so placed under an arrangement between powers the interests of which are involved in the disposition.

"Unlike a community under the suzerainty of another state, the rights of a protected state are rather residuary than delegated in their nature, and the presumption therefore is in favor of any international capacity claimed by it. Unlike a suzerain community, also, a protected state always retains a certain international capacity and is, therefore, a subject of international law. The establishment of a protectorate usually takes place when a weak state places itself under the guardianship and protection of a more powerful state, handing over to the latter the management of its more important foreign relations.

The most recent example of the kind was the establish. ment of a protectorate by Japan over Korea in 1904. The degree of the control exercised by the protecting state varies widely and depends upon the particular facts of each case, the terms and conditions upon which the protectorate is maintained being embodied in a treaty between the protected state and the protector.

Some, like the French protectorate of Indo-China, are nothing more than colonies; while others have practically complete control over their internal and external affairs. The citizens or subjects of a protected state retain their own distinct nationality, and must remain neutral in a war between the protecting state and a third power.

In the case of the Ionian Islands, which were under the protection of Great Britain from 1815 to 1863, the control exercised by the protector included only the management of the foreign relations of the islands and the appointment of the executive. The islands were declared to be a "free and independent state, "were not included in British treaties unless especially named, received consuls from other states, and had their own commercial flag.

The only protected states in Europe to-day are the petty republics of Andorra, under the joint protection of France and Spain, and of San Marino, under the protection of Italy, and possibly the principality of Monaco, which is theoretically under the protection of Italy. Inasmuch, however, as the right of protection in the latter case has not been exercised since the establishment of the Italian kingdom, Monaco is claimed by some to be an independent state.

In Africa there are various petty states under the protection of European powers, among which may be mentioned Zanzibar and Tunis, under the protection of Great Britain and France respectively. Until 1896 Madagascar was a French protectorate, but in that year it was annexed to France as a colony.

INEUTRALIZED STATES

A state whose independence and integrity have been guaranteed by the joint action of other states and placed in a condition in which it is forbidden to engage in offensive war is said to be neutralized. Its immunity from attack on the part of other states is usually guaranteed by way of compensation for the restriction placed upon its freedom of action with regard to making offensive war.

The status of neutralization may be conferred upon a weak state at its own request as a means of protection against ambitious and unscrupulous neighbors; or it may be conferred without regard to its own wishes by other states out of considerations affecting the general peace or the balance of power. Small states so geographically situated that they are in danger of being overrun by contending armies and of having their neutrality otherwise disregarded by opposing belligerents, are those which have usually been neutralized by the collective action of other states. The method by which neutralization takes place is usually by international treaty between the powers concerned.

The state so neutralized must abstain from engaging in hostilities against other states except as a matter of defense and must avoid any act which would involve it in war with another state. In all other respects it is fully sovereign and independent, and can enter into treaties of all kinds, except possibly those of alliance and guarantee, and can of course maintain armies and navies for purposes of defense.

Examples of neutralized states are: Switzerland, whose permanent neutrality was recognized and guaranteed by the Powers through the act of the Vienna Congress in 1815; Belgium, whose neutrality was guaranteed by the Treaty of London in 1831 and renewed by a similar treaty in 1839; the Grand Duchy of Luxembourg, neutralized by the Treaty of London in 1867; and the Congo Free State, whose neutrality the signatory powers of the General Act of the Berlin Congo

Conference of 1885 agreed to "respect "provided the power in possession of the Congo territory should proclaim its neutrality.

This the king of the Belgians did, and his act was recognized by the powers. Finally, by a treaty signed at Christiania, November 2, 1907, Great Britain, France, Germany, and Russia, "animated by a desire to secure to Norway... her independence and territorial integrity, as also the benefits of peace, "obligated themselves to "recognize and respect "the integrity of Norway, and agreed in case the integrity of the Norwegian kingdom was "threatened or impaired by any power whatsoever, "they would afford the Norwegian government their support with a view to safeguarding the integrity. Norway was also a party to the treaty, and agreed not to cede any portion of its territory to any power.

INTERNATIONAL UNIONS

For the accomplishment of certain common objects and the promotion of mutual interests, states not infrequently associate themselves by formal agreement into unions. Such unions in the past have been numerous and diverse in character. They have differed not only as regards their legal nature, but also as regards their purposes, objects, and duration.

Juristically considered, the basis of the union may be: first, the principle of equality or coordination, according to which each member retains its sovereignty and independence unrestricted; second, the principle of inequality according to which some of the members stand in the relation of superiority to others, the latter occupying a status of subordination; and, third, the principle of equality among the associated members, all of which have the same power, but are subordinate to a central government.

According to Brie and Jellinek international unions may again be classified as *unorganized* and *organized*. An unorganized union is one in which more or less permanent relations are established for the promotion of common policies or the maintenance of certain relations, but in which there is no common governmental organization for the exercise of a common will, or for purposes of administration. Jellinek enumerates as examples of unorganized unions: alliances of various kinds, leagues of friendship, loosely connected federations, and a certain kind of composite state which he describes by the term *Staatenstaat*; that is, a so-called state composed not of individuals, but of inferior states, which receive their powers from a superior. Examples of the *Staatenstaat* were the feudal states of the Middle Ages and the old German Empire after the Peace of Westphalia.

Other examples were the Christian states of the Mohammedan Empire; the vassal states of the Ottoman Porte, such as Egypt and Tunis; such relationships as those between the United States and the Indian tribes, and between Nicaragua and the Mosquito Coast; the tributary states of Asia; the native states of India; the relation of Holland to Java; the relation between China and Siam; etc.

The organized union differs from the unorganized union in possessing the element of permanency, an independent administrative organ, and a common will. Examples of this type of union are:

- The various international administrative unions;
- Real unions;
- Confederations; and
- Federal unions

Of these all except the first mentioned have already been described.

Among the more important international administrative unions may be mentioned:

- The International Postal Union, established by treaty in 1874, for the creation of a single postal territory for the reciprocal exchange of mails between the member states;
- The International Rhine Navigation Commission, created by the Vienna Congress for the enforcement of common regulations governing the navigation of the river Rhine;
- The European Danube River Commission, created in

1856 by the Treaty of Paris for a similar purpose and having permanent offices at Galatz;

- The International Telegraph Union, created in 1865 by the Conference of the Powers at St. Petersburg;
- The International Metric Union, created in 1875, and having as its common organ the International Bureau of Weights and Measures, with permanent offices at Sèvres, near Paris;
- The International Union of Railway Freight Transit, created in 1893, and having a central bureau at Berne;
- The International Union for the Protection of Literary and Artistic Property, with a permanent central bureau at Berne;
- The International Association for the Protection of Labour, with an international office at Berne;
- The Intenational Sugar Commission, with a bureau at Brussels;
- The International Commission of Insurance, with a bureau at Brussels;
- The International Prison Association, with a secretariat at Berne;
- The International Sanitary Association, with an office at Paris;
- The International Bureau of American Republics at Washington, created in 1890 and reorganized in 1906;
- The Congress of Hygiene and Demography, with a permanent commissioner at Brussels;
- The International Seismological Association;
- The International Office of Public Health, created by an international convention signed at Rome in December, 1907; and
- The International Institute of Agriculture at Rome, created by an international convention signed at Rome, July 7, 1905. It is announced that an International Bureau of Wireless Telegraphy is to be established in the near future. Most of these unions have been created by international agreement, and some of them, like the Postal Union, embrace

practically all the civilized states of the world. Provision is made in the acts creating some of them for the holding of congresses at periodic intervals at which each member state may be represented and entitled to one vote.

Thus a congress representing the Telegraph Union is held every three years; the Postal Congress meets every five years; the Union of Weights and Measures holds a congress every six years. Most of them maintain a central administrative bureau or office, usually at Berne.

The river commissions have inspectors to supervise the execution of common arrangements, and the common expenses are borne by the members of the union in some proportion agreed upon.

Chapter 6

Forms of Government

MONARCHIES, ARISTOCRACIES, AND DEMOCRACIES

Having examined the several forms of states and associations of states, we come now to consider the forms of government, keeping in mind that government is not the state, but, as Francis Lieber has remarked, merely the instrument or contrivance through which the state acts in all cases in which it does not act by direct operation of its sovereignty. Following the same principle observed in the classification of states, namely, the number of persons in whom the supreme power is vested, we shall find that governments may be classified as monarchical, aristocratic, and democratic.

If the supreme governing authority is vested in a single person, however numerous his subordinates, the form of government is said to be monarchical. Popular usage, however, considers any government having a hereditary executive to be a monarchy, even though its legislative department rests upon a popular basis.

In short, popular usage makes the test the nature of the executive tenure and the tenure of the titular executive at that. Thus most of the governments of Europe are commonly styled monarchies, when in reality only the executive part of the government is constituted on the monarchical principle. The modern term "monarchy, "as Sidgwick observes, is largely used to denote governments in which only a share of power is left to the single individual called the monarch.

If the supreme governing authority is intrusted to a small

group or class of the population, the government is said to be aristocratic. It is a government in which only a minority of the citizens have a share, the rest of the population, as Montesquieu remarks, being in respect to the former the same as the subjects of a monarch in regard to the sovereign. If the great mass of the adult male citizens share in the government, either through the choice of its agents, through participation in the enactment of law by means of the so-called initiative or referendum, or through a popular assembly of all the citizens, we have a democratic form of government or a democracy. Professor

Seeley defined democracy more broadly as a government in which every one has a share. John Austin said it signified any government in which the governing body is a comparatively large fraction of the entire nation. Sir Henry Maine said it could be most accurately described as "inverted monarchy. "

The classification of governments as monarchical, aristocratic, and democratic is identical with the classification of states given in the preceding chapter, but it does not follow that the form of government in any given state is necessarily identical with the form of state, though usually they are similar in form and spirit.

A democratic state, for example, is apt to have a government in which democratic or popular elements predominate. But while this is the natural and usual condition, it is quite possible that a democratic state should have a government organized upon an aristocratic basis. Indeed, it is difficult to see why such a system is not the nearest approach to the ideal, provided the aristocracy is one of real merit rather than one which is artificial in character. Strictly speaking, there are no longer any pure monarchical governments in Europe.

What are loosely and popularly called such are in fact mixed governments, that is, governments composed of monarchical, aristocratic, and democratic elements combine. The truth is, as Rousseau remarks, all governments are in a sense mixed. There is no modern civilized state in which the governing power is vested wholly in the hands of a single person. In the typical monarchies, so called, of Europe, there is an hereditary chief of state and a legislative body, containing usually both aristocratic and democratic elements. Only in certain absolute states of Asia and Africa do we find anything approaching pure monarchical government, that is, one in which the ruling power is vested in the hands of a single person.

On the basis of the source or tenure of the executive, monarchies may be classified as hereditary or elective, or they may be a combination of both. All of the monarchies of the present day are hereditary, though there have been many exceptions in the past.

The early Roman kings were elective, as were the kings of the ancient monarchy of Poland. The head of the Holy Roman Empire, as is well known, was chosen by a small college of electors, though usually from the same family. Under the Treaty of Berlin, of 1878, the reigning prince of Bulgaria owed his throne to election. In general, it may be said that the installation of dynasties in newly formed states usually takes place through election, though the crown thereafter. is generally transmitted according to certain rules of hereditary succession.

It may also be stated as a general proposition that in the early history of states kings were generally chosen or in some way accepted in the first instance, though the hereditary feature was so strong that the elective principle was gradually pushed into the background.

Speaking of the election of the early English kings, Stubbs observes that "the king was in theory always elected and the fact of election was stated in the coronation service throughout the Middle Ages in accordance with the most ancient precedent. ""But, "he adds, "it is not less true that the succession was by constitutional practice restricted to one family, and that the rule of hereditary succession was never, except in great emergencies and in most trying times, set aside. "In a sense, of course, the English monarchy is still elective, since Parliament claims and exercises the right to regulate the law of succession at its pleasure.

Again, monarchy may be either of the absolute type, in which case the monarch is sovereign, and state and government, legally and politically speaking, are identical, or it may be constitutional or limited in form. In the former case the monarch is bound by no will except his own; in the latter case he is bound by the prescriptions of a constitution which he has sworn to support, and hence the royal office is nothing but an organ of government.

No examples of the former type of monarchy, as has been said, are found to-day outside of Asia and Africa. All of the so-called monarchies of continental Europe now have written constitutions, framed either by national assemblies representing the people, or granted by ruling sovereigns and accepted by the people. Monarchies may of course be still further subdivided, but little or nothing would be gained by extending the classification beyond hereditary and elective, absolute and limited types.

Aristocracies, like monarchies, may likewise be of several varieties. There may be aristocracies of wealth, and these may be based either on ownership of land or of all property in general; or they may be hereditary and hence based upon birth or family connection; or they may be official in character, that is, composed mainly of those who hold or have held public office; or they may be military or a combination of some or all of the above elements.

Democracies are of two kinds: pure or direct, and representative or indirect. A pure democracy is one in which the will of the state is formulated and expressed directly and immediately through the people acting in their primary capacity. A representative democracy is one in which the state will is ascertained and expressed through the agency of a small and select number who act as the representatives of the people.

A pure democracy is practicable only in small states where the voting population may be assembled for purposes of legislation, and where the collective needs of the people are few and simple. In large and complex societies, where the legislative wants of the people are numerous, the very necessities of the situation make government by the whole body of citizens a physical impossibility. In the city states of antiquity pure democracies were not impossible, and they were not uncommon; but in the states of the modern world and under modern conditions they are impossible. The only surviving examples to-day are found in four of the petty and largely primitive cantons of Switzerland. What is in substance a representative democracy is sometimes called a republic or a republican government.

Although restricted by modern usage to a government conducted through agents popularly chosen, yet the term "republic, "as Hamilton and Madison pointed out in "The Federalist, "has often been employed to describe governments which popular usage to-day would designate as monarchical or aristocratic. Thus Sparta, Athens, Rome, Carthage, the United Netherlands,

Venice, and Poland have all been described by political writers as republics, though none of them possessed that full representative character which we to-day consider to be the distinguishing mark of a republic. Rome, for example, was organized on a military basis, Venice was an oligarchy of hereditary nobles, Poland was a mixture of aristocracy and monarchy. France under the constitution of the year XII was styled a republic, though the chief of state bore the title and rank of emperor, and the crown was hereditary in the Napoleonic family.

The constitution of the United States imposes upon the national government the duty of guaranteeing to the component states a republican form of government, but it does not attempt to define the essential characteristics of such a government, simply assuming that they are too well understood to admit of a difference of opinion. Madison in "The Federalist "said it was a government in which there was "a scheme of representation. "It was, he said, "a government which derives all its powers, directly or indirectly, from the great body of the people and is administered by persons holding their offices during pleasure, for a limited period or during good behaviour.

"The two "great points of difference, "said Madison,

"between a republic and a democracy are: first, the governing power in a republic is delegated to a small number of citizens elected by the rest; and, second, a republic is capable of embracing a larger population and of extending over a wider area of territory than is a democracy.

In a democracy the people meet and exercise the government in person; in a republic they assemble and administer it by their representative agents. "Madison rightly regarded hereditary tenures as inconsistent with modern notions of republican government, although he considered good behaviour tenure for the judiciary at least admissible.

It is also essential to the republican idea that the principle of representation shall be based upon a reasonably wide suffrage.

A suffrage so restricted, for example, as that which existed in France under the restored monarchy, when the number of voters did not exceed 300, 000 Out of a total population of 10, 000, 000 would hardly be considered consistent with republican governnment.

Republics have been classified as aristocratic and democratic; as monocmtic and plutocratic; unlimited, mixed, and limited; as corporate, oligarchic, aristocratic, and democratic; as federal and confederate; as centralized and unitary; as hereditary and elective, etc.

The classification of governments as monarchies, aristocracies, and democracies has lost its former importance and now possesses little interest for the political scientist. To speak of a government as monarchical or aristocratic conveys little or no idea of its structural organization or processes of action.

Many so-called monarchies are such only in name, and there is no fundamental difference in principle between aristocracies and democracies, the only distinction being one of degree. Such a classification puts governments as widely different as those of Great Britain, Prussia, Russia, and Turkey in the same class, others as different as those of France and the United States in another and the same class.

It is necessary, therefore, to find other principles of

classification in order to be able to classify governmental forms in any satisfactory or consistent manner.

OTHER CLASSIFICATIONS; CABINET AND PRESIDENTIAL GOVERNMENT

Montesquieu classified governments as republics, monarchies, and despotisms. He defined a republican government as one in which the whole body or a part of the people exercises supreme power; a monarchy as one in which a single person governs by fixed and established laws; a despotism as one in which a single person directs everything by his own will and caprice.

The principle underlying this classification is partly numbers and partly the spirit and character of the government. Woolsey classified governments as monarchies, aristocracies, democracies, and "compound states. ". Other writers recognize only two forms, namely, monarchies and republics, the latter comprehending both aristocracies and democracies.

The fault with most classifications of governments is, as was said of the classifications of states, that they do not rest upon any consistent scientific principle which will serve as a basis for the differentiation of governments with respect to their fundamental characteristics. No single classification can be of much value; there must be as many classifications as there are points of view from which the government may be considered.

A well-known authority on political science adopts the following canons of distinction in classifying governmental forms: first, the identity or non-identity of the state with its government; second, the nature of the official tenure, including the method of constituting the official relation; third, the relation of the legislature to the executive; and fourth, the concentration or distribution of governmental power.

Upon the basis of the identity or non-identity of the state with the government, they may be classified as primary or representative. The pure democracy, where the citizens assemble in mass meeting and enact the laws of the state and frame administrative regulations, is, of course, the nearest approach to what we have called primary government. Where, on the other hand, the sovereign has delegated to an organ or organs the power to act for it in matters of government, as is now the almost universal practice, we have representative government in some form, though not necessarily popular government.

Considered from the standpoint of the nature and source of the official tenure, governments may be classified as hereditary and elective. Hereditary government is that form in which the source of office is inheritance according to some rule or principle governing the transmission of political honors and titles.

Elective government is that form in which the choice of those who exercise public power devolves upon the citizens or rather that portion of them who constitute the electoral body. The method of election may be direct, or, as is sometimes said, election in the first degree; or it may be indirect, or in the second degree. In either case it may be by an electorate constituted on the basis of a restricted suffrage or by one on the basis of what is popularly designated as universal suffrage.

With respect to the relation of the executive to the legislature, governments may be classified as cabinet (the terms "ministerial, ""parliamentary, "and "responsible "are sometimes preferred); and what, for lack of a more suitable term, has been called presidential or congressional government.

Cabinet government is that system in which the real executive — the cabinet or ministry — is immediately and legally responsible to the legislature or one branch of it (usually the more popular chamber) for its legislative and administrative acts, and immediately or politically responsible to the electorate; while the titular or nominal executive — the chief of state occupies a position of irresponsibility.

The members of the ministry are usually members of the legislature and the leaders of the party in the majority, but whether they are members or not, they have the privilege of occupying seats therein and of participating in the deliberations. In short, the ministerial office is not incompatible with legislative mandate. On the contrary, the cabinet system presupposes the double character of minister and member, and thus executive and legislative functions are inextricably commingled. "There is, "observes Courtenay Ilbert, "no such separation between the executive and legislative powers as that which forms the distinguishing mark of the American Constitution "but the relation is one of intimacy and interdependence.

The nominal or titular executive, according to a legal fiction, is incapable of doing wrong, in a political sense, and is, as it were, under the guardianship of his ministers, who assume the responsibility for his official acts. Collectively they constitute the "government "; they prepare, initiate, and urge the adoption by the legislature of all the more important legislative projects; and from their seats in the legislature they defend their policies from attack, and when called upon must give an account of their official conduct.

They are the heads of the great administrative departments as well as the political chiefs and parliamentary leaders of the country, and are charged with administering the laws which they propose and have enacted. So long as their policies and official conduct command the support of the majority of the members of the legislature, or rather of that chamber to which they are responsible they continue to hold the reins of office and govern the country.

But as soon as the legislature manifests in no uncertain language its want confidence in the ministry, through a vote of censure or by a refusal to pas its measures, the ministry either resigns office in a body or it dissolves the chamber to which it owes responsibility, orders a new parliamentary election, and appeals to the electorate to sustain it by returning a new parliament which is in sympathy with its policies and acts.

If the results of the election are favorable to the ministry, it continues in office; if adverse, it resigns as soon as the results are fully known or when the new parliament has assembled and by positive vote has made known its want of sympathy. In a typical cabinet system like that of Great

Britain the ministry is taken wholly from the ranks of the party having a majority in the popular chamber, and thus possesses the character of homogeneity.

In legal theory the ministers are chosen by the nominal or titular executive, though where the system of responsibility to the legislature is fully developed they are in reality chosen by the legislature, and the designation by the chief of state is little more than a ceremonial function of investing them with the symbols of office.

The number of ministers is rarely fixed either by law or by custom, and hence the size of the ministry is uncertain and variable, the exact number in any case being usually determined by the premier or by executive decree. In Great Britain the number (*i. e.* of the cabinet) in recent years has been in the neighborhood of twenty; in France, it is now twelve; in Italy, eleven; in Belgium, ten.

The cabinet system originated in England and was the product of history rather than of invention. From England it spread little by little to Holland, France, Belgium, Roumania, Sweden, Norway, Denmark, and the British Colonies, until it has become, says Esmein, "the principal system of government in the world. "It has made little headway in Germany, however, and none at all in Switzerland or North America, and but little in Latin America. The cabinet system has received its fullest development in Great Britain, and there its workings have been attended with the most satisfactory results.

Among the cabinet systems of the continent, that of Belgium most nearly resembles the British system, though the crown plays a more important role in that country than in England. The responsibility of ministers to the king is more real than in England, and he may direct and dismiss them with more freedom than the British sovereign may. As there are generally recognized parliamentary leaders, the king rarely has any real choice, however, in the selection of his ministers.

In Belgium, as in England, ministers without portfolios are sometimes appointed as a means of introducing into the government eminent persons whose support and experience the government desires to avail itself of, yet who would hesitate to assume the burden of a cabinet portfolio. As in England, ministers are chosen not from the ranks of technical administrators, except in the case of the minister of war, who is always a soldier and usually an active general, but from the members of parliament and from the chamber of deputies rather than from the senators. All ministers, whether members or not, have full entree into either chamber.

Cabinet government was introduced in France by the charter of 1814; it became fully established under the July monarchy, was practically abandoned in 1848, but was reestablished with the third republic, though it has never attained the success there that it has in England. In France there is no incompatibility whatever between ministerial office and legislative mandate, and neither law nor custom requires a member of parliament appointed to the cabinet to resign his seat and seek a reelection, as is the rule in England.

Custom now requires that all cabinet portfolios shall be given to members of parliament, though until recently this rule did not apply to the ministers of war and marine. The English and Belgian practice of appointing ministers without portfolios has not been followed in France since 1868, though undersecretaries are sometimes appointed, there being four such at the present time.

Ministers are usually regarded as being responsible to the chamber of deputies only, though the constitutional law of February 25, 1875, expressly declares that they shall be solidly responsible to the *chambers* for the general policy of the government and individually responsible for their personal acts. In legal theory they are appointed by the president of the republic, but in fact circumstances usually determine who shall be members, so that the president has little freedom of choice.

Owing to the existence of many groups in France the task of constructing a cabinet is often one of great difficulty. Hardly any single group or coalition of groups ever possesses a majority in the popular chamber, and it not infrequently happens that there is no recognized leader to whom the chief of state may turn and intrust the task of constituting the cabinet. Under such circumstances the premier is sought from the old cabinet which has been condemned. Consequently it nearly always happens that a new cabinet in France contains several members of the old one, a condition that almost never happens in England, especially when there has been a change of parties. The principal difficulty encountered in constructing a stable cabinet in France arises from the necessity of giving the different groups a sufficient number of members so as to satisfy them.

This requires skill and tact, and even when the task is well done such a ministry is weak and unstable because it is heterogeneous instead of homogeneous. Where there are more than two political parties in a state having the cabinet system of government, coalition cabinets, with their traditional weakness and instability, are inevitable. They are weak and unstable because it is next to impossible for a ministry representing such widely different interests to pursue a common policy for any great length of time. The result is that ministries are short-lived in France and cabinet government has not produced satisfactory results.

In Italy the conditions under which cabinet government is conducted are similar in many respects to those prevailing in France. As in France, the chambers are always divided into a number of political groups or factions, unstable, but sharply differentiated and well-disciplined. Under such circumstances it is difficult for one man to rally the support of a majority to any measure concerning which there is any considerable opposition. Enormous difficulties, even more so than in France, are consequently encountered in forming a cabinet.

Hardly any leaders are designated by circumstances as the representatives of public opinion, and hence there is no certainty that the ministerial leaders chosen will be able to command the support of the chamber on any measure. As in France, widely different groups must be given representation in the cabinet, and each must be placated whenever it shows signs of disaffection. Cabinets formed after long and laborious negotiations, says Dupriez, sometimes go to pieces over the first question which provokes debate.

The Italian parliamentary system differs in some particulars from both those of England and of France. In the first place, the action of the chamber in determining the selection of the ministers is less than it is in either England or France. In Italy the king enjoys a much larger freedom and discretion in choosing his ministers, a fact which sometimes leads to the "disorganization and confusion of the parliamentary assembly.

"In theory the cabinet is responsible to the king and the parliament combined, but the parliament, we are told, has "obsequiously surrendered its powers of control, so that the responsibility is now due mainly to the king. "The ministers are generally taken from the chamber of deputies, the premier practically always.

The ministers of war and marine are usually army and navy officers respectively, and if not already senators, they are made such by royal appointment at the time they are chosen to the cabinet. Ministers without portfolios are sometimes appointed, and since 1888 each minister has had under his control an undersecretary, who takes no part in the deliberations of the cabinet, but may represent the minister before the chamber and defend the acts of the government.

In Germany there exists what may be called ministerial, but not parliamentary, responsible government. Both in the imperial and state governments ministers are appointed by the executive without reference to the political complexion of the legislature or without regard to the wishes of the majority. In short, the executive is free to choose whom he will.

Technical administrative experts who have had long experience in the service and have risen by degrees to be heads of departments, rather than parliamentary leaders or political chiefs, are usually preferred. They are not generally required by the constitution to be taken from either chamber, though, whether members or not, they are given *entree* thereto with the right of debate.

They are not chosen exclusively from one or the other party, though certain groups are usually recognized in the construction of a cabinet, for homogeneity is not considered a necessity. Legally and theoretically they owe no responsibility to parliament, but are responsible for their acts only to the king or the prince who appointed them. Their tenure, legally speaking, is dependent upon the royal favor and not upon the will of either chamber.

The policies of state are determined by the king and carried out by the ministers, who are theoretically at least the servants of the royal will. Generally, in cabinet governments, the role of the cabinet is not determined by positive law, but by usage and custom. In Prussia, however, this is not the practice. There the relations between king and ministers, between the ministers themselves, their control over the administration, etc., are all fixed by royal ordinances.

There is no such officer as prime minister who exercises the power of direction over his subordinates. though there is a minister-president who acts as a moderator during the absence of the king, and who frequently presides over the meetings of the cabinet.

Cabinet government is most commonly found in so-called monarchical states, where the conditions most favorable to its success are more generally present than elsewhere. Nevertheless it is sometimes found in republics, particularly those like France, in which monarchical traditions are strong. It has also been introduced into some of the Latin-American republics, notably Chile, Haiti, San Domingo, and Venezuela; but in none of them has the system received anything like a perfect development or attained any high degree of success.

Presidential government as contradistinguished from cabinet or parliamentary government is that form in which the executive is constitutionally independent of the legislature as regards his tenure and to a large extent also as regards his policies and acts. The executive may be, and generally is, responsible to the legislature or one chamber of it for certain grave crimes and sometimes even for lesser offenses, and may be impeached and upon conviction be removed from office; but he is politically irresponsible to the legislature and cannot be removed from office except upon impeachment.

This is the system which prevails in the United States, both in the national and local governments, in Switzerland, and in most of the Latin-American republics, and in a modified form in Germany. Where the presidential system prevails, no distinction exists between what we have denominated the titular or nominal executive and the real or actual executive.

There are ministers upon whom the chief work of the administration devolves, to be sure, but they are not members of the legislature and rarely have entree to either chamber; they do not assume responsibility for the acts of the executive; they are appointed by the executive without regard to the political complexion of the legislature or the wishes of the majority in control of either chamber; they are, within the limits of the law, controlled and directed by the executive and may be dismissed by him at will.

They are, in short, the ministers of the executive, not of the legislature, administrative chiefs rather than parliamentary leaders. They neither prepare, introduce, nor advocate before the chambers the adoption of legislative measures, except in so far as they may do so through the agency of members of the legislature who are in sympathy with their policies. Votes of censure or of want of confidence by the legislature do not affect them, and when the legislature refuses to enact the measures which they suggest, instead of resigning they continue to govern as though they were in complete harmony with the majority. It not infrequently happens, of course, that they belong to a different political party from that which is in control of one or both of the chambers of the legislature, in which case the presidential system would break down were their tenure dependent upon the support of the majority.

From this it will be seen that the one feature which distinguishes presidential government from the parliamentary or cabinet system is the almost complete isolation of the executive branch from the legislature, and its independence of the same body in respect to its tenure and powers.

UNITARY, FEDERAL, AND CONFEDERATE GOVERNMENT

Considered from the point of view of the concentration

or distribution of power, governments may be classified as unitary and federal. If the powers of government are concentrated in one supreme organ or organs that are located at one common centre, and from which all local governing authorities derive their existence and powers, the government is both unitary and centralized.

In such a system there is a single common source of authority, and hence but one supreme will is exerted. For convenience of administration the territory of the state may be subdivided into circumscriptions or districts, in each of which a local government may be established and to which certain powers of a local character may be delegated by the central government; but so long as the local organizations are the mere creations of the central power and exist at its will and derive their powers from it and it alone, the governmental system is unitary in character.

These local organizations are nothing more than parts of the central government, created to act as its agents; in short, they have no independent wills of their own. In such a system there is no local self-government existing independently of the will of the central government, but only such as the latter may choose to allow. Examples of such systems of government are those of England, France, Spain, Portugal, Italy, and most of the other states of Europe.

In none of them do we find a constitutional distribution of powers between a central government and a number of local governments, each with a constitution and political organization of its own creation. There are local governments, to be sure, such, for example, as the counties in England, the departments and communes in France, the provinces in Belgium and Italy, etc.; but all such governments are nothing but the creatures and agents of the central authorities and enjoy little or no constitutional protection against central interference and control.

If, on the contrary, the government of the country is distributed by the constitution between a central organization and a number of local organizations, the latter of which are not ordinarily the creatures or agents of the former, but owe their existence to the general constitution in the sense that their spheres are determined by it, the government is said to be federal in character. Federal government may be defined as a system of central and local government combined under a common sovereignty, both the central and local organizations being supreme within definite spheres, marked out for them by the general constitution.

It is dual government as contradistinguished from unitary government, and implies local self-government as opposed to centralized government. It represents a sort of compromise between unitary government and confederate government. Contrary to the principle which underlies unitary government, the local organizations under the federal system are not the direct creations of the central government; but in most federal systems the reverse is true, that is, the central government has been created by the local organizations through the act of federation.

The territorial areas of these local organizations are not therefore mere administrative districts, but autonomous and, in a certain sense, self-created political communities, having their own constitutions and political systems. The central and local governments are not, however, totally separate and disconnected from each other in organization. Federal government is not, as is often loosely said, the central government alone, but it is a system composed of the central and local governments combined.

The local governments are as much a part of the federal system as the central government is, though neither is subject to the control of the other. In most federal systems the component parts participate in the organization of the central government. In the German Empire and the United States, for example, the upper chambers of the national legislature are composed of members chosen by a branch of the state government rather than by the people. Thus a connecting link between the central and local governments is established, which serves to minimize the tendency to mutual jealousy and to strengthen good feeling between them.

The principle upon which the powers of government are

distributed between the central and local organizations in a federal system is, that those affairs which are of common interest to all the component parts of the federation and which require uniformity of regulation should be placed under the control of the central government, while all matters not of common concern should be left to the care of the local governments. In short, there should be one government for national affairs and a number of local governments for local affairs. In respect to the former, therefore, federal government resembles unitary government, while in respect to the latter it is more like confederate government.

Opinions differ, however, as to what affairs require uniformity of regulation and what should be left to local regulation, and hence the line of separation between general and local matters is in practice drawn differently in different federal systems.

In most states having the federal form of government, however, such affairs as foreign relations and international intercourse, war and peace, interstate and foreign commerce, coinage of money, patents and copyrights, have been placed under the control of the central government. In international relations the local governments are non-entities and are officially unknown, though, as will be pointed out later, they have shown themselves able in certain instances to interpose obstacles in the way of the successful prosecution of a common foreign policy by the central government.

In the more recently established federal systems of Europe and Latin-America the notion of what requires uniformity of regulation and what will permit of variety of control is somewhat different from that which has prevailed in the United States, and, consequently, the principle of distribution has been different. In these states many affairs are treated as being of general interest and hence requiring uniformity of regulation, which in the United States are left to local regulation.

Thus, in Canada and the German Empire the whole body of civil, criminal, and commercial law and the law of procedure, as well as the law of marriage and divorce, is national, not local; that is, instead of separate and widely varying legal systems in these domains, there is a single uniform code for all the component parts of the empire. The evils that have arisen in the United States in consequence of the extraordinary variety of legislation, especially in respect to certain businesses and occupations that are really national in scope rather than local, have recently aroused discussion in many quarters in favor of increasing the powers of the national government along various lines.

Two methods have been followed in distributing the powers of government between the central and local organizations, where the federal system prevails. In most such states the powers intrusted to the central government are specifically enumerated. To the local governments are reserved all the remaining powers except such as may be specifically prohibited.

The central government is thus an authority of delegated powers, while the local governments are authorities of residuary powers. In other words, the competence of the central government is *positively* determined by the constitution, while that of the local governments is *negatively* determined. The presumption of law in case of doubt, therefore, is against the existence of any power claimed by the central government and in favor of any power claimed by the local governments. In the federal system of Canada, however, a somewhat different principle of distribution prevails.

There the local governments are authorities of delegated powers, while the central government is one of both delegated and reserved powers. Whatever may be the method or principle of distribution, or the nature and extent of power delegated or reserved to either government, neither may enlarge its competence or distribute the powers of government differently from the way in which they have been distributed by the constitution.

Only the sovereign itself can do that. In some federal systems, however, the central government is given a limited control over the organization and acts of the local governments. Thus, in the United States it is made the duty of the national government to see that only republican governments shall be maintained by the individual states, from which it may be inferred that the national government may prohibit such local organizations as may not in its judgment conform to this requirement.

In Canada the Dominion government has the power to disallow the acts of the provincial legislatures; likewise in the federal republic of Venezuela the national government may veto the acts of the local legislatures. Both in Germany and Switzerland the central authorities have a sort of *jus suprema inspectionis* over the operations of the local governments, especially when they are charged with carrying out the acts of the central government. In the German Empire the imperial government may by the process of federal execution compel a delinquent or recalcitrant member of the empire to perform its obligations to the empire.

Confederate government is that form of government in which, as to territory and population, the state is coextensive in its own organization with the organization of the local government. In a confederate system, as in the federal system, there is a central organization; but instead of a single sovereignty there are as many sovereignties as there are local governments.

The central government is merely the agent of the states composing the confederacy, and its jurisdiction is limited to a very few concerns. In operation its commands extend, as has been said, not to the individuals who inhabit the confederacy, but are addressed to the confederated states themselves and reach the individuals for whom they are intended only mediately and indirectly, through the medium of the state organizations.

A confederacy in reality has no citizens or subjects who owe it direct and immediate allegiance. Its jurisdiction generally includes only such matters as relate to foreign relations, defensive war, and possibly a few matters of an interstate character. Usually it possesses no power over the sources of its own revenue supply, but is dependent upon the voluntary contributions of the confederated states. Finally, it lacks stability and permanence, and its existence is precarious, since it belongs to the component members to withdraw from the confederation at will or refuse to be bound by its acts and resolutions. It is a transitory form of political organization which usually develops into the federal system or dissolves into its constituent elements.

BUREAUCRATIC VERSUS POPULAR GOVERNMENT

From the standpoint of the organization and spirit of the administrative service, governments may be classified as *bureaucratic* and *popular*. A bureaucratic government is one which is composed of administrators especially trained for the public service, who enter the employ of the government only after a regular course of study and examination, and who serve usually during good behaviour and retire on pensions.

Under such a system the governmental service acquires the character of a profession, its officials are subject to a rigid discipline, and they tend to acquire an *esprit de corps* somewhat similar to that found among the soldiers of a regular army. They devote their entire time to the discharge of their public duties and have no other occupation. They therefore tend to become a class

apart from the rest of the population, possessing different ideals and interests. In a large measure such government is irresponsible to the people, and is little affected by public opinion — it is, in short, very largely a government of men rather than of laws. It is marked by an excessive formalism, is inclined to parade and pomp, and has a tendency to overemphasize administrative routine rather than conditions and principles — in short, it tends, as Burke remarked, to think more of forms than of substance.

The most extreme example of a bureaucracy which the world has seen in modern times, perhaps, was that which existed in Prussia from 1720 to 1808. A bureaucracy of a less absolute character was that which existed in France under Napoleon for a time after 1808. In varying degrees of development it exists to-day in all the so-called monarchical states of Europe, especially in Prussia and Russia, and to a less degree in England. Commonly thought of only in connection with monarchical states, its forms and methods, and to some extent its spirit, are, nevertheless, found in the governmental systems of many republican states as well.

The chief merit of bureaucratic government is that it represents high skill and ability. Its officials are specially trained for the public service. It is thus more efficient than popular government; and if skilled, efficient, and economic administration were the only or the main end of government, little fault could be found with such a system. "It accumulates experience, "says John Stuart Mill, "acquires well-tried and well-considered traditional maxims and makes provision for appropriate practical knowledge in those who have the actual conduct of affairs. "

But as we have attempted to show, efficiency of administration is not the sole end to be attained in any governmental system. The education of the people in political matters, the stimulation of popular interest in public affairs, and the cultivation of loyalty and patriotism on the part of the masses should be among the important aims of every political system, and this cannot be accomplished by the bureaucratic system.

It is not favorable to the development of patriotism, self-reliance, or loyalty. Moreover, it is not without defects inherent in its own nature. "The disease, "said Mill, "which afflicts bureaucratic governments and of which they die is routine. They perish by the mutability of their maxims and still more by the universal law that whatever becomes a routine loses its vital principle. "Such a government, he said, tends to become a "pedantocracy. "It is the only government, some one has remarked, for which the philosopher can find no defense.

Contradistinguished from bureaucratic government is popular government, that is, government by persons drawn at regular intervals from the ranks of the people, who after a brief service return to the private walks of life. Generally they are without special training; not infrequently they serve without pecuniary compensation; and often they are during the term of their public service engaged in other occupations.

Under such a system most of the offices are open to all without preliminary preparation or examination; few or no professional qualifications are required, and the official class never develops a caste system or loses touch with the people. The officers are more or less influenced by public opinion, and in the discharge of their duties are more often subject to legislative than administrative control.

Finally, from the point of view of their functions and sphere of activity, governments may be denominated as *individualistic* and *paternal*. A government of the former type is one whose activities are limited mainly to the simple police functions of maintaining the peace, order, and security of society and the protection of private rights. A paternal government is one whose functions are not limited merely to restraining wrong-doing and the protection of private rights, but which goes farther and endeavors to promote by various means the social well-being of the people.

It undertakes to perform for society many services which might be performed as easily through private initiative, on the ground that they can be more efficiently and economically done by the government than by private individuals. Such a government may own and operate various industries, conduct businesses like insurance, provide pensions for the old, the sick, and the infirm, and in various ways care for the social interests of the people.

SUCCESSION OF GOVERNMENTAL FORMS

No state has retained the same form of government throughout its whole history. Governments, like living beings, are constantly changing their forms so as to adapt themselves to the altered conditions of a new environment. Thus, Athens was first ruled by kings, then by an aristocracy, later by tyrants, then by a democracy, and finally again by kings. So Rome went through a circle of political transformations. It began as a city kingdom, then it became a republic, and finally an empire ruled by Caesar.

The government of France within half a century passed through the forms of an absolute monarchy, a republic, an empire, a kingdom, again a republic, again an empire, and for the third time a republic.

Many of the early writers undertook to reduce the successive transformations through which governments pass to a regularly ordered sequence or rule of general application. There existed in early times a popular belief that there was a natural order of political development through which all states must pass in the course of their history. Plato, for example, taught that the natural course of evolution was from aristocracy, the rule of the best, to timocracy, the rule of the military, then to oligarchy, then to the rule of the mob, and finally to tyranny.

Aristotle, while differing from Plato as to the order of development, nevertheless believed that forms of government followed one another according to a regular order of succession. According to his rule the state began as a hereditary monarchy, which in time passed into an aristocracy. The latter in the course of time became an oligarchy, the oligarchy became a tyranny, and the latter ultimately passed into a democracy.

Ordinarily after an unsatisfactory experience with democracy a monarchy would be reestablished, and the cycle thus begun again would be passed through as before. Polybius taught that in the beginning the strongest person physically in the state ruled, that is, the state began originally as a monarchy. Then followed a period when justice rather than physical power became the basis of the right to rule, during which time a form of government called by Polybius "royalty "prevailed.

This form in time degenerated into tyranny, only to be overthrown eventually, and an aristocracy set up in its place. This in the course of time was succeeded by oligarchy, which in turn was overthrown by the people and a democracy was established. "Machiavelli laid down almost the same rule regarding the order of natural succession in respect to the political forms of ancient states.

The noted German scholar Schleiermacher asserted that political transformations are determined largely by the spread of political self-consciousness. At first, he said, political consciousness was not highly developed in any minds, though diffused equally among the masses. The democratic form of government naturally corresponded to this condition and was therefore the first state form. In the course of time a higher state consciousness developed and concentrated itself in a few minds.

This led to the establishment of aristocracy. Finally the state consciousness concentrated itself in a single individual, and monarchy, the highest form of state, succeeded. There is a residuum of truth in the principle of Schleiermacher's law, but the weight of opinion is against the order in which he conceived political consciousness to have spread. It is more reasonable to believe that it existed at first in but one or at best only a very few minds, and that it grew and spread slowly and became diffused throughout the mass of the population rather late in the life of the state.

It seems more probable, therefore, that the order of succession was the reverse of that which Schleiermacher laid down; that is, the state began with a monarchical form of organization, which in time became aristocratic, and finally, when political consciousness became general, the organization of the state became democratic. History, indeed, shows that this has generally been the order of development.

Bluntschli, a critic of Schleiermacher, held that the normal forms of government succeeded each other in the following order: first, theocracy; second, monarchy; third, aristocracy; and fourth, democracy; while the abnormal forms succeeded each other in the following order: hierarchy, tyranny, oligarchy, and ochlocracy. Each of these forms not infrequently passed through several transformations. For example, monarchy began in its pure form, then it became aristocratic in character, and finally, democratic. Republics likewise passed through monarchical, aristocratic, and democratic stages.

Regarding the merits of the rule laid down by the early writers in respect to the succession of state forms, there can be but one conclusion, namely, that such changes do not follow each other in accordance with any law such as reigns in the physical world. History furnishes abundant evidence of this truth. For example, the early monarchies did not always pass into tyrannies, but often the latter resulted from strife among the leaders of an aristocracy. Not infrequently monarchies have been transformed into democracies, aristocracies into monarchies, and democracies into aristocracies. Bodin, in his treatise on the republic, gives numerous historical examples of such transformations.

In modern times monarchies have more often been succeeded by democracies than by aristocracies. During the sixteenth and seventeenth centuries in many states of Europe monarchical governments of an absolute type were erected upon the ruins of feudal aristocracies. A study of the subject indeed will show that the exceptions are more numerous than the rule. There are, of course, certain laws of political evolution, but no such sequence of succession as was described by the early writers. Not all states have passed through the same stages or undergone the same transformations.

The changes that have occurred in some have been the result of internal revolution, in others the result of conscious adoption or imitation. Woolsey justly remarks that if there were such a law of succession as described by Polybius, it would afford a most hopeless prospect to the world. It would, in short, mean the reign of fatalism and of death in the domain of politics.

MERITS AND DEMERITS

MONARCHICAL GOVERNMENT

FROM a consideration of the various forms of government, from the standpoint of their structural organization, we come next to consider, in the light of reason and experience, the elements of strength and weakness of each. Of all the types considered, the oldest and most widely distributed is the so-called monarchical form. It has existed from the earliest times and is to-day universal in Asia and nearly so in Europe. Until the latter part of the eighteenth century it was widely believed to be the nearest approach to a perfect form of political organization that could be devised by the ingenuity of man. Of its merits the English philosopher and historian David Hume wrote near the middle of the eighteenth century:

"Though all kinds of government be improved on in modern times, yet monarchical government seems to have made the greatest advance to perfection. It may now be affirmed of civilized monarchies, what was formerly said of republics alone, that they are a government of laws, not of men. They are found susceptible of order, method, and constancy to a surprising degree.

Property is there secure; industry is encouraged; the arts flourish; and the prince lives among his subjects like a father among his children. "And, he adds, there are more "sources of degeneracy "to be found in free governments like England than in France, which was then, in Hume's estimation, "the most perfect model of pure monarchy, "a judgment which Sir Henry Maine pronounces to be quite lacking in the essential element of truth. "All the world, "said Bossuet, "began with monarchy, and almost all the world has been preserved by it in the most natural state. "It has its foundation, continued the same writer, in the paternal empire, that is, in nature itself.

In judging of the merits of monarchical government we must distinguish between the two forms in which it manifests itself; namely, that form in which the monarch is both sovereign and executive, and that form in which he is executive only, and usually only titular executive at that. In the former the whole power of government, the whole source of authority, is in the hands of a single person, however numerous may be his subordinates.

In favor of this form of government may be mentioned the elements of strength, vigor, and energy of action, unity of counsel, promptness of decision, and simplicity of organization. "Where such a system prevails, "said Rousseau, "the will of the people and the will of the prince, the public force of the state and the individual force of the government, all respond to the same motive power; all the springs of the machine are in the same hand, all look to the same end. There are no opposing movements which destroy each other, and no sort of constitution can be imagined in which a slight effort produces greater action. "Rousseau goes on to compare a skillful monarch governing his people throughout a vast state and making everything move while seeming himself immovable, to an engineer seated tranquilly on the shore of a sea and setting in motion without difficulty a huge vessel upon the waters.

In the early stages of civilization monarchy is undoubtedly well adapted to the needs of a people who have not yet developed a high political consciousness and who therefore lack the capacity themselves for participating actively in the management of public affairs. Perhaps no better form could be devised for disciplining uncivilized peoples, leading them out of barbarism and inculcating in them habits of obedience. John Stuart Mill has well remarked that "despotism is a legitimate mode of government for dealing with barbarians, provided the end be their improvement and the means be justified by actually effecting that end.

"Liberty, "he observes, "as a principle, has no application to any state of things anterior to the time when mankind have become capable of being improved by free and equal discussion. Until then there is nothing for them but implicit obedience to an Akbar or a Charlemagne, if they are so fortunate as to find one. "The absolute monarchies of the medieval and early modern times justified their existence through their work of consolidation and nationalization.

Popular government could make no headway until provinces were consolidated into kingdoms, classes and races into nations, and conflicting jurisdictions were unified. It was the mission of absolute monarchy to establish the sovereignty of the national state in the place of the rival authorities of the church, of feudalism, of free cities, and of other obstacles which stood in the way of the development of the modern state. No other agency than absolute monarchy could have wrought out so important a result and thus paved the way for constitutional government.

But when all is said that can be said in favor of the pure

monarchical form of government, the fact remains that it is absolute government; that is, government in which the people for whose protection and benefit governments are instituted have no share. Having exhausted its mission, its *raison d'être* no longer exists. It is government organized and administered by a single person according to his own sense of what is best and right for those over whom he reigns, and history abundantly confirms the truth of the assertion that such governments have more often been administered in the interests of the monarch himself than in the interests of his subjects.

"It has long been a common form of speech, "says John Stuart Mill, "that if a good despot could be insured, despotic monarchy would be the best form of government. "But, as he goes on to remark, it is a most "pernicious misconception of what good government is. "Assuming for the sake of argument that absolute power in the hands of one individual would never be abused, but on the contrary would insure a virtuous and intelligent administration of the government; granting that good laws would be enacted and enforced, that justice would be dealt out to all, that the public revenues would be wisely and judiciously expended; in short, that the despotism were the wisest and most benevolent conceivable, there are still other considerations which render it far from being the ideal polity. Administrative efficiency is only one of the tests of a good government.

No government which does not rest upon the affections of the people, which does not stimulate among them an interest in public affairs and create an active, intelligent, and alert citizenship, can be called ideal; and, certainly, no government from which the participation of the people in some form is excluded will ever be able to produce such a body of citizens.

The merits and demerits of the second type of monarchy, that is, the form of monarchy in which the reigning prince is not sovereign, but merely an organ of government, are mainly, though not wholly, those which are associated with the principle of hereditary tenure in the organization of the executive. It is this principle which mainly distinguishes the so-called constitutional monarchy to-day from the republic. About all that can be said in favor of the hereditary principle is that it tends to secure an uninterrupted and orderly succession in the executive office without the recurring dangers and inconveniences, the tumults and disorders, which are almost inseparable from the method of popular choice. It also tends to promote continuity of executive polity in the conduct of the government.

The inherent weakness in the hereditary principle is that it affords no guarantee that a strong, vigorous, or trained person will succeed to the office, but allows the choice to be determined by the accident of birth. Thus, as a method for securing fitness and character in the executive office it has no merits. To intrust one man with the government of the people, not because he is the wisest or the best, but because he is the son or heir of another person, as a principle of politics has little to commend it.

History affords numerous examples of immature, feeble-minded, and incompetent rulers succeeding to thrones under the operation of such a principle. France, for example, was governed for more than five hundred years by kings who had not reached the age of twenty-five years at the time of their accession to the throne, and for nearly one hundred years by kings who had not attained the age of twenty-one.

ARISTOCRATIC GOVERNMENT

In order to form a proper estimate of the merits and demerits of aristocratic government we must distinguish between the several forms under which it manifests itself. There are or have been, as we have seen, aristocracies of birth or family; aristocracies of wealth, and these may be of two kinds; aristocracies of culture and education; aristocracies of elder statesmen; priestly and military aristocracies;

natural and artificial aristocracies; etc. Manifestly they do not all possess the same virtues or the same vices, nor the same elements of strength or of weakness. Whatever may be the method or basis of classification or the form which aristocracy may take, the general political principle is the same, namely, that aristocratic government is government by a comparatively small portion of the population.

If as a form of government it meant what the etymological derivation of the word implies, it would, as De Parieu remarks, undoubtedly be the most perfect as well as the most widely prevalent kind of government in the world. Interpreted in the sense of the best, it is the government par excellence, the only government in fact which can be defended on sound and rational principles.

It ought to be readily granted by all that only the good should govern; but, as Seeley observes, if "good "is only a euphemistic name, meaning simply a quality possessed by the wealthy or well-born, then aristocracy is only a euphemistic name for oligarchy, which is itself a perverted or "diseased "form of aristocracy.

The Greek notion of aristocracy was that of government by the "best, "not necessarily by the wealthy or powerful. Originally it was one of the most respected, as it was one of the most widely distributed, of all forms of political organization; but in recent years the name has come to have an unsavory if not a disreputable ring about it.

The ancient writers like Aristotle, as has been said, carefully distinguished between aristocracy, which they defined as government by the "best, "and oligarchy, which they described as government by a wealthy minority in their own interest. But with modern notions concerning government by the few the distinction has largely disappeared, so that aristocracy has come to possess the same disagreeable meaning which the ancients associated with oligarchy. In short, the two, as forms of government, are now regarded as substantially the same.

One of the distinguishing characteristics of aristocracy is that it emphasizes quality rather than quantity, character rather than mere numbers. It assumes that some are better fitted to govern than others, attaches great weight to experience and training as political virtues, and seeks to reward special talent and attract it into the public service.

It is preeminently conservative government; it honors

authority, especially when it has had the sanction of long acquiescence, and has great reverence for longestablished custom and tradition.

It strikes its roots deep in the past and distrusts innovation, especially when it would lay violent hands upon institutions which have become venerable with age. Where it is associated with monarchy and democracy, it acts as a tempering and restraining element. It curbs the passions of democracy and holds in check the absolute tendencies of monarchy. In this sense it is, said Lord Brougham, a necessary part of a governmental system, since "nothing else can protect liberty from an arbitrary sovereign or from the more insupportable tyranny of the irresponsible multitude.

"The very soul of it, said Montesquieu, is moderation founded on virtue. It possesses an inherent vigor, he declared, unknown to democracy. Naturally jealous of its exclusive privileges and fearful of its own security, it has every reason for refraining from an unwise and immoderate use of its power. Thus it avoids rash political experiments and advances only by cautious and measured step. If the principle of selection were always that of genuine merit, it is difficult to see what could be said against aristocratic government *qua* government.

Considered from the standpoint of the quality, of the government itself, without reference to its effect upon the masses who are permanently excluded from participation in political affairs, government by the most capable few undoubtedly possesses elements of strength and efficiency which are conspicuously absent from a system in which the untrained and ignorant masses hold the reins of power. John Stuart Mill has well remarked that "the governments which have been remarkable in history for sustained mental ability and vigor in the conduct of affairs have generally been aristocracies, "though, as he adds, they have been "without exception aristocracies of public functionaries — that is, of men who have made public business an active profession and the principal occupation of their lives. "

But the weakness of aristocracy as a practical system of

government lies in the difficulty of finding any safe and just principle of selection by which the fittest, politically speaking, may be differentiated from the unfit and, when this is done, of providing any adequate security against the temptation of the former class to exercise their powers in their own interest. It is now generally agreed that the most capable and fit of the population cannot be selected by conferring the power to govern upon certain families and their descendants, for political capacity and probity are qualities not always transmitted from father to son.

There are still, however, some highly respected writers who defend under certain limitations aristocracies constituted on the hereditary principle. Sir Henry Maine, for example, has expressed the opinion that the chances of getting capable persons into the service of the state are as great under the principle of hereditary succession as under a system of popular election.

"A man, "said Professor Seeley, "who is the son of a statesman, who has grown up in the house of a statesman, may be presumed to have learnt something, if only some familiarity with public questions, some knowledge of forms of routine which others are likely to want; and there is a fair probability that he may have acquired more and a certain possibility that, as the younger Pitt, he may have acquired very much and also inherited very much. "

The late W. E. H. Lecky, in a defense of the English aristocracy, commenting on a saying of Benjamin Franklin that there was no more reason for hereditary legislators than for hereditary professors of mathematics, and that it was absurd to expect that the eldest son of a single family should always display exceptional or even average capacity, remarked: "But it is not absurd to expect that more than five hundred families, thrown into public life for the most part at a very early age, animated by all its traditions and ambitions, and placed under circumstances exceedingly favorable to the development of political talent, should produce a large amount of governing faculty....

The qualities required for successful political life are, not like poetry or the higher forms of philosophy, qualities that are of a very rare and exceptional order.

They are for the most part qualities of judgment, industry, tact, knowledge of men and of affairs, which can be attained to a high degree of perfection by men of no very extraordinary intellectual powers.... Few persons, I think, will dispute the high average capacity for government which the circumstances of the English aristocratic life tend to produce.

"Of the value of such an aristocracy to the state Lecky goes on to say: "It is of no small importance that a nation should possess a class of men who have a large stake in the prosperity of the country, who possess a great position independent of politics, who represent very evidently the traditions and the continuity of political life, and who, whatever may be their faults, can at least be trusted to administer affairs with a complete personal integrity and honor.

In the fields of diplomacy and in those great administrative posts which are so numerous in an extended empire, high rank and the manners that commonly accompany it are especially valuable, and their weight is not the least powerfully felt in dealing with democracies. "But when all is said that can be said in favor of birth as the principle of selection, the fact remains, as Seeley readily admits in his defense of the system, that it works for the false aristocracy as well as the true and that the worse traits are transmitted as well as the best.

The possession of property, whether of land or personalty, is an equally unsatisfactory test of political capacity, especially if it be inherited wealth. If gained by honest toil, thrift, and wise management it is, however, a sign of the possession by the owner of qualities which undoubtedly fit him for some participation in public affairs, though obviously there are many men equally capable and worthy who are not property owners.

In other words, property, like birth, is not the only criterion, and therefore the governing power cannot wisely be restricted to either class or to both combined. And so with all other tests which do not rest upon intrinsic merit. Yet to prove that no just or adequate tests can be found really proves nothing against aristocracy itself. The question of whether there ought to be a test by which the fitness of men to exercise a share in the government, as Seeley observes, is not answered by showing that wealth is not such a test or that birth is not such a test. The trouble is not with the aristocracy, but with the test upon which it is constituted.

Rousseau and Jefferson, both champions of democracy in their respective countries, pointed out the distinction between what they called natural aristocracies and artificial or "sham "aristocracies. Rousseau considered elective aristocracies to be the only natural ones, and these he pronounced the "best of all governments, "since they insured "probity, enlightenment, experience, and all the other guarantees that the government would be wisely administered. "In a word, he said, the best and most natural order is where the wisest govern the multitude, if them is any guarantee that the government will be conducted for the benefit of the people and not for themselves.

Jefferson agreed with Rousseau in declaring al aristocracies based on wealth or birth to be not "only useless but mischievous and dangerous "though he was a strong defender of those based on "virtue and talent. "Contrary to the popular belief, he was a believer in aristocratic government, when the aristocracy was of the latter kind. "There is, "he said, "a natural aristocracy founded on talent and virtue which seems destined to govern all societies and all political forms, and the best government is that which provides most efficiently for the purity of the choosing of these natural aristocracies and their introduction into the government.

"Artificial aristocracies have always been hated by the masses because they are constituted on the theory that some are born to rule and others to be their subjects. All of them, whether natural or artificial, are apt to be narrow and exclusive, and are inclined to arrogance and excessive conservatism which at times retards wholesome progress.

Public opinion toward aristocracies in recent times has

been so unfavorable that no example of a pure aristocracy has survived the middle of the nineteenth century. The ancient aristocracy of Rome gave way to democracy. The medieval aristocracies of Germany and Italy were superseded by the growing power of the princes, and the royal governments which they established were in time overwhelmed by the rise of the democracy.

In modern times they survive only in part, being associated wherever they exist with democracy and monarchy. We are entitled by deductions from history, say Woolsey, to lay down the principle that aristocracy is ordinarily capable of no long continuance, when it is the sole governing or by far the strongest power in the state.

Aristocracy is a very common form of government in the infancy of states, when political consciousness manifests itself only in the minds of a few. As this consciousness spreads, the state becomes democratic, and as a matter of fact most of the aristocracies of history have fallen before the advance of democracy.

Aristocracy proper is a principle which all states have admitted and to some extent followed in practice. In all ancient states, democracies and aristocracies alike, large classes of persons were excluded from participation in public affairs. The laboring classes everywhere have been enfranchised only in comparatively recent years.

In England, at the beginning of the eighteenth century one of the freest of states, all the lower classes and a large proportion of the middle classes were excluded from all share in the government of the country. And the same was true to a less degree in America for a considerable period after the colonies became independent. Modern democracies no longer exclude the laboring classes, yet practically all of them apply standards of fitness, even if they sometimes apply them indirectly and in a manner unconsciously.

In this sense the governments of most states are aristocratic. Modern government is such a difficult art and requires so much skill and special knowledge that the whole number of persons really qualified is very small. In short, it must from the very nature of the case be largely government by specialists.

DEMOCRATIC OR POPULAR GOVERNMENT

Democratic or popular government is, as has been pointed out, that form in the constitution and administration of which the great mass of the adult population have a direct or an indirect share. The democratic governments of to-day are founded on the theory that any honest and self-supporting male citizen is, on the average, as well qualified as another for participating in the business of government. They rest, said Jefferson, on confidence in the self-governing capacity of the great mass of the people, and in the ability of the average man, or of average men, to select rulers who will govern in the interest of society.

But it must not be overlooked that, however democratic the basis of government may be, the actual business of governing must be restricted to a comparatively small number of persons — that is, it must be aristocratic. "The whole people cannot operate the government any more than the whole of twenty people in an omnibus can drive the horses. Some one must drive as some one must govern. "

The chief merits of popular government consist in its beneficial effects, first, on the character of the public service itself; and second, upon the citizens who share in its control and administration. Under the first head it is claimed for popular government that it is the only form which responds readily to the needs and desires of the people for whom it is instituted — is, in short, the only form in which responsibility to the governed can be effectively enforced.

Always subject to popular control and immediately responsible to the electorate, it is largely free from the temptation to govern in its own interest or that of a class. Responsibility in any form of government is the soul of efficiency, and governments organized so as to secure in an effective manner the one are likely to possess the principal elements of the other.

By no one has the strength of democratic government in

its representative form been so ably set forth as by John Stuart Mill, who defined it as that form in which "the whole people, or some numerous portion of them, exercise the governing power through deputies periodically elected by themselves.

"There is no difficulty in showing, he asserts, that the ideally best form of government is that in which the supreme controlling power in the last resort is vested in the entire aggregate of the community, every citizen not only having a voice in the exercise of that ultimate sovereignty, but being at least occasionally called on to take an actual part in the government, by the personal discharge of some public function, local or general.

The only government, he continues, which can fully satisfy the exigencies of the social state is one in which the whole people participate, and the degree of participation should everywhere be as great as the general degree of improvement of the community will allow, and ultimately all should be admitted to a share in the sovereign power of the state.

So far as the welfare of the community is concerned, the superiority of popular government, Mill goes on to say, rests upon two principles of as universal truth and applicability as any general proposition which can be laid down respecting human affairs. The first is that the rights and interests of the individual can only be safeguarded when he is able to "stand up "for them himself; the second is that the general prosperity attains a higher degree and is more widely diffused in proportion to the amount and variety of the personal energies enlisted in promoting it.

But the greatest glory of democratic government in the opinion of its votaries does not flow so much from its own inherent excellence as a political contrivance, as from its influence in elevating the masses of the people, developing their faculties, stimulating interest among them in public affairs, and strengthening their patriotism by allowing them a share in its administration. Democracy refuses to concede that some are born to rule and others to obey, and that some should be citizens and others subjects.

It recognizes no privileged classes, but puts all on a footing of political equality. "No man is free in the political acceptation of the word, "says Laveleye, "if he does not have some share in the government of his country, and he who is governed, not by functionaries whom he has helped to choose, but by authorities constituted without his consent, is a subject, not a citizen. "For a government in which the masses have no share they naturally show little readiness to make sacrifices. Democracy strengthens the love of country because the citizens feel that the government is their own and that magistrates are their servants rather than their masters.

The French people, to quote Laveleye again, never began to love France until after the Revolution, when they were admitted to a share in its government, since which time they have adored it. Popular governments, resting as they do on the consent of the governed and upon the principle of equality, are more immune from revolutionary disturbances than those in which the people have no right of participation. De Tocqueville has justly remarked that almost all revolutions which have changed the face of the world have had for their purpose the destruction of inequality.

The same author, in his study of democracy in America, dwelt repeatedly upon the interest which the American people take in public affairs, their high state of intelligence in regard to political matters, and their natural patriotism. He pointed out that one of the great advantages of a democracy is that it serves as a sort of training school for citizenship. Mill likewise laid great stress upon the influence of democracy in elevating the character and intelligence of the masses.

The "most important point of excellence, "he said, "which any form of government can possess is to promote the virtue and intelligence of the people themselves, and the first consideration in judging of the merits of a particular form of government is how far they tend to foster intellectual and moral qualities in the citizens. "The government which does this best, he continues, is likely to be the best in all other respects. Government is thus an agency of education as well as an organization for managing the collective affairs of the community.

The faults and weaknesses of democracy as a form of government have been emphasized by many writers in the past, and have more often been exaggerated than impartially stated. First of all, it is said that democracy emphasizes quantity rather than quality, in that it does not give proper consideration to worth and special fitness, qualities that count for so much in other fields of human activity. It rests on the false principle that one man is as capable of governing as another, in short, that all men are specialists when it comes to the business of government.

Yet government really done well, as the late Mr. Justice James Fitzjames Stephen aptly remarked, requires an immense amount of special knowledge and the steady, restrained, and calm exertion of a great variety of the highest talents which are to be found. The results of ignorance and incapacity can no more be avoided in the difficult art of government than in private business; they are as disastrous in the one as in the other. Both Montesquieu and Mill admitted that democratic government was practicable only where the citizens possessed a high amount of virtue and intelligence.

Democracy stands for short tenures, rotation in office, honorary as contradistinguished from professional service, and the extension of the privilege of officeholding to all without qualification — principles certainly not conducive to strength and efficiency in government. Burke once criticised democracy for the overconfidence of those who participate in the government and for their sense of irresponsibility. If a blunder or a wrong be committed, he said, the share of each individual in the responsibility or infamy is infinitesimal. Each man's approbation of his own acts has to him the appearance of a public judgment in his favor.

"A perfect democracy, "he affirmed, "is the most shameless thing in the world, and as it is the most shameless it is also the most fearless. "Some writers have attempted to show that democratic societies are not favorable to art, science, and culture because their governments do not encourage such things either by direct aid or through the maintenance of conditions under which they naturally flourish.

Two of the most vigorous criticisms of democracy to be found in English literature are those of Sir Henry Maine, in his work on "Popular Government, "and Professor W. E. H. Lecky, in his "Democracy and Liberty. "Maine, after a review of the history of popular government, concluded that "it affords little support for the assumption that it has an indefinitely long future before it. "

Experience, he asserted, rather tends to show that it is a form of government characterized by "great fragility, "and that since its appearance in the world "all forms of government have become more insecure than they were before. ""Popular governments, "he declared, "have been repeatedly overturned by mobs and armies in combination; of all governments they seem least likely to cope successfully with the greatest of all irreconcilables, the nationalists; they imply a breaking up of political power into morsels and the giving to each person an infinitesimally small portion; they rest upon universal suffrage, which is the natural basis of tyranny; they are unfavorable to intellectual progress and the advance of scientific truth; they lack stability; and they are governments by the ignorant and unintelligent. "

"Of all the forms of government, democracy, "he declared, "is by far the most difficult. Little as the governing multitude is conscious of this difficulty, prone as the masses are to aggravate it by their avidity for taking more and more powers into their direct management, it is a fact which experience has placed beyond all dispute. It is the difficulty of democratic government that mainly accounts for its ephemeral duration.

The inherent difficulties of democratic government, he goes on to say, are so great and manifold that in large complex modern societies it could neither last nor work if it were not aided by certain forces which are not exclusively associated with it, but of which it greatly stimulates the energy. The prejudices of the people are far stronger than those of the privileged classes; they are far more vulgar and they are far more dangerous because their opinions are apt to run counter to scientific conclusions.

Maine denies that there is any real connection between

democracy and liberty, and asserts that in case there is and the choice has to be made between them, it is better to remain a nation capable of displaying the virtues of a nation than even to be free. "By a wise constitution, "says Maine, "democracy may be made as calm as the water in a great artificial reservoir; but if there is a weak point anywhere in its structure, the mighty force which it controls will burst through it and spread destruction far and near. "

Lecky likewise dwells upon the dangers of government by the "poorest, the most ignorant, the most incapable, who are necessarily the most numerous. "The idea of government by such a class reverses, he declares, all the past experience of mankind. "In every field of human enterprise, in all the computations of life, by the inexorable law of nature, superiority lies with the few and not with the many, and success can be obtained by placing the guiding and controlling power mainly in their hands.

"Democracy insures neither better government nor greater liberty; indeed, some of the strongest democratic tendencies are adverse to liberty. On the contrary, strong arguments may be adduced both from history and from the nature of things to show that democracy may often prove the direct opposite of liberty. "Ancient Rome and modern France, for example, seem to furnish evidence of the truth of Lecky's assertion.

The French despotisms, which had their foundations on plebiscites, were quite as natural forms of democracy as republics, yet liberty can hardly be said to have been one of their virtues. To place the chief power in the most ignorant classes is to place it in the hands of those who naturally care least for political liberty and who are most likely to follow with an absolute devotion some strong leader.

The upper and middle classes have shown the greatest devotion to liberty and have been its most ardent defenders, while democracy has often enough sought to dethrone it. Speaking of the United States, he declares, as De Tocqueville did before him, that in hardly any other country does the best life and energy of the nation flow so habitually apart from politics, and is the best talent so rarely chosen to the public service. Likewise he adopts the view of De Tocqueville, Laveleye, Bluntschli, and Maine that democracy is unfavorable to the development of the higher forms of intellectual life, such as literature, art, and science, in short, that democracy levels down quite as much as up.

Speaking of the alleged equality upon which the American democracy rests, Maine declares that there has hardly ever been a community in which the weak have been pushed so piteously to the wall; in which those who have succeeded have so uniformly been the strong, and in which, in so short a time, there has arisen so great an inequality of private fortune and domestic luxury.

"Laveleye, in his work entitled argues similarly to show that democracy does not necessarily produce equality any more than it produces liberty, and that it is, besides, the enemy of both wealth and culture. Inequality of conditions and the struggle of classes, he declares, were responsible for the fall of the ancient democracies. If the people are ignorant and incapable, democracy must inevitably degenerate into anarchy and despotism, and both equality and liberty will be lost.

Concerning the future of democratic government there is no longer any considerable difference of opinion. The adverse opinions that used to be so commonly expressed have slowly dwindled in number and respectability until only here and there are serious doubts raised, though warnings are still frequently heard. Sir Henry Maine, who ventured the opinion twenty-five years ago that the history of popular government did not warrant the assumption that it had an indefinite future, admitted that the example of the United States had done much to raise the credit of democratic republics and to reveal their possibilities.

Lecky, who, like Maine, feared and distrusted democracy, also admitted that it was "likely to dominate, at least for a considerable time, in all civilized countries, "and that the only questions to be met were those relating to the form which it should take and the means by which its characteristic evils could be best avoided. The most remarkable political phenomenon of the latter part of the nineteenth century, as

Lecky observes, has been the "complete displacement of the centre of power in free governments. "Democracy has advanced until it has spread over the greater part of the civilized world.

It has in effect wrought a profound and far-reaching revolution throughout Europe and America, though in most instances it has been effected without acts of violence or change in the external framework of the government. Its continued spread is inevitable and irresistible, and no hand can stay its advance.

For more than half a century the opinion has been steadily gaining ground that the masses are as well qualified for governing and more worthy to be trusted than any small minority, however respected or highly trained. Democracy represents for us, as Sidgwick aptly remarks, not merely a depressingly prevalent political fact, but a widely and enthusiastically accepted political ideal. Lecky is charitable enough to say that the

American democracy is not a failure, but he asserts that it carries with it at least as much of warning as of encouragement. One thing is absolutely essential to its safe working, he concludes, namely, a "written constitution, securing property and contract, placing difficulties in the way of organic changes, restricting the power of majorities, and preventing outbursts of mere temporary discontent and mere casual coalitions from overthrowing the main pillars of state.

"He might also have added to his list of essentials an intelligent and virtuous citizenship, for upon this strong foundation, more than upon anything else, the future of democracy throughout the world depends. Happily the widespread interest in public education and civic honesty offers an encouraging prospect for its future.

What has been said above concerning the strength and weakness of democracy has reference mainly to representative democracy. The pure or direct type exists in too rare and restricted a form in the modern world and is too impracticable to merit extended consideration. Sufficing for the simple needs of the few communities where it still survives, it is wholly unsuited to the conditions of the complex states of to-day. Nevertheless recent years have seen the growth of popular dissatisfaction with the representative system, and a demand for more direct participation of the masses in the government, particularly in the legislative function.

This growing self-consciousness of the masses has found expression in a variety of new institutional forms of democracy, such as the referendum, the initiative, proportional representation, the recall, etc. The introduction of these new forms of direct democracy into the constitution of many states bids fair to work important changes in the character of the representative system.

FEDERAL GOVERNMENT

Federal government, like all other forms, has its elements of strength and of weakness, its advantages and its disadvantages. Among the more conspicuous merits of the federal system may be noted, first of all, that it affords a means of uniting into a powerful state commonwealths more or less diverse in character and having dissimilar institutions, without extinguishing wholly their separate existences.

It furnishes the means of maintaining an equilibrium of centrifugal and centripetal forces in a state of widely different tendencies. Federalism has been the means of bringing together many petty states in the past which, but for this, would have remained forever apart. It has thus proved a powerful unifying force where other forms of government have repelled. Again, it excels all other forms of government in the effectiveness with which it combines the advantages of national unity and power with those of local autonomy.

It secures at the same time all the advantages of uniformity in the regulation of affairs of general concern with those of diversity in the regulation of local affairs. Instead of concentrating the power of the state in a single organ or set of organs, as is the case in the unitary state, federalism distributes it between a common central government and a number of local governments, and thus prevents the rise of a single despotism absorbing all political power and menacing the liberties of the people. By securing the advantages of selfgovernment for the people in those affairs which are peculiarly local to them, it reconciles them to the loss of power which they have sustained through the surrender of their control over other affairs to the general government. Furthermore, through the right of local self-government, the interest of the people in local affairs is stimulated and preserved, they are educated in their civic duties, and this in turn reacts upon the character of the local administration.

Federalism, observes Bryce, allows experiments in local legislation and administration which could not safely be tried in a large country having a unitary system of government. At the same time it supplies the best means of developing a new and vast country by allowing the particular localities to develop their special needs in the way they think best.

The excellencies of federal government have been widely and frequently dwelt upon by political writers during the last half century. John Fiske declared it to be the only kind of government which, according to modern ideas, is permanently applicable to a whole continent.

Sidgwick, an English writer, predicts that we shall see an extension of it even in western Europe, where the example of America will be followed. The German writer Brie, who has made an elaborate study of federal government, declares that it represents the highest realization of the state idea; while Westerkamp, whose researches have been along the same line, dwells upon its excellencies and points out that it has spread until it embraces a portion of the globe equal to three times the territorial area of Europe.

In recent years, however, owing to changed conditions under which its success has been less marked, there has been an increasing disposition to dwell upon the weaknesses as well as the virtues of federal government. These weaknesses are coming to be more apparent as economic and industrial conditions of society become more complex and require uniformity of regulation.

As one writer has recently said: "Federal government has very decided limitations, serious faults of structure, unheeded perhaps at the time of its inception, but likely to break down under the altering strain of a new environment. Politically and on its external side it has proved itself strong, but economically and in its internal aspect it is proving itself weak. "

First of all, in the conduct of foreign affairs federal government possesses an inherent weakness not found in unitary government. The experience of the United States in particular has shown that the individual members of the federal union, by virtue of their reserved powers over the rights of person and property, may embarrass the national government in enforcing its treaty obligations in respect to aliens residing in the United States.

Likewise in the domain of internal affairs federal government has given evidence of weaknesses which have grown enormously in recent years. It means division of power between coordinate authorities in many fields of legislation and administration, and division of power always produces weakness, whatever other advantages it may secure.

Particularly as respects such matters as commerce and transportation, marriage and divorce, labour, and industries which are national in their scope of operation, federalism usually means variety of regulation where there ought to be uniformity. It is here that some of the most serious faults of the United States federal system have shown themselves. In the domain of military affairs federalism is of course entirely out of place, and usually where the federal system of government exists the unitary principle prevails in military administration.

Concerning the future of federal government there is, of course, a difference of opinion. Some writers maintain that it is only a transitory form and will ultimately give way to the unitary form, just as confederate government has nearly everywhere been superseded by the federal system. It was established, its critics assert, out of sheer pressure of external necessity rather than from its own inherent excellence; and it marks merely a transition stage through which many states have been obliged to pass in order to attain a more perfect organization.

But this pressure having been removed, and the preliminary stage having been passed through, the principal purposes of federal government will have been accomplished, and it will give way to a more efficient system - one better adapted to the conditions and needs of the present civilization.

THE TEST OF A GOOD GOVERNMENT

Some writers have endeavored to lay down certain general principles concerning the best form of government for all societies and all conditions of men. Others have adopted the view of the poet: "For forms of government let fools contest, That which is best administered, is best. "

We are safe in saying that no single form of government is adapted to all conditions and stages of society. In determining what are the characteristics of the best government for any particular society we must take into consideration the stage of development which the society has attained, the intelligence and political capacity of the people, their history and traditions, their race characteristics, and a variety of other elements.

"To attempt, "says John Stuart Mill, "to say what kind of government is suited for every known state of society would be to compose a treatise on political science at large. "Monarchy is undoubtedly a desirable system for certain purposes; aristocracy is better adapted to certain others; while democracy is still better suited to other societies. Universal suffrage may be well suited to certain stages of society, while in others it would lead to a breakdown of government. Federal government is excellently adapted to certain stages of political development, while unitary government is better suited to others. Confederate government and even theocracies, as we have tried to show, have their places in the development of the state.

No single form of government is adapted to all societies any more than a suit of clothes can be made to fit all men. The system best suited to Sparta was not the best for Athens; what is best for a large empire is not necessarily the best for a state of small area. What was the best for England in the time of the Tudors is not the best for England to-day. If mere security of life and property are the main objects to be attained, then a very different kind of government will suffice from that which is necessary when the promotion of the social well-being of the people is considered a necessary object. "If, "says Lieber, "the object is to reform and reorganize the debased and nerveless population of a large country in a tropical climate as that of Egypt, the government must essentially differ from that of an industrial people who, like the Dutch, must battle with the sea.

"Government is like a house which must be adapted in construction to its peculiar purposes and needs. The most that can be done is to lay down a few general principles, and these will be determined by the point of view or prejudices of the writer. Alexander Hamilton declared that the "true test of a good government "was its "aptitude and tendency to produce a good administration. "John Stuart Mill said "the first element of a good government "was the "promotion of the virtue and intelligence of the people.

"The first question to be considered, he said, was "how far does the government tend to foster the moral and intellectual qualities of the citizens? "The government which does this best, he maintains, is likely to be the best in other respects. The main criterion of a good government, in other words, is the degree to which it tends to increase "the sum of good qualities "in the governed, collectively and individually, rather than the efficiency of the government itself as an administrative body.

DEFINITIONS AND DISTINCTIONS; LEGAL VERSUS POLITICAL SOVEREIGNTY; DE FACTO VERSUS DE JURE SOVEREIGNTY

THE one mark which fundamentally distinguishes the state from all other human associations is supremacy of will and action — the supreme power to command and enforce obedience. It is not enough that the state should have a single collective will — other associations have that — but its will must dominate all other wills and override them in case of conflict. There is in every independent political community not in the habit of obedience to a superior, as Sir Henry Maine has observed, some single person or some combination of persons which has the power of compelling other minds to do exactly as it pleases, and, he adds, this person or agency may be found as certainly as the centre of gravity in a mass of matter. To this power, legally speaking, all interests are potentially subject, and all wills subordinate. We call this attribute or power sovereignty.

The study of its nature and characteristics constitutes one of the most important, if not the most important, topic in political science. The term "sovereignty "(*souverainete*) is derived from the Latin *superanus* (supreme, sovereign), and was first employed by Bodin in his celebrated work "*De la Republique,* "published in 1576. The idea, however, is as old as Aristotle. Since Bodin first introduced the term into the literature of political science, the word and the idea, observes Bluntschli, have exercised a vast influence on the development of constitutions and on the whole politics of modern times.

Definitions of sovereignty, like definitions of the state, are almost infinite in number. Bodin, the first writer to employ the term, defined it as "*the summa in cives acsubditas legibusque soluta potestas* " — the supreme power of the state over citizens and subjects, unrestrained by law.

Grotius, who wrote half a century later, defined it as "the supreme political power vested in him whose acts are not subject to any other and whose will cannot be over- ridden. "Blackstone conceived it to be "the supreme, ir-resistible, absolute, uncontrolled authority in which the *jura summi imperii* reside. "Jellinek has defined it as "that characteristic of the state in virtue of which it cannot be legally bound except by its own will or limited by any other power than itself.

"The French publicist Duguit defines it simply as the power of willing and commanding. Bur-gess characterizes it as "original, absolute, unlimited power over the individual subject and over all associations of subjects. "Again he calls it "the underived and independent power to command and compel obedience. "

Before proceeding with a discussion of the attributes of sovereignty it will be well for us to differentiate between the several meanings which the term has come to possess. In the first place, we may note the distinction between titular and actual sovereignty. Titular sovereignty is the supremacy fictitiously attributed to a ruling prince, who personifies the power and majesty of the state and in whose name the government is conducted, the real sover- eignty being in other hands. Thus the crowned heads of Europe are officially designated as "sovereigns, "though of course they are only such in a nominal or titular sense.

Again, we must distinguish between legal and political sovereignty. The former represents the lawyer's concep- tion of sovereignty, that is, sovereignty as the supreme law- making power. The legal sovereign, therefore, is that determinate authority which is able to express in a legal formula the highest commands of the state; that power which can override the prescriptions of the divine law, the principles of morality, the mandates of public opinion, etc.

This is the only sovereignty recognized by the courts Behind the legal sovereign, however, is another power, legally unknown, and incapable of expressing the will of the state in the form of legal command, yet, withal, a power to whose mandates the legal sovereign must in practice bow and whose will must ultimately prevail in the state.

This is the political sovereign. In a narrower sense the electorate constitutes the political sovereign, yet in a wider sense it may be said to be the whole mass of the population, including every person who contributes to the molding of public opin-ion. Powerful as it is, however, it cannot itself express its will in the form of a legal rule, except where the principle of the pure democracy prevails, though it may command the legislature to do its bidding, and if the command is clearly pronounced and fully understood, it will not be lightly dis-regarded.

Where the will of the legal sovereign and the political sovereign conflict, the former must, however, take prece-dence, since only that which has been embodied in legal form will be enforced by the courts, however much more in accordance with the principles of expediency or abstract justice the mandate of the political sovereign may seem to be. The legal sovereign, observes a well-known writer, is the lawyer's sovereign *qua* lawyer, the sovereign beyond which lawyers and courts refuse to look.

For the lawyer a law may be good law, legally, though passed by a parliament which has been condemned by the political sovereign, the electorate. With the wishes or feelings of the electors the lawyer as lawyer has nothing to do. He may take into consideration their opinions and wishes, but until the latter have been embodied in a written legal command they are for him mere ***brutum fulmen***. James Bryce has remarked that the distinction between legal and political sovereignty is largely the result of the difference between the juristic and the popular conception of sovereignty.

"To an ordi-nary layman, "he says, "the sovereign is that person or body of persons which can make his or their will prevail in the state, who is acknowledged to stand at the top, who can get his own way and make others go his. For the lawyer, however, a more definite conception is required. To him the sovereign is no other person or body than him to whose directions the law attributes legal force, the person or body in whom resides as of right the ultimate power of laying down general rules. This person or body is the legal sover-eign and represents the juristic conception. "

Some writers reject the distinction between legal and political sovereignty on the ground that it seems to involve the recognition of a dual sovereignty in the state. A little reflection, however, will show that the distinction between legal and political sovereignty does not rest upon the principle of a divided sovereignty, but rather upon the distinction between two different manifestations of one and the same sovereignty through different channels.

As has been said, the one may not harmonize with the other, that is, the expressed will of the legal sovereign may not be that which the political sovereign has commanded, in which case the legal sovereign ought to be reorganized or reconstituted by a new election, otherwise the will of the electorate cannot be made effective. This is nothing more than saying that law ought to conform to public opinion when properly expressed; that the legislator ought to obey the mandate of the electorate; and that when he does not, the electorate and the legislature are out of harmony and should be "reharmonized "by new elections.

The problem of good government, says Professor Ritchie, is largely the problem of the proper relation between the legal and the ultimate political sovereignty. Of course, where the principle of the pure democracy prevails, the possibility of this divergence between the will of the legal and political sovereigns is eliminated, for under such conditions the two are identi-cal.

In a pure democracy the expressed will of the elec-torate is not mere opinion or mandate, but law itself. Ordinarily, however, the legal sovereign is organized separate and distinct from the political sovereign, and is either some determinate organ like the British Parliament or a constituent body called into existence for the specific purpose of formulating and expressing the sovereign will.

The distinction between legal and political sovereignty is most prominent in those countries like Great Britain whose constitutional enactments proceed from the legislature, where, in consequence, there is no legal distinction between constitutional and statute law. In Great Britain the Parliament is both the ordinary legislative body and the constituent assembly. It is legally omnipotent and subject to no restraints except those of a moral and physi-cal character.

There is no person or body of persons in Great Britain capable of making rules which can override or derogate from an act of Parliament. The British Parlia-ment is so omnipotent, legally speaking, says Dicey, that it can adjudge an infant of full age; it may attaint a man of treason after death; it may legitimize an illegitimate child, or, if it sees fit, make a man a judge in his own case. By the act of 1716 it did what only a sovereign body can do, when it prolonged its own existence from three to seven years.

It can alter the constitution by the same legal processes that are followed in the enactment of an ordinary statute. No court will listen to an argument against the va-lidity of an act of Parliament, even though it be contrary to the most sacred prescriptions of the constitution. It is clear, therefore, that the legal sovereignty of the British state is in the Parliament, and hence there is no legal authority in existence which can restrain it or override its acts.

Yet there is a sense in which the English Parliament is not sovereign. There is a power above Parliament whose mandates it must obey and whose will must ultimately prevail in all governmental matters. This is the will pronounced by the electorate at a general parliamentary election. The lawyers do not recognize this sovereignty and the courts do not take notice of it, and even the Par-liament itself might for a time lawfully resist it, but in the end, if the electorate insists upon obedience, Parliament must bow before the popular will and enact its commands into law. In this sense the electorate and not Parliament is sovereign.

While attempting to justify the existence of that sover-eignty which has no legal basis, we must not, however, over- look the limitations and conditions under which it is entitled to recognition. The "general will, "the "sovereignty of the people, "or whatever we may choose to call the controlling power behind the organ through which the will of the state is given legal formulation, are rather vague and loose expressions and when not used with proper discrimination lead to misconception and even to mischief.

As Professor Sidgwick has well said, "There is a certain sense in which the mass of the people in any community may be said to be the ultimate depository of supreme political power, though it is misleading to say that the people are everywhere sovereign. "To maintain the doctrine of popular sovereignty without restriction is to ignore the fundamental distinction between power legally exercised and power usurped and illegally exercised. The will of the people expressed otherwise than through legally constituted channels is not sovereign any more than the unofficial opinions of the members of a legislative body are law. The sover- eignty of the people has a meaning and is entitled to legal recognition only when it is the sovereignty of the people organized in their legislative bodies or constituent assemblies.

In the next place a distinction may be made between the sovereignty which is actually obeyed by the inhabitants of the state, though it may be without legal basis, and the sovereignty which according to legal right is entitled to the obedience of the people, but of which in fact the bearer may be temporarily dispossessed or which for other reason is incapable of making its will prevail.

That person or body of persons who is in fact dominant in the state, who for the time receives the actual obedience of the great mass of the in- habitants, who constitutes the strongest power in the state, is the actual or *de facto* sovereign, though not necessarily the legal sovereign. This sovereign may be a usurping king, a self-constituted assembly, a military dictator, or even a priest or a prophet; in either case the sovereignty rests upon physical power or spiritual influence rather than upon legal right.

History abounds in examples of such sovereignties. Cromwell, after he had dissolved theLong Parliament, Napoleon, after he had overthrown the Directory, the English convention which offered the crown to William and Mary, the French assembly which made peace with Germany in 1871, the Southern Confederacy from 1861 to 1865, are instances of actual sovereignties which rested upon no legal basis, though some of them ultimately became *de jure* sovereignties through the ac-quisition of a legal status.

The temporary occupation of the part of a state's territory by a hostile army when the commander displaces the local authority and exacts obe- dience from the inhabitants is another example of *de facto* sovereignty of which history affords many instances. In some of the instances cited above, the usurping sovereign expelled the legal sovereign from his rightful seat and by force compelled the obedience of the inhabitants.

It is an established rule of public law that the adherents

of the *de facto* sovereign in case of a war between it and the *de jure* sovereign do not incur the penalties of treason and under certain limitations the obligations assumed by it in behalf of the country or the public acts performed by it will be respected by the *de jure* sovereign when it is re- stored to its rightful place.

It is also a rule that where the *de facto* sovereign gives evidence of his ability to main- tain his supremacy and command the obedience of the great mass of the people, he shall be morally entitled to receive the recognition of foreign states. Other examples of *de facto* sovereignties occur where the power of the legal sovereign has been superseded by the moral influence of some per- son, body of persons, or government. Such was the power wielded by the former Shoguns in Japan, and such is the power exercised by the British government in Egypt to- day.

De jure sovereignty, on the other hand, has its foundation in law, not in physical power, and the person or body of persons by whom it is exercised can always show a legal right to rule. This is the sovereignty which the law recog- nizes and to which it attributes the right to govern and exact obedience. It does not depend for its validity upon obedience actually rendered, for the law assumes the obe-dience to be enforceable.

As a matter of fact it may not be the actual sovereign, for it may be expelled, as has been said, from its rightful place or may have temporarily disappeared through disorganization or disintegration; but, however this may be, it has legal right on its side and is lawfully entitled to command and exact obedience. Mani-festly, every consideration of expediency, however, requires that the sovereign in actual control should be legally entitled to rule, that is, physical power and mastery ought to rest upon legal right.

In reality the sovereign who succeeds in maintaining his claim to rule usually becomes in the course of time the legal sovereign, through the acquies-cence of the people or the reorganization of the state, somewhat as actual possession in private law ripens into legal ownership through prescription.

On account of the manifest advantages which flow from the exercise of power resting on strict legal right rather than upon mere physical force, the new sovereign sometimes has his *de facto* claim converted into a legal right by election or ratification. This was done, *e. g.*, by William the Conqueror in 1066 and by Napoleon III of France in 1852. Such an act on the part of the new sovereign by thus establishing a legal basis for his power strengthens his moral claim to the obedience of the people and diminishes the danger of conspir-acies and rebellions on the part of the adherents of the displaced sovereign. There is, as Bryce well observes, a natural and instinctive opposition to submission to power which rests only on force.

THE ATTRIBUTES OF SOVEREIGNTY

We may enumerate the distinguishing attributes of sovereignty as permanence, exclusiveness, all-comprehensiveness, absoluteness, inalienability, and unity. By the quality of permanence or perpetuity, we mean that quality in virtue of which the sovereignty of the state continues without interruption so long as the state itself exists. It does not cease with the death or dispossession of the temporary bearer, or the reorganization of the state, but shifts imme- diately to a new bearer, as the centre of gravity shifts from one part of a physical body to another whenever it undergoes external change.

By exclusiveness we mean that quality in virtue of which there can be but one supreme power in the state, entitled to the obedience of the inhabitants. To hold otherwise would be to deny the principle of the unity and organic nature of the state and to recognize the possibility of an imperium in imperio.

Sovereignty is coextensive in its operation with the jurisdiction of the state and comprehends within its scope all persons and things in the territory of the state. The modern state does not recognize the existence of any staatlos person within its jurisdiction. For reasons of public policy and international comity civilized states voluntarily re- linquish the exercise of jurisdiction over the diplomatic representatives of foreign states residing within their ter- ritories, but this rule of extraterritoriality, as it is called, is no exception to the principle stated above. The fact that states have until comparatively recent times declined to recognize the principle of extraterritoriality, and that even now any state may expel a diplomatic representative from its territory and thus deprive him of his immunity, are evidences of the truth of the proposition that the sover-eignty of the state is all-embracing and all-comprehensive.

By the quality of absolutism we mean simply that sovereignty is legally unlimited, that is, it is subject to no higher power — an attribute which results from the very nature of the thing itself. To hold otherwise would be to assume the existence of a higher power by which the sovereign is limited.

By the quality of inalienability we mean that attri-bute of the state by virtue of which it cannot cede away any of its essential elements without self-destruc-tion. Sovereignty can no more be alienated, says Lieber, than a tree can alienate its right to sprout, or a man can transfer his life or personality to another without self- destruction. Rousseau holds the same view, though he admits that *power* may be transferred. A few writers, however, take the contrary view. Professor Ritchie, for example, declares that the doctrine of inalienability is belied by the facts of history.

Of course it is not meant that where a state parts with a portion of its territory it retains its sovereignty over the territory alienated. His-tory abounds in examples of territorial cessions involving the alienation of the sovereignty of the state over the territory ceded, but that is a different thing from saying that the state may cede away its sovereignty as such; that is, part with a constituent element without which it could no more exist than a man without heart or blood. Nor does the principle of inalienability mean that the person or per- sons in whom the sovereignty is for the time reposed may not abdicate.

The British Parliament, for example, might dissolve itself without making any provision for calling another Parliament, or the Czar of Russia might voluntarily relinquish his rights of sovereignty in favor of a Duma, as he seems to have in fact lately done; but there would not be in either case an alienation, but only a shifting of the re-pository or abiding place.

Implied in the principle of inalienability of sovereignty is that of imprescriptibility, according to which sover-eignty cannot be lost by mere lapse of time, as prop-erty in land may be lost by prescription at private law. There is an old doctrine held by some writers that originally the people were sovereign everywhere, but through the long and uninterrupted usurpation of sovereign power by kings it was gradually lost to the people by operation of the principle of prescription. But the theory has little evidence to support it.

THE ABSOLUTISM OF SOVEREIGNTY; THEORY OF LIMITATIONS

Among the characteristics of sovereignty which merit a more extended consideration than we have given in the preceding section is the quality of absolutism. Sover-eignty cannot be limited; it is an original, not a de- rived power. As it is the supreme power in the state, there cannot, legally speaking, be any authority above it, and to speak of it as being limited by some higher power is a contradiction of terms. Sovereignty, as Jellinek re- marks, can be bound only by its own will, that is, it can only be self-limited.

While from the very nature of the case sovereignty cannot be subject to legal restrictions, many writers rec- ognize the existence of certain moral limitations on the power of the sovereign, arising from the natural and inherent rights of man — rights which, according to the views of some authorities, exist independently of the state and cannot therefore be restricted or limited by it.

Thus, observes a well-known writer, "although... some of those who have written on sovereignty described the sov-ereign as being subject to no restraint whatever, his sole will being absolutely dominant over all his subjects, there has never really existed in the world any person or even any body of persons enjoying this utterly uncontrolled power, with no external force to fear and nothing to regard except the gratification of mere volition. "The same assertion is made by Bluntschli, who declares that "there is no such thing on earth as absolute independence.... Even the state as a whole is not almighty, for it is limited externally by the rights of other states and internally by its own nature and by the rights of its individual members. "

Some writers maintain that the sovereignty of the state is limited by the prescriptions of the divine law, or by the power of some superhuman authority. The Russian publicist Martens, for example, in his definition of sovereignty recognizes in God a "legal superior "over a state otherwise "entirely sovereign. "Bluntschli asserts that nations are "respon-sible to the eternal judgments of God "as well as to "the facts of history. ""There is above the sovereign, "says the German writer Schulze, "a higher moral and natural order, the eternal principle of the moral law. "

The doctrine that the state is absolutely supreme and incapable of do-ing wrong is, he says, fallacious and dangerous. Other alleged limitations on sovereignty are those arising from the law of nature, the principles of morality, the teachings of religion, the principles of abstract justice, immemorial custom, long-established traditions, etc. To these have been added the limitations imposed by the rules of inter-national law, the particular restrictions imposed by conventions between states, and limitations imposed by states themselves by their fundamental law, such, for example, as the method of procedure for altering their constitutions.

It must of course, be admitted that in a certain sense the exercise of sovereignty is subject to restrictions. The most despotic monarch respects the opinions of his subjects on certain questions and often bows to their wishes. Probably no sovereign, whether monarch or assembly, ever existed who assumed and exercised the right to change any law, custom, or institution at his pleasure without regard to the opinions of the mass of the popula- tion.

All sovereignty, in short, must be conditioned upon the ready obedience or acquiescence of those over whom it is exercised. The sultan of Turkey, for example, abso- lute as he is, would hardly dare interfere with the religion of his subjects; the British Parliament, with power legally unlimited, would hesitate to tax the colonies, or to pass a decennial act, or to establish the Episcopal Church in Scot- land; it is doubtful if any Roman emperor would have dared to subvert the national religion of Rome; Louis XIV, who is credited with having boasted that he was the state, would probably never have been able to force Protestant- ism on his subjects.

An examination of these limitations, however, will show that legally they are no restrictions on sovereignty at all. The law of nature, the principles of morality, the laws of God, the dictates of humanity and reason, the law of nations, the fear of public opinion, and all the other alleged restric- tions on sovereignty have no legal effect, except in so far as the state chooses to recognize them and give them force and validity. They are not such limitations as the courts will ordinarily enforce in the decision of legal controversies.

Thus, if the English Parliament, which is the legal sovereign in the British Empire, should pass an act opposed tothe principles of morality or contrary to the rules of inter- national law, however repugnant the statute might be to the moral sense of the people or their ideas of justice and good faith, it would not be legally invalid. The courts would presume that Parliament did not intend to violate the rules of morality or the principles of international law, and they would not listen to an argument which rested on the assumption that Parliament had exceeded its author- ity.

If in any case the limitations of the divine law are recognized, the state in the last analysis must be the interpreter of the divine will, so that in fact the restriction is nothing but a self-limitation. In other words the principles of morality, of justice, of religion, etc., so far as they constitute limitations on the sovereign, are simply what the consciousness of the state decides them to be, for there can be no other legal consciousness than that of the state.

Regarding the so-called limitations on sovereignty imposed by the principles of international law, we are forced to the same conclusion, namely, that in the last analysis they are nothing more than "self-limitations. "The subjects of international law are sovereign states, and in the last resort they must be considered as the interpreters of their own rights and of their obligations to other states.

There is no higher legal power to enforce the obligations which the public opinion of the civilized world may declare to be binding upon them. States are subject only to their own wills, not to any outside will. Juristically speaking, the state has an undoubted right to refuse to be bound bya particular usage of international law, and as a matter of fact the courts of most countries are bound to give prece- dence to municipal statutes in preference to the prescrip- tions of international law, even though the former are contrary to the latter.

And so as regards the obligations of the state which it may have imposed upon itself by ex- press convention with other states. They are not legal limitations on the sovereign power, but conventional agree- ments which the state may disregard or even repudiate so far as its legal right to do so is concerned. The same may be said of the alleged limitations set by the state upon the manner in which its powers shall be exercised, such, for example, as the method of procedure which it may have prescribed for making changes in its own constitutional organization.

Such rules of procedure cannot be considered as legal restrictions upon the sovereignty of the state, and it is a matter of common knowledge that such provisions have in the past been time and again set aside for other methods.

The inevitable conclusion, therefore, to which we are led, is that all attempts to place legal restrictions upon sovereignty are futile and useless. Whoever or whatever can impose limitations on the power of the state is itself the sovereign, and not until we reach that power which is unlimited do we come into the presence of the sovereign. Supreme power, limited by positive law, says Austin, is a flat contradiction in terms.

The doctrine of unlimited sovereignty is sometimes criticised on the ground that it leads to the legal despotism of the state. But granting *arguendo* that sovereignty may be limited in the interest of liberty or good government, we are no better off. We are still brought face to face with another sovereign, namely, that which imposes the limitation – the very thing from which we are seeking to escape. John Austin, with his usual clearness and incisiveness, stated the matter correctly when he said:

"The power of the superior sov- ereign imposing the restraints on the power of some other sovereign superior to that superior would still be absolutely free from the fetters of positive law. For unless the imagined restraints were ultimately imposed by a sovereign not in a state of subjection to a higher or superior sovereign, a series of sovereigns ascending to infinity would govern the imagined community, which is impossible and absurd. "

It is difficult to see what is to be gained by trying to avoid such a conclusion. It is necessary to recognize in the state a power to which all things and all wills are po- tentially subject, otherwise the state is no different funda- mentally from the other associations and organizations into which mankind is grouped. But this recognition does not imply an admission of the moral right of the state to control and regulate all the interests and activities of the people over whom sovereign power potentially exists.

In all modern states there is a large group of interests, a wide domain of human conduct, which are in fact exempt from all governmental interference. There is no likelihood that the state will ever exercise all of the power which legally belongs to it. Considerations of expediency, to say nothing of justice, require that in practice the greater part of its power should exist only *in potentia,* and that the individual should be left free from governmental control within a certain sphere. Any sovereign, whether monarch or assembly, which should attempt to exercise its un- doubted legal power to regulate all the interests and relations of human life would soon be overthrown by revolution.

It is difficult to see how the doctrine of unlimited sover-eignty is inconsistent with the idea of the widest liberty. It does not require profound thinking to we that the more fully and completely sovereign the state, the more secure and permanent must be the liberty of the people. During the eighteenth century the sovereignty of the state was generally confused with the absolutism of particular kings, and therefore the doctrine of unlimited sovereignty had few defenders except among those who, like Hobbes, were the apologists of certain princes who sought to rule with- out regard to constitutional restrictions.

With the dis-appearance of absolutism in government and the general introduction of constitutionalism, however, the theory of the unlimited sovereignty of the state came to have more advocates than opponents. When the state came to be organized outside of the government and sovereignty was understood in its true light, namely, as an attribute of the former rather than of the latter, it became an easy matter to reconcile the doctrine of an unlimited sovereignty with that of a limited government.

THE INDIVISIBILITY OF SOVEREIGNTY

Another characteristic of sovereignty which requires more detailed consideration is the quality of unity. Being the highest will in the state, it cannot be divided without producing several wills, which is, of course, inconsistent with the notion of sovereignty. The existence of several supreme wills, each capable of issuing commands and of exacting obedience, would obviously result in conflicts and an ultimate paralysis of the state.

If the several supposed wills were co-ordinate, obviously neither could be sovereign; if one were superior and the others subordinate, manifestly the former would be sovereign and the latter subject, and what would appear to be a division of sovereignty would in fact be no division. By no one has this truth been more forcibly set forth than by the American statesman John C. Calhoun, in his

"Disquisition on Government, "written in 1851. "Sovereignty, "he declared, "is an entire thing; to divide it is to destroy it. It is the supreme power in a state, and we might just as well speak of half a square or half a triangle as of half a sovereignty. "But this view is by no means universally accepted by publicists and politi- cal writers of to-day. The existence of a large number of petty states on the continent of Europe during the six- teenth and seventeenth centuries, which were practically, though not theoretically, independent, contributed to the spread of the popular belief in the distinction between part-sovereign and fully sovereign states — a distinction which rests in fact on the notion of a divided sovereignty. In more recent times the organization of so-called composite states, confederations, real unions, and federal states, and the establishment of such relationships as are involved in the creation of protectorates, have powerfully strengthened the divisibility theory.

The question of a dual sovereignty first became a con-troversy of practical politics in the United States of America toward the middle of the nineteenth century. Under the Articles of Confederation each member of the union expressly retained its own sovereignty, so that the possibility of misunderstanding was avoided.

But the constitution of the federal union of 1789 was silent on this all-important subject, hence, the questions were left open as to whether sovereignty remained in the individual states where it had formerly rested, whether it was in the united state created by their joint agency, or whether it was divided between the individual states on the one hand and the union on the other. This casus omissus was doubtless the result of a compromise between the conflicting forces of particularism and nationalism in the convention which framed the con- stitution.

The theory of a dual sovereignty under the American federal system was generally held by publicists in America at the time of the adoption of the constitution, it was enunciated in the "Federalist "by Hamilton and Madison, and was adopted at an early date by the Supreme Court, which held that the United States was sovereign as to the powers which had been conferred upon it, and that the states were sovereign as to those which were reserved to them, and this view is still maintained by the court.

It has received the approval of such eminent

constitutional lawyers as Judges Cooleyand Storyand political writers like De Tocqueville, Wheaton, Halleck, Hurd, Bliss, and many others.

"There is no question, "says Hurd,. "that the statesmen of all sections who made the constitution of the United States understood that political sovereignty was capable of division according to its subject and powers. "Their view was that the sovereignty was divided between what they called the "nation "on the one hand and the states on the other; that is, each was sovereign within the sphere marked out for it by the constitution of the union.

This theory of a dual sovereignty was vigorously combated by the Southern statesman John C. Calhoun, in his "Disquisition on Government, "where, as already stated, he enunciated the doctrine that sovereignty was a unit, in- capable of division, and that it existed unimpaired and in its entirety in the separate states composing the union. The question, so far as the United States was concerned, was finally settled by the armed conflict of 1861-1865, but there is still a difference of opinion among able writers as to whether the power which is left to the states is sover-eignty or mere local autonomy.

Among foreign publicists we find the same diversity of opinion regarding the divisibility of sovereignty. The Eng- lish historian Freeman asserts that "the complete division of sovereignty we may look upon as essential to the absolute perfection of the federal ideal. "The French scholars De Tocqueville, Esmein, and Duguit have expressed substantially the same views; and many German publicists support the theory so far as it relates to sovereignty in federal states.

The "father "of the divisibility doctrine in Germany was the noted scholar Waitz, and among his followers may be mentioned the names of Von Mohl, Bluntschli, Brie, Wester- kamp, Jellinek, Bornhak, Schulze, Rüttiman, and others. After the founding of the empire, however, and the triumph of nationalism over particularism, the theory of a divided sovereignty found less favor among the German jurists and philosophers, and the unity theory has come to have more advocates than formerly.

According to the latter view, sovereignty in the German Empire reposes in the totality of the German states regarded as a single personality instead of being divided between the empire, on the one hand, and the states composing it, on the other. When the latter became members of the empire, they gave up their sovereignty, receiving in exchange, as Bismarck ex- pressed it, a share in the joint sovereignty of the empire.

While the better opinion is in favor of the theory that sovereignty is a unit and therefore incapable of division, there is no reason why the expression of the powers of sovereignty, its emanations or manifestations, cannot be divided and expressed through various mouthpieces and carried out through a variety of organs.

Thus, said Rous- seau, power may be divided, though will never can be. It is a unit and indivisible. Those who maintain the divisibility theory, as Rousseau points out, really confuse sovereignty with its emanations. The same idea was expressed by Calhoun, who said with evident truth: "There is no difficulty in understanding how powers appertaining to sovereignty may be divided and the exercise of one portion be delegated to one set of agents and another portion to another, or how sovereignty may be vested in one man, in a few, or in many. But how sovereignty itself, the supreme power, can be divided... it is impossible to conceive. "

Applying this principle to the so-called federal state, we shall find that the sovereign will expresses itself on certain subjects through the medium of a central government, and on certain other subjects through the organs of the indi- vidual political units composing the federation. But there is no partition of sovereignty, no division of the supreme will. There is a division by the sovereign itself of governmental powers and a distribution of them among two sets of organs, but no division of the will itself.

To say that the component members of a federal union are partly sovereign, or sovereign within their particular spheres, is an abuse of the term "sovereignty. "Juristically it is just as logical to say that a municipal corporation or a religious society is sovereign within the sphere assigned to it by the law. "There is no middle ground, "says an able writer, speaking of the nature of sovereignty in the American federal system; "sovereignty is indivisible, and either the central power is sovereign and the individual mem- bers not, or vice versa. They are not states, for that would be imperia in imperio, but they are administrative districts with larger powers of autonomy than are given others — an autonomy which amounts to practical local self-government in matters not of general concern.

"Legally this is an absolutely correct statement of the status of the so-called states of the American federal republic. That power and that power alone is sovereign in a federal union which can in the last analysis determine the competence of the central authority and that of the component states, and which can redistribute the powers of government between them in such a way as to enlarge or curtail the sphere of either. That power is not in the cen- tral government nor in the states; it is over and above both, and wherever it is, there is the sovereign. The task of "running the sovereign to cover, "especially in the "composite "states of to-day, is not always easy, and when discovered it is not always recognized.

It is extremely difficult to place one's finger on the exact spot where it reposes. The constitutional lawyer and the layman do not always travel the same path in the search for it, and they do not always find it in the same place. But it is always present somewhere in the state; and if in the search we push our inquiry until we find that authority which has the power to say the last word in all matters of authority, we shall find ourselves in the presence of the sovereign.

INTERNAL VERSUS EXTERNAL SOVEREIGNTY

The fact that the state has an international personality and exerts a will in relation to other states has given rise to the common distinction between external and internal sovereignty, between sovereignty as a concept of inter- national law and sovereignty as a concept of constitutional law. Those who recognize the distinction conceive internal sovereignty to mean the supremacy of the state within its own territory as over against the wills of all persons or associations of persons therein; while external sovereignty is conceived to be the supremacy of the state as against all foreign wills, whether of persons or states. The one has reference to the exclusive power of the state viewed from within, the other to the immunity of the state from outside control. Many writers, especially those on inter- national law, maintain that the two sovereignties are separate and distinct, and that the state may possess one without the other; that is, the state may be internally sovereign without being sovereign in its external relations.

The logical conclusion is that states may be sovereign as to certain things and non-sovereign as to others; in other words, that sovereignty is divisible and admits of differ- ent degrees of perfection — a conclusion which we have already shown to be untenable. Georg Meyer, a noted German scholar, distinguishes between constitutional sov-ereignty and international sovereignty; the former being the power of "unrestrained political action, "as regards internalaffairs, the latter being independence of foreign control. But if a state possesses the power of unrestrained po-litical activity in internal affairs, it cannot at the same time be dependent upon an outside will. That would, as Jellinek remarks, be a contradiction adjecto..

The distinction between international or external sovereignty on the one hand, and internal or constitutional sovereignty on the other, is, according to strict logic, unsound. The former is but the outward reflex action of the highest power in the state, the manifestation of its supremacy in a particular direction. In other words, external and internal sovereignty are simply different aspects or manifestations of one and the same thing. One may be considered the positive side of sovereignty, the other its negative side. Or, to state it in a different form, one is the supremacy of the state viewed from the exterior, the other the same supremacy looked at from within.

IS SOVEREIGNTY AN ESSENTIAL ELEMENT OF THE STATE

Many able writers, particularly among the Germans,

maintain that while sovereignty is a common attribute of the state it is not an essential constituent; in other words, that states and sovereign states are not necessarily identical concepts. Sovereignty, they assert, may or may not be present in the state; it may constitute the basis of recognition in international law, but is in itself an insuffi- cient test of statehood.

They distinguish between sover- eignty, the power of the state to determine the limits of its own competence, and state power, or the right to rule, which is possessed by every state, while only certain states possess the former. Communities, like the component members of federal unions, for example, which were once independent and which have never surrendered their essential marks of existence, but have only delegated certain powers of gov- ernment to a central authority, are cited as examples of states without sovereignty. In becoming parts of a new union they have ceased to be sovereign but have not ceased to be states.

Thus Jellinek maintains that a community which exercises political power according to its own right, that is, power which is original rather than de- rived and which can lay down binding legal norms, is in a juristic sense a state, whether it possesses full sovereignty or not. They are, he says, public law corporations, have their own constitutions, their own independent spheres of action, and retain their magisterial rights. Other authorities who hold the view that sovereignty is not a vital principle in the constitution of the state are Laband, Rehm, Georg Meyer, There are sovereign and non-sovereign states. "von Mohl, Le Fur und Posener, Hermann Schulze, Brie, Anschütz, Bluntschli, and the French writers Michoudand Lapra- delle.

According to these writers the distinguishing characteristic of the state is, as has been Intimated, not sov-ereignty, not the original power of the state to deter- mine its own competence, but the power to command and compel obedience. A community which rules and governs in its own right, says Jellinek, is a state, and non-sovereign as well as sovereign communities may do that. There were many communities during the Middle Ages, he says, which were tributary or vassal, like the great feudal seignories of France, yet were recognized as states.

But if the possession of political power is a sound test of statehood, it is difficult to see why provinces possessing large autonomy, or self-governing colonies like Australia, Canada, or New Zealand, do not equally possess the quality of states. Whether sovereignty is an essential characteristic of the state depends mainly upon our notion of the thing itself and our conception of the nature of the state.

If we accept the theory of a divided sover-eignty, or the distinction between perfect and imperfect states, we need have no trouble in accepting the doctrine that a community in which sovereignty is partly lacking may nevertheless be considered as a state. But if we ad- here to the test laid down elsewhere in this work, no non- sovereign community, however great its local autonomy, is entitled to be treated as a state. We agree with Zorn and Burgess that sovereignty is not only an essential element, but the first and highest conceivable mark of the state; and with Willoughby that it is the one characteris-tic which serves to distinguish the state *in toto genere* from all other human associations.

There are many communities, among them the constituent members of some federal unions and the great English self-governing colonies, which have an autonomy amounting almost to independ- ence in the management of their local affairs, yet they are not free to determine their own competence or the limits of their own autonomy. It would seem, therefore, more accurate to treat such communities not as states, but as parts of states, possessing some, but not all, of the marks of real states.

AUSTIN'S THEORY OF SOVEREIGNTY

A conception of sovereignty which has been the subject of wide discussion and which has exerted an important influence upon the legal thought of the last half century is that enunciated by the analytical school of jurists of which John Austin was the most conspicuous representative. Austin's views were based largely on the teachings of Hobbes and

Bentham, and were first made public in his "*Lectures on Jurisprudence,* "published in 1832. His theory was conditioned mainly upon his view of the nature of law, which he defined in a general way as a "com-mand given by superior to an inferior. ""If a determi-nate human superior, "he declared, "not in a habit of obedience to a like superior receive habitual obedience from the bulk of a given society, that determinate superior is sovereign in that society, and the society (including the superior) is a society political and independent. ""Furthermore, "he continued, "every positive law, or every law simply and strictly so-called, is set, directly or circuitously, by a sovereign person or body to a member or members of the independent political society wherein that person or body is sovereign or supreme. "

The test of sovereignty, then, according to Austin, is habitual obedience to a superior who owes no obedience to a like superior — not obedience by all the inhabitants, but by the "bulk "of the members of the community. This superior cannot be the general will, as Rousseau taught, nor the people in the mass, nor the electorate, nor some abstraction like public opinion, moral sentiment, the common rea-son, the will of God, and the like; but it must be some "determinate "person or authority which is itself subject to no legal restraints.

Austin's theory that sovereignty must reside in a determi-nate body has found many critics among the historical ju-rists like Maine, Clark, Sidgwick, and others. In the first place, the theory is criticised on the ground that it is inconsistent with the present-day idea of popular sovereignty — is in fact the complete antithesis of Rousseau's doctrine that sovereignty is the general will, a doctrine which lies at the basis of the modern democratic state.

Again, it ignores the power of public opinion, and takes no account of what we have described as political sovereignty. Thus, says Sir Henry Maine, it is a historic fact that sovereignty has repeatedly been for a time in the hands of a number of persons not determinate, and, he adds, "it is asserted by some writers that this is true of the abiding place of sover-eignty in the republic of the United States. "Furthermore, Austin's notion of law as a command emanating from a determinate superior — a conception which lies at the basis of his theory of sovereignty — has been criticised by the historical jurists on the ground that it ignores the great body of customary law which has grown up through usage and interpretation, and which never had its source in the will of a determinate superior; that it errs in treating all law as being merely command; and that it exagger-ates the single element of force to the neglect of obvious historical facts with which Austin could not have been unacquainted.

Austin apparently foresaw the objections that would be urged against his definition of law, and he sought to antici-pate them by one of those legal fictions common among lawyers, namely, by extending the scope of his definition to include customary law. Custom, he argued, is law only when sanctioned by the sovereign, and what the sovereign permits he commands; hence, customary law is a legal command, and he who permits it to continue as law is the sovereign. But, like most legal fictions, this is rather unsatisfactory, if indeed it does not prove too much for his doctrine.

Another objection sometimes urged against the Austinian theory is the absolutism which it attributes to sovereignty. Like Hobbes, Austin held that the fountain and source of law could not be limited by any higher law, and hence sovereignty involved legal despotism.

There cannot, he said, be a hierarchy of supremacies nor a coordination of creators nor a series of sovereigns ascending to infinity. He frankly admitted that there was no escape from the conclusion that sovereignty is legally unrestrainable, and hence the sovereign is, legally speaking, a despot, however benevolent he may be in fact. But he pointed out, what is obviously true, that it does not follow that because the sovereign is unlimited in its powers the government through which it expresses itself is necessarily subject to no restriction.

Of the merits of Austin's theory we venture the opinion that his chief error consisted in unduly emphasizing the purely legal aspects of sovereignty, and in overlooking the forces and influences which lie back of the formal law — a very natural mistake for a lawyer to make. It may also be said that his theory was probably inapplicable to all states of society, such, for example, as Maine described in his work on the "*Early History of Institutions.* "But as a conception of the strict legal nature of sovereignty, Austin's theory is, on the whole, clear and logical, and much of the criticism directed against it has been founded on misapprehension and misconception.

The nature of sovereignty has not always been understood, nor is it now.

It has often been the subject of much loose thinking by statesmen and of dogmatism by political writers. Powerful constitutional controversies concerning its location have shaken more than one state in the past and have some- times even led to civil commotion.

While there is now a substantial consensus of opinion among the best political writers concerning its fundamental characteristics, there are still differences of opinion regarding its place of abode. in some of the complex states of the present day.

Chapter 7

Theories of State Functions

THE INDIVIDUALISTIC OR LAISSEZ-FAIRE THEORY

THE doctrines concerning the sphere of the state, if we exclude those of the anarchists, who profess to believe that the state should be done away with entirely, may be roughly grouped into three classes, which we may designate as the individualistic theory, the socialistic theory, and the compromise theory.

The individualist, unlike the anarchist, considers the state to be a necessity, though he is pretty nearly at one with the anarchist in regarding it as essentially an evil, and hence its sphere of activity should be restricted to the narrowest possible limits, consistent with the maintenance of peace, order, and security. The individualistic doctrine regards all restraint *qua* restraint as an evil and every extension of the power of the state as so much taken from the domain of individual liberty. It holds that the state is a necessity simply because of the inherent egoism and ignorance of man, which lead him to disregard the rights of his fellow men for his own selfish purposes.

A noted Frenchman, Jules Simon, expressed the individualistic idea in extreme form when he said the state ought to strive to make itself useless and prepare for its own demise. The same idea was ex- pressed by the historian Freeman, in language which has a decided anarchistic ring, when he remarked that "the ideal form of government is no government at all; the existence of government in any shape is a sign of man's imperfection.

The state exists, argue the individualists, merely because crime exists, and its principal function, therefore, is to restrain, not to direct and promote. When the state undertakes to own and operate agencies for transporting freight and passengers; when it undertakes to carry parcels for private individuals; send telegrams; subsidize theaters and give concerts; maintain libraries, museums, art galleries, hospitals, zoological gardens, parks, playgrounds, bath and wash houses; erect dwellings for the poor; provide schools and colleges for the education of the young; and send out scientific expeditions, —it not only undertakes to do what is not necessary for the protection of the individ- ual, which is the only excuse for the existence of govern-ment, but it is encroaching upon the domain of private enterprise or otherwise interfering with the liberty of the individual.

The individualists therefore condemn public education; sanitary, vaccination, and quarantine laws; laws regulating the conduct of trade and industry; pure food laws; and indeed all legislation the effect of which is to impose restrictions upon industry or business or to interfere with the social habits of individuals. In short, its sole function in regard to industry is to leave it alone.

"The modern state attempts to do entirely too many things, say the individualists. "Ne pas frop gouverner; ""laissez faire, laissez passer, "expresses their conception of its legitimate duty. It should be nothing more than a police organization to enforce contracts, keep the peace, and punish crime; and when this is done, its functions are exhausted.

Individualism as a political doctrine had its origin in the latter part of the eighteenth century as a reaction against the evils of over government in Europe. It was one of the leading tenets of the physiocratic school of economists that the state ought not to interfere with the economic activities of the people by prescribing conditions under which industry should be carried on, but should confine its functions to the simple protection of the laws of nature under which production would best regulate itself if left alone.

They accordingly attacked the prevailing notions

regarding the omnipotence of the state and de-manded freedom of trade and industry. This doctrine received a powerful stimulus from the publication of Adam Smith's *"Wealth of Nations "*, which was largely a plea for the policy of non-interference by the state in economic matters. Smith denounced the laws then in force restricting the free interchange of the products of labour and interfering with the free employment of labour, as mischievous and destructive of their own purpose.

Later the doctrine of natural liberty in economic matters was defended by various other English economists, notably Cairnes, Ricardo, and Malthus; by French writers like Bastiat, De Tocqueville, Dunnoyer, Leon Say, and M. Taine; and by the German philosophers Kant, Fichte, Wilhelm Humboldt, and the Baron Eotvos. Still more recently the individualistic doctrines have found earnest advocates in Laboulaye, Michel, and Leroy-Beaulieu in France, and in Herbert Spencer, John Stuart Mill, Earl Wemyss, the Duke of Argyle, Bruce Smith, Wordsworth Donisthorpe, and others in England.

One of the earliest and ablest arguments in favor of the "governmental minimum "was written by a Prussian, Wilhelm Humboldt, in 1791, but for political reasons it was not published until 1852, after the author's death. It was entitled. "Humboldt laid down the proposition that the state should "abstain from all solicitude for the positive welfare of the citizens and ought not to proceed a step farther than is necessary for their mutual security and protection against foreign enemies.

"For these purposes only should it impose restrictions upon individual liberty. "The grand point to be kept in view by the state, "he said, "is the develop-ment of the powers of all its single citizens in their perfect individuality; it must, therefore, pursue no other object than that which they cannot procure for themselves, viz. security; and this is the only true and infallible means to connect, by a strong and enduring bond, things which at first sight appear to be contradictory — the aim of the state as a whole and the collective aims of all its individual citizens. "

The most elaborate defense of the individualistic view of the sphere of the state has been made by Herbert Spencer in a series of essays published under the collective title *"Social Statics and Man versus the State,* "a work which has done more to elucidate and popularize the laissez-faire doctrine than any other political treatise.

Spencer starts out with the assertion that the existence of the state is the result of man's inherent perversity and egoism and that in reality it is an aggressor rather than a protector. "Be it or be it not true, "he says, "that man is shapen in iniquity and conceived in sin, it is unquestionably true that government is begotten of aggression and by aggression. "Being instituted merely for the purpose of curbing his wicked propensities and protecting him from the violence and fraud of his fellows, it follows that in a morally perfect condition of society government can have no *raison d'être.* "Have we not shown, "he asks, "that government is essentially immoral?...

Does it not exist because crime exists, and must government not cease when crime ceases, for very lack of objects on which to perform its functions? "He goes on to say that "it is a mistake to consider that government must last forever.... It is not essential, but incidental. As amongst Bushmen we find a state antecedent to government, so may there be one in which it shall have become extinct. "The doctrine that the state is justified in doing whatever seems to those in authority to be "expedient, "or whatever tends to produce the "greatest happiness, "or which will subserve the "general good, "

Spencer denounces as governmental despotism, since there is no standard or test for determining what is expedient or what is for the general good except the opin- ions of the governors themselves.

He dwells upon what he calls the *militant* type of society, with its excessive regimentation and its army-like organization; he compares this with the *industrial* type, contrasts the condition of the individual under the regime of status with his condition under a regime of contract, as he calls it, and emphasizes the advantages of voluntary over compulsory

cooperation and of negative *versus* positive regulation. The experience of the past, he affirms, proves that the acquisition of happiness does not come through state action, but through being left alone. Cut- ting away men's opportunities on one side in order to add to them on another is nearly always accompanied by loss, he says, through the friction of administrative mechanism.

The sphere of government should be "negatively regulative, "that is, its functions should be to redress evils, not to try to make men happier by helping them to do what they can do as well or better themselves. "To administer justice, to mount guard over men's rights, "are the only proper functions of the state; and when it does more, it defeats its own ends. The duty of the state is to formulate in law pre-established rights, not to create them, and to enforce them instead of intruding on them like an aggressor. The individual has but one right, the right of equal freedom with everybody else, and the state but one duty, the duty of protecting that right against violence and fraud.

Spencer inveighed against all legislation for the regulation of commerce and trade; against sanitary legislation, such as quarantine, vaccination, and registration laws; against public education; against poor relief by the state; and even against state-managed post offices and currency issued by the state. Every attempt to mitigate the suf- fering of the poor through state intervention, he declared, "eventuates in the exacerbation of it. "The sums de- voted to the support of paupers should go to support la- borers in new reproductive works.

In regard to education by the state, he observes that "taking away a man's property to educate his own or other people's children is not needful for the maintenance of his rights and hence is wrong. "State intervention is legitimate only for the protection of violated rights, and the rights of children are not violated by neglect of their education. The idea that it is the duty of the state to undertake to protect the health of the people Spencer combats with equal ardor, though he admits that the state may suppress nuisances.

All taxation for sanitary superintendence must, he says,

be condemned. He goes to the length even of maintaining that it is a "violation of the moral law "for the state to "interpose between quacks and those who patronize them, "or to forbid unlicensed persons from prescribing for the sick, since it is the inalienable right of the individual to "buy medicine and advice from whomsoever he pleases, "and the unlicensed practitioner should have the same right to sell to whomsoever he will.

Regarding the right of the state to monopolize the issue of money, he maintains that it cannot justly forbid the issue of or enforce the ac-ceptance of certain notes or coin in return for other things, since that would be an infringement of the natural right of exchange and a violation of the law of equal freedom. Finally, Spencer condemns the construction of public works by the state except such as may be necessary for the national defense and rejects its right to a monopoly of the postal service, since "it is clear that the restriction thus put upon the liberty of trade by forbidding private letter-carrying establishments is a breach of state duty. "

Much of Spencer's case against the state is based upon the errors and blunders of particular governments in the past. The statute books, he laments, are a record of unhappy guesses. ""Nearly every parliamentary proceeding is a tacit confession of impotence, for the great majority of legislative measures introduced are designed to amend and improve existing laws. "In an essay entitled *"The Sins of Legislators,* "Spencer reviews much of the unwise legislation of the past, dwells upon the evils which resulted from it, and concludes that because much of this legislation was in time repealed or modified it ought never to have been enacted.

He protests against what he calls the worship of the legislature and asserts that as the great political superstition of the past was the divine right of kings, that of the present is the divine right of parliaments. And the divine right of parliaments means only the divine right of the majority, for the minority has no right to be respected. Some men actually seem to think, he remarks, that individuals can be made moral by an act of the legislature and that which is economically unsound can be made sound and wise by the fiat of the state.

Some of Spencer's followers, like Donisthorpe and Auberon Herbert, go to even greater lengths in their opposition to state regulation. They not only oppose education by the state; poor relief; inspection of factories, mines, and workshops; the regulation of injurious trades; compulsory vaccination laws; quarantine and health regulations; the requirement of official oaths; Sunday legislation; laws regulating public amusements; restrictions upon the sale of liquor, etc., — but they even deny to the state the right to regulate the marriage relation or restrict in any manner individual liberty in social matters except in so far as it is absolutely necessary to protect each man from the positive aggressions of his fellows.

DEFENSE OF THE LAISSEZ-FAIRE THEORY

In defense of the individualistic conception of the sphere of state activity it is argued, in the first place, that considerations of justice require that the individual shall be let alone by the state in order that he may realize fully and completely the ends of his existence. This particular line of argument has had the powerful support of such scholars as Kant, Fichte, Humboldt, and John Stuart Mill.

According to their views it is necessary to the harmonious development of all the powers of the individual that he should be interfered with as little as possible by the state, because every restriction upon his freedom of action tends to destroy his sense of initiative and self-reliance, weaken his responsibility as a free agent, impair his energies, and blunt his character.

"The true end of man, or that which is prescribed by the immutable dictates of reason, "observed Humboldt, "is the highest and most harmonious development of his powers to a complete and consistent whole. "Over government Humboldt goes on to say, not only diminishes freedom, but "super induces national uniformity and a constrained and unnatural manner of action "by its tendency to reduce society to a dead level. The same line of argument is pursued by Mill, who asserts that an excess of government, especially of the meddling and inquisitorial sort, "starves the development of some portion of the bodily or mental faculties, when it deprives one from doing what one is inclined to do or from acting according to one's judgment of what is desirable.

"Free competition develops in the individual the highest possibilities, sharpens and strengthens his powers of initiative, and increases his sense of self-reliance; while over government not only hampers enterprise and interferes with the natural development of trade, but it strikes at the development of character, tends to crush out individuality and originality by interfering with the natural struggle between individuals, and leads to a general lowering of the social level. The highest civilization, say the laissez-faire advocates, has been developed under individualism, a system which has produced more material and educational progress than could ever have been produced under paternalism.

Spencer dwells upon the fact that in an over governed state "everybody is like everybody else. "Government management and control of industry, he complains, is "essentially despotic"; it "unavoidably cramps "by diminishing liberty of action, "angers, "leads to discontent, "galls by its inefficiency, and restrictions, "offends by professing to help those whom it will not allow to help themselves and vexes by the swarm of dictatorial officials who are forever stepping in between men and their pursuits. The "evils of officialism "and of "socialistic meddlings, "he declares, prevent the healthy and natural development of a people, while freedom develops and strengthens individual character and conduces to human progress.

"A people among whom there is no habit of spontaneous action for a collective interest, "said Mill "who look habitually to their government to command and prompt them in matters of joint concern — who expect to have everything done for them except what can be made an affair of mere habit and routine — have their faculties only half developed; their education is defective in one of its most important branches. "

The laissez-faire principle, say its advocates, rests also upon sound considerations of a scientific character. It is in harmony with the principle of evolution, since it is the only system that will lead to the survival of the fittest in the economic struggle. It assumes that self-interest is a universal principle in human nature, that each individual is a better judge of what his own interests are than any government can possibly be, and that if left alone he will follow them.

It holds that each individual should be allowed to stand alone or fall according to his worth, unaided by the props and supports of the state, and should be left to work out his own destiny without the guidance and tutelage of government. By leaving each individual to do unaided that for which he is best fitted, the strong and fit classes survive, the unfit elements are eliminated, and thus the good of society is promoted.

Again, and this is most important in the arguments of the laissez-faire theorists, the policy of non-interference rests upon sound economic principles. Better economic results, it is asserted, are obtained for society by leaving the conduct of industry as far as possible to private enterprise. Adam Smith, in his "*Wealth of Nations,* "pointed out that the system of natural liberty tends toward the largest production of wealth. The self-interest of the consumer will lead to the demand for the things that are most useful to society, while the self-interest of the producer will lead to their production at the least cost. In the economic struggle the individual is animated mainly by motives of self-interest.

If, therefore, he is allowed to use his capital as he pleases, to dispose of his labour to the best advantage, to exchange the products of his toil freely, and to have prices fixed by the natural laws of supply and demand, better results, not only to himself, but to the whole society, will be secured. Unrestricted competition stimulates economic production, tends to keep wages and prices at a normal level, to prevent usurious rates of interest, to secure efficient service and the production of better products than can be obtained by state regulation or state management.

The experience of the past, say the laissez-faire advocates, abundantly establishes the wisdom of the non-interference principle. History is full of examples of attempts to fix by fiat of the state the prices of food and clothing and of many other commodities; of laws regulating the wages of labour, prohibiting the wearing of certain kinds of apparel and requiring the wearing of certain other kinds, forbidding the exportation of divers commodities, forbidding certain kinds of machinery in manufacturing processes, restricting the manufacture of certain articles to apprentices, prescribing the location of factories; laws aiding and encouraging certain industries by means of bounties and discouraging certain others by prohibitive taxes; laws prohibiting combinations among laboring men, fixing the hours of labour, restricting certain trades exclusively to members of guilds; and even laws prescribing the cut of one's dress, the number of meals which one should eat, the sizes of buttonholes, the length of shoes, the making of pins, and the kind of material in which the dead should be buried.

As late as 1795 magistrates in England had the power of fixing the rate of wages according to the price of bread, and it was not until the same year that a workman could travel out of his parish in search of work. Until 1824 there was in force an act of Parliament which forbade manufacturers from locating their factories more than ten miles from the royal exchange.

Throughout the seventeenth and eighteenth centuries the state everywhere exercised a strict and at times arbitrary control over many forms of industry. It determined who could work and where, the materials with which they should work, and the conditions generally under which various trades should be carried on. Legions of inspectors, measurers, and commissioners saw that the conditions prescribed by the state were observed.

Regulations prescribing the quality and dimensions of manufactured articles were defended on the ground that consumers were not competent judges of their own needs. Industry was deprived of its natural freedom by laws forbidding skilled labour except by apprentices or by monopolies which limited the right to engage in certain trades to those who had exclusive privileges. Most of such legislation was mischievous and destructive of the ends which it was intended to secure, and the results which were sought for could have been more effectively obtained by allowing every man to sell his labour and goods whenever and wherever he wished.

Speaking of those who were responsible for this sort of legislation, Buckle observed that "they went blundering along in the old track, believing that no commerce could flourish without their interference, hampering that commerce by repeated and harassing regulations, and taking for granted that it was the duty of every government to benefit the trade of its own people by injuring the trade of others. "The extent to which the governing classes have interfered and the mischief which that interference has produced are so remarkable, he concludes, as to make thoughtful men wonder how civilization could have advanced in the face of such repeated obstacles.

Finally, the laissez-faire theorists argue that it is a false assumption which attributes omniscience and infallibility to the state and which regards it as better fitted to judge of the needs of the individual, and to provide for them than he is himself. There is, they assert, a common belief that governments are capable of doing anything and everything, and of doing it more efficiently than it can be done by private initiative, when, in reality, experience and reason show the contrary to be the fact.

The state has no greater powers of invention or of initiative than the individuals who compose it; it is not a creative organ, but an "organ which acts only by means of a complicated apparatus, composed of numerous wheels and systems of wheels subordinated one to another "; it is an organ of criticism, of generalization, and of coordination, from which it follows that the state cannot be the first agent, the primary cause of progress in human society, but only an auxiliary or agent of propagation.

Every additional function, observes Mill, means a new burden imposed on a body already overcharged with duties; the result is that most things are ill done; and much is not done at all, because the government is not able to do it without delays. The great majority of things are worse done, he declares, when done by government than when done by individuals who are most interested, for the people understand their own business better and care for it better than any government can; all the faculties which a government enjoys of access to information, all the means which it possesses of remunerating and therefore of commanding the best available talent in the market, are not an equal for the one great disadvantage of an inferior interest.

CRITICISM OF THE LAISSEZ-FAIRE DOCTRINE

The individualistic theory of state functions has been criticised upon various grounds. First of all, the assumption that the state is an evil has not been borne out by the experience of mankind under the regime of state organization. History, in fact, shows unmistakably that the progress of civilization in the past has been promoted to a very large degree by wisely directed state action, in short, that the state is a positive good.

It is true, of course, that at times the ends of the state have been perverted to the detriment of the public good, but this is no more reason for condemning it as an evil than for saying that railroads are an evil because their operation sometimes results in accidents. Spencer's doctrine that the state exists only because crime exists and that it would subserve no purpose in a society of morally perfect beings cannot be accepted. The function of the state in the complex civilization of to-day is not merely repressive, not simply "negatively regulative "; it has a higher mission than that of restraint and punishment.

The State is not an Evil

So long as men live in groups they will have collective wants which can only be satisfied through state organization, and hence there is no reason for believing that the necessity for the state will ever disappear or that the role which it now plays in the life of human societies will ever diminish. On the contrary, all the signs indicate that with the increasing complexity of modern civilization the need for state action will become stronger and its role more extensive.

In comparatively recent years a strong reaction against

the individualistic movement of the earlier nineteenth century has everywhere taken place, due largely to the conditions resulting from the growth of manufactures, the congestion of the population in the cities, the growth of corporate wealth, and changed economic and social conditions generally, all of which have thrown the laissez-faire theories into disrepute.

"The higher the state of civilization, "observes Huxley, "the more completely do the actions of one member of the social body influence all the rest, and the less possible is it for any one man to do a wrong without interfering more or less with the freedom of all his fellow-citizens. So that even upon the narrowest view of the functions of the state it must be admitted to have wider powers than the advocates of the police theory are disposed to admit.

"Laveleye points out in the same manner that as civilization progresses men become more dependent on one another and upon society as a whole, and hence the role of the state must increase correspondingly in order to satisfy their common wants. The individualism of Spencer, as Laveleye rightly concludes, is wholly inadmissible under the conditions of modern society.

The view of the laissez-faire advocates that state intervention in the interest of the common good necessarily involves a curtailment of individual freedom rests on an assumption that is true only within very restricted limits. It is a very narrow view indeed which sees in a factory act, a pure food law, or a quarantine regulation nothing but an infringement upon the domain of individual liberty. "The rights of all are enlarged and secured by wise restrictions upon the actions of each. It is somewhat like pruning a fruit tree or trimming a vineyard; it means a loss of some fruit, but better fruit is produced so that all are gainers in the end.

The weakest point in the argument of the laissezfaire advocates is the assumption that the state is necessarily hostile to freedom, that government and liberty represent antithetical ideas, that in proportion as the functions of government are multiplied the domain of individual liberty is restricted, — in short, that a maximum of government means a minimum of freedom. In reality wisely organized and directed state action not only enlarges the moral, physical, and intellectual capacities of individuals, but increases their liberty of action by removing obstacles placed in their way by the strong and selfseeking, and thus frees them from the necessity of a perpetual struggle with those who would take advantage of their weakness. In this way the latent abilities of the individual are liberated, and his opportunities increased. It is manifestly wrong to assume that all restraint is an evil.

In truth the state emancipates and promotes as well as restrains. The doctrine that governmental regulation tends to impair individual character by weakening the sense of individual initiative, self-reliance, and self-help, and by preventing the full and harmonious development of the faculties of the individual, has been greatly exaggerated by the laissez-faire advocates.

Many of the individualistic writers like Mill, Humboldt, and Spencer have, in fact, confused individuality with eccentricity and oddity of character, qualities which in themselves have nothing of value. Character is developed not through freedom alone, but quite as much through discipline and restraint. It is not true that as the functions of government are extended the individual becomes weaker and less self-reliant. The

be trusted in the future; or that because sumptuary laws are wrong, factory and sanitary legislation must be wrong as well; or that because municipally constructed sewers have sometimes produced typhoid fever, cities in the future should leave the construction of their sewer systems to private enterprise; or that because some poor laws have proved ineffective, the state should abandon altogether the policy of poor relief. The laissez-faire writers never tire of parading and exaggerating the mistakes which governments have made in the past, and when they are all collected and put on exhibition, they constitute what to some is a strong indictment against state interference.

"The state lives in a glass house, "observes Huxley; "we see what it tries to do, and all its failures, partial or total, are made the most of. But private enterprise is sheltered under good opaque bricks and mortar. The public rarely knows what it tries to do and only hears of its failures when they are gross and patent to all the world.

"We may well ask, with Lord Pembroke, "What would private enterprise look like if its mistakes and failures were collected, and pilloried in a similar manner? "It may readily be admitted, observes an able writer, that government is weak and inefficient at times and obedient to private interests, but it does not follow from such an admission that government ought to be made "weaker, corrupter, and more inefficient by practicing the illogical doctrine of laissez faire. "

The laissez-faire assumption that each individual knows his own interests better than the state can know them, and is therefore the best judge of what is good for him and if left to himself will follow those interests, is true only in a limited sense, and is still less true of classes. This is readily admitted by some individualist writers like Mill.

Sidgwick, an unusually fair and judicial writer, discussing this assumption, well says: "But it seems to me very doubt. ful whether this can be granted; since in some important respects the tendencies of social development seem to be rather in the opposite direction. As the appliances of life become more elaborate and complicated through the progress of invention, it is only according to the general law of division of labour to suppose that an average man's ability to judge of the adaptation of means to ends, even as regards the satisfaction of his everyday needs, is likely to become continually less.

"If every man, observes the Belgian writer Laveleye, could see clearly and judge accurately of his own interests, rights, and duties, then pursue them, and do voluntarily what he ought to do and nothing that he ought not to do, the necessity for state intervention would disappear and we should enjoy the reign of liberty.

But the very point of the matter is that ignorant people cannot take precautions against dangers of which they are ignorant. No one lives in a badly drained house, drinks water polluted with sewage, or eats adulterated food because his interest leads him to do so, but generally because he is ignorant of the real character of the service or article which he consumes or because he cannot help himself.

Not only is the individual not always a competent judge of his own interests as an economic consumer, but in affairs of personal conduct he is often not to be trusted, particularly in matters relating to his health or safety or moral welfare. The truth is the state may be a better judge of a man's intellectual, moral, or physical needs than he is himself, and it may rightfully protect him from disease and danger against his wishes and compel him to educate his children and to live a decent life.

The practice of all modern states is in fact in harmony with this view. Few, if any, governments leave their citizens to find out for themselves what is healthy food; what physicians, surgeons, and druggists are qualified to practice; or what conditions of work are safe or dangerous. Most governments prescribe conditions under which certain dangerous occupations shall be carried on and refuse to permit them to be dispensed with even with the consent of those who would be endangered.

All governments prohibit the exercise of certain callings of a quasi-public character, except by persons who are able to show by examination or otherwise that they possess the requisite qualifications to insure the public against incompetent service. Evidence of competency is generally required of physicians, apothecaries, engineers, pilots, and even of barbers and plumbers. The state goes even further and undertakes to protect the individual against the consequences of his own acts, as where it limits the number of hours of labour in mines and factories, and prohibits women and children from engaging in certain injurious trades.

Much of the individualistic distrust of government is due, as Sir Frederick Pollock has pointed out, to the failure to distinguish between centralized government and local self-government. A good deal of the objection which the individualists urge against government would be justified if it were centralized government that is complained of, but the objection is not always well founded, when directed against local government, through local bodies directly under the eye of the people concerned.

There is a vast difference, for example, between the "nationalization "and the "municipalization "of an industry, and there is an equal difference between national regulation of individual conduct and control by locally elected bodies. Manifestly the same objection cannot be urged against a local health regulation that would be applicable to a national quarantine law.

Individualists, likewise, in their wholesale condemnation of government usually overlook the distinction between government, popularly constituted and controlled, and bureaucratic, irresponsible government. It is difficult to see, in many cases, why a public utility owned by the government, but under immediate control of the people of the locality, should be more feared and distrusted than one under the management of a private company not amenable to public opinion or popular control.

Spencer's doctrine of "negative regulation, "which would limit the function of the state to redressing rather than preventing wrongs, would in many instances defeat the ends of the state. This, if the only security provided by the state against unsanitary plumbing, adulterated foods, incompetent practitioners of medicine or apothecaries, consisted of the right to sue the negligent plumber, the dishonest milk dealer, or the incompetent physician or druggist, instead of requiring plumbers to give bonds for the efficient discharge of their duties, physicians and druggists to pass examinations or otherwise furnish evidence of capacity, milk to be inspected, etc., the protection afforded would in many cases be inadequate, since the injury could not be redressed by a mere suit for damages.

We agree with Sir Frederick Pollock that if it is negative and proper regulation to say that a man shall be punished for building his house in a city so that it falls into the street, it cannot be positive and improper regulation to say that he shall so build it that it will not appear to competent persons likely to fall into the city street. If it is purely negative regulation, and therefore proper, to punish a man for communicating an infectious disease by neglect of common precautions, it is not improper to require precautions, where the danger is known to exist, without waiting for somebody to be actually infected.

The individualists show a distorted notion of liberty when they contend, as they do in effect, that the individual has a right, if he wishes to keep his premises in an unsanitary condition, to discharge his sewage where he will, to spread disease among his neighbors, to sell unwholesome food and drugs to whomsoever will buy. If the state has the right and duty to protect by preventive measures the individual against violence and fraud, it has the same right and duty to protect him against acts the consequences of which will be to inflict upon him injuries which cannot be redressed.

There is, as Huxley well says, no very great difference between the claim of an individual to go about threatening the lives of his neighbors with a pistol, and his claim to keep his premises in a condition which threatens the health and lives of his fellow men. The same is true of the right and duty of the state to protect the individual against the dangers incident to modern in dustrial processes, such as those resulting from dangerous machinery, from bad ventilation, from unsanitary workshops, from fire, and even from unfair contracts of labour.

The freedom of contract is a taking phrase, as has been aptly remarked, and to many it is a conclusive argument against state intervention in industrial matters; but when it refers to an agreement between a capitalist and an ignorant laborer who is at the mercy of his employer, there is no equality. The doctrine of freedom has no sanctity in such cases. There is really no iilegitimate interference with the freedom of contract when the state undertakes to prescribe the conditions under which contracts shall be entered into between parties one of whom is really not on a free and equal footing with the other.

Nevertheless, when all is said against the laissez-faire doctrine that can be said, it must be admitted that up to a certain point the weight of evidence is on its side. The proposition that the individual is the best judge of what contributes to his own happiness and that he will prosper most under a system of liberty and free competition is in most cases a sound one and ought in practice, as Sidgwick and Cairnes have shown, to be deviated from only in special cases where there are strong empirical reasons for believing that the general assumption is not true.

The doctrines of the individualists, while in many cases productive of harm, have not been entirely without a good effect. They have, as an able economic writer has observed, "taught the people not to confound public morality with a state church, public security with police activity, or public wealth with government property.

"They have "taught men that, as society develops, the interests of its members became more and more harmonious; in other words, that rational egoism and rational altruism tend to coincide. "The principal fault with them has been their disposition to exaggerate the completeness of this coincidence in the existing imperfect stage of human development, and in assuming that freedom will do everything for society, economically and morally.

THE SOCIALISTIC THEORY

Directly opposed to the laissez-faire theory of state functions is what, for lack of a more suitable term, we may call the socialistic theory, which contends for a maximum rather than a minimum of government. The supporters of this theory, instead of distrusting the state and looking upon it as an evil whose functions should be restricted to the narrowest possible limits, regard it as a supreme and positive good; and hence its mission should include the promotion of the common economic, moral, and intellectual interests of the people.

"A socialist, "says Professor Ely, "is one who looks to society organized in the state for aid in bringing about a more perfect distribution of economic goods and an elevation of humanity; the individualist regards each man, not as his brother's keeper, but as his own, and desires every man to work out his own salvation, material and spiritual. It must not be understood, however, that the advocates of state socialism attach any less importance to individual freedom than do the individualists. On the contrary, they regard it as all important and differ from the individualists only in holding that it can be better secured through state action than through the laissez-faire policy, which permits unrestricted competition.

Those who advocate a wide extension of state activity may be grouped into several classes according to the nature and extent of the role which in their opinion the state should play. First, there are the extreme socialists, who advocate collective ownership and management of all industries, including land and capital, and the instruments of production and transportation.

They would substitute state management of industry in the place of private management, and joint ownership of the instruments of production in the place of individual ownership, thus making of the state a vast compulsory cooperative commonwealth in which the means of production, distribution, and exchange are under the control of government. Under such a system the state would become the principal owner of the wealth of the country, and there would be no private property except perhaps in things actually used by each individual.

Socialism of the present time, says an able writer on the subject, extends the state's intervention from those industrial undertakings it is best fitted to manage well to all undertakings of whatever character, and from the establishment of those securities for the full use of men's energies to the attempt to equalize in some way the results of their use of them. It may be less shortly described as aiming at the progressive nationalization of industries with a view to the progressive equalization of incomes.

Some extreme socialists, indeed, would have the state guarantee work to everybody, lend them money without interest, furnish them with the implements of labour, build houses for them, give them farms, strike bargains for them, provide pleasures for them, and in fact supply all their wants, economic, social, intellectual, or otherwise. The socialists of the United States in their national platform demand that the machinery of production shall be owned by the people in common; that the national government shall obtain possession of the mines, railroads, canals, telegraphs, telephones, and other means of public transportation and communication, which shall be operated on the cooperative plan under the control of the federal government; that the municipal governments shall obtain possession.

Of the local railways, ferries, waterworks, gas works, electric light plants, and all industries requiring municipal franchises, to be operated on the cooperative plan under municipal control; that inventions shall be free to all; that education shall be free and compulsory; that the state shall assist poor school children with food, clothing, and books; and that employment on the public works shall be provided by the state for the unemployed.

The principal arguments advanced in favor of the socialistic state are the following: Under the present system of economic organization, the laboring man does not receive the fruits of his toil. A large part goes to reward capital or to pay for the services of those who direct and supervise the employment of labour, or to speculators and middlemen, and too little to those who are the real producers. In short, society under the present system is organized in the interests of the rich and leads to grave inequalities of wealth and of opportunity.

The means of production are being monopolized by the few who exploit the masses; if indeed private competition has not been largely eliminated through the organization of trusts and combinations. The state should therefore take control of all the land and capital or means of production now being used for the exclusive benefit of the owning class. Under the individualistic regime industrial competition has become so fierce that the industrially weak have no chance of success and cannot survive in competition with the rich; they are growing relatively poorer and becoming more dependent upon the employing class, while the rich are growing richer and becoming more independent.

The theory of socialism, it is argued, is founded on principles of justice and right. The land and the mineral wealth contained therein should belong equally to all, not to a few. They are nature's gift to the human race, and ought not to be appropriated by the few any more than sunlight, air, or water. The same is true as regards the instruments of production.

Competition under the present system not only leads to injustice and the crushing out of the small competitor, but it involves enormous economic waste and extravagance in the duplication of services. The system of unrestricted competition leads to lower wages, overproduction, cheap goods, and unemployed workers. The only remedy for such a condition, say the socialists, is the abolition of competition and the substitution of the cooperative principle, under which equality of opportunity and equality of reward and economy of production will be secured.

Under the socialistic regime, it is asserted, a higher type of individual character will also be produced and a larger degree of real freedom. Such industrial competition as we have to-day tends to beget materialism, unfairness, dishonesty, and a general lowering of the standard of individual character. Man is naturally weak and inclined to depravity, and the present system of economic individualism serves to accentuate his weakness and dishonesty. He needs, therefore, to be guided and aided by the state and protected against his own inherent frailties.

The doctrine of socialism, moreover, is really in harmony with the organic theory of the nature of the state, which teaches that society is an organism, not a mere aggregation of individuals, that the good of all is paramount to that of a few, and that in order to secure the good of the greatest number the welfare of the individual as such must be subordinated to that of the many.

Finally, it is argued by the socialists that the state has already abolished competition in certain fields and introduced in its place the cooperative principle and has demonstrated its success as an industrial manager to the entire satisfaction of all candid and thoughtful men.

Government management and control of the postal service, government coinage, government ownership and operation of railroads, telegraphs, mines, and other industries of a public nature in various countries have all established the advantages of collective management over private management, and thus fully justified the wisdom of the principle of socialism.

Then why should the state not go further and occupy the entire field? Why should it not organize all labour as it has already done a part, and apportion the products of industry on the basis of each man's rightful share as the principles of justice require? Collective ownership and management, it is maintained, is thoroughly democratic; indeed, socialism is the "economic complement of democracy "; it rests upon both ethical and altruistic principles and is the only system under which efficiency and justice in production can be secured and under which a full and harmonious development of individual character can be realized.

Against the socialistic theory the chief argument advanced is the difficulty, if not the impossibility, of realizing in practice the system which it advocates. The ideas of the extreme socialists are in many respects fantastic and would prove impracticable, both on account of reasons of an economic character and for others which are inherent in the constitution of human nature itself. There have always been some men who believed that the state was both omniscient and omnipotent and that it has only to issue a decree saying, "Let misery and inequality be abolished, "and it will be done forthwith.

The socialistic theory starts from a false premise when it maintains that private property in land and the instruments of production is not only wrong morally but also economically. To substitute collective ownership for private ownership, even if it were practicable, would tend to destroy one of the most powerful mainsprings of human endeavor and the chief incentive to individual effort and industry.

Take away the right of the individual to acquire property and to accumulate the product for his own use, say the opponents of socialism, and you make an end of all progress by destroying the incentive to labour. The saying of Sir James F. Stephen that to try to make men equal by altering social arrangements is like trying to make the cards of equal value by shuffling the pack, is hardly less true of all efforts to make men equal in economic matters.

Socialism, says Laveleye, rests on the principle that the able, industrious, and provident should share with the stupid, the idle, the improvident, whatever may be obtained as the reward of their energy and virtues. It is a system, says another critic, "which requires the state to do work it is unfit to do in order to invest the working classes with privileges they have no right to get.

"The doctrine that each man should be rewarded according to his labour, when labour is understood to mean simply work with one's hands without reference to capital or skill, cannot be defended upon any rational principle of justice. Even if account should be taken of the difference in the productive capacity and hence of the value of the service of different workers, the practical difficulty in applying any such rule of distinction would be insurmountable under a system of socialism.

On what principle would it be possible to distribute the rewards of industry to each worker according to his share in producing when he works side by side with machines, with unskilled and skilled laborers, and with directors and supervisors? Socialism will never be practicable until there is a fundamental change in human nature, to some of whose deepest principles it runs counter.

We agree with Professor Ely that it is a "glorious ideal, but it will never become a reality this side of the golden gates of Paradise. "The state may provide for the poor and the infirm, and even furnish employment to the idle, but it ought not to take away from the former the motive for making voluntary provision for old age or from the latter the incentive to search for work.

One error of the socialist is that he entirely overestimates the state's capacity and efficiency. He assumes that every business managed by a joint stock concern can be as well managed by the state and ought therefore be taken over and operated by it in the interest of the public. But experience and reason are against such a view. Government in most cases is better fitted to restrain the evils of monopoly and regulate the conduct of a business which affects the public interest than it is to manage the business itself.

The more numerous and diverse the functions of government, the greater the difficulties. The business of a joint stock company is usually limited to one or a few activities, while under a socialistic regime the business activities, of the state would be legion. It goes without saying that there are some industries that can be better conducted by private management and to overcharge the government with the conduct of the whole complex volume of industrial activity in a modern society would lead to inefficiency, if not to a complete breakdown.

The problem of providing all the necessaries of life for the people of a populous state, of managing the labour and distributing the products, would be a task which no government could perform satisfactorily. Under a socialistic regime, moreover, nothing would be produced except as it pleased those in authority. It would be necessary to persuade the state to produce many things that are now produced under private competition.

Production would no longer be regulated by the law of supply and demand, but it would determine demand, contrary to every existing principle of political economy. Besides, the calculations of the government would constantly be upset by various circumstances. Everything would depend on the pleasure of the governors.

A diminution in the quantity and quality of production might be expected to result from the withdrawal of the stimulus of private incentive. Government managers would be languid and without interest in the result, laborers would be without incentive and the state timid, from which there would result, says one writer, "a diminished rate of progress, decreased production of wealth, with, finally, in all probability, a diffused poverty, which, besides being an evil in itself, is one that threatens all the higher human interests. Finally, socialism would involve, not an enlargement, but a restriction of individual freedom, and a deterioration of individual character. This point has been ably emphasized by Mill, Spencer, and others. Under a socialistic regime society would have to be organized and controlled to some extent like an army.

In the absence of all selfinterest and incentive individuals would have to be disciplined and driven to the discharge of their duties, and in the place of freedom we should, according to some writers, have virtual slavery. If all industry and commerce must be managed by a central authority which has to calculate and regulate everything, observes McKechnie, it follows that all deviations from the appointed and expected routine on which these calls are based must be strenuously put down.

No travesty of a healthy state, McKechnie concludes, is more deplorable than a practical socialism in the form of an absolute government directing with inquisitorial and irresistible sway every detail of human life. "Such are some of the arguments that have been advanced by various writers against the theories of socialism as popularly understood.

The ideas of socialism in the form in which it has been described above have never been realized in practice in any state. The Amana and Icarian communities in Iowa, the Shakers and the Harmony Society of Pennsylvania, and various others represent attempts to realize in practice communistic principles; but they all resulted in failure and left behind only "buried hopes and aspirations. "These communities, says Rae, led to the same results as in England, namely, a slackening of industry and a deterioration of the general level of comfort

While socialism in its extreme form has never been attempted by any modern state, all states perform various functions that are socialistic in character, some more than others; and one of the marked political tendencies of the time has been the drift in this direction.

The movement has been strongest on the continent of

Europe, particularly in Germany, since the founding of the empire. There the state operates and controls many businesses that in America are left to private enterprise, and regulates many of the details of individual conduct that elsewhere are left uncontrolled by the state.

In various countries of Europe the state owns and operates railroads, mines, banks, and breweries; monopolizes the manufacture of certain commodities like brandy, tobacco, and gunpowder; owns and operates or subsidizes theaters and opera houses; aids and encourages literature, science, and art; insures people against sickness, accidents, and old age; owns and operates wholly or in part the instrumentalities of communication and transportation; and through the local governments manages many public utilities such as waterworks, gas and electric light plants, and street railways.

In England, until recently, state socialism had made little headway, but in recent years a "profound change has come over the spirit of English politics "and the state is running fast in the direction of socialism. Indeed, says Laveleye, England is now leading the nations of the Old World in this respect. England is changing from the old trust in individualism and liberty to a new trust in state regulation and from the French doctrine of laissez-faire to the German doctrine of state socialism.

During the last few years the English Parliament has enacted a large volume of social legislation, such as factory acts, health legislation, laws providing dwellings for the poor, employers' liability acts, workingmen's compensation acts, old age pension acts, etc., while the local governments have gone farther than those of any other country toward the municipalization of public service industries such as the water and light supply and the means of local transportation. Throughout England to-day the cities generally own and operate their own gas, electric light, and water systems; in many cases they own and manage the street railway utilities; and own public washhouses, libraries, music halls, etc.

The state now operates not only the postal service but also the telegraph and to a large extent the telephone service, operates a parcels post system, conducts postal savings banks, and performs many other services that were formerly left to private enterprise. Most of the state intervention in England, however, has been in the interest of better moral and social conditions rather than for the promotion of economic interests. Most of it, in short, has been guided by ethical rather than by economic considerations.

In some of the English colonies, particularly in Australia and New Zealand, where private capital has been lacking, the activities of the state have been multiplied to an extent not equaled anywhere else in the world. There a large part of the tillable land is owned by the state and rented to tenants; the coal mines and forests are likewise under state control; so are the railroad, telegraph, and telephone systems; there is also a government parcels post system and there are government savings banks.

The state makes loans to farmers at low rates and constructs improved dwellings for workingmen. There is a system of state insurance, not only against death and old age, but against loss by fire. The government maintains labour bureaus and a system of compulsory arbitration in labour disputes; regulates the hours of labour in various occupations and in some instances undertakes to regulate the wages of labour; constructs public works by direct labour rather than by contract, and, through the municipalities, generally owns and operates the public service industries.

The state, in short, approaches more nearly the socialistic ideal than any other in the world. It is a vast landlord and employer; it engages in banking, farming, insurance, the express business, mining, and other industries. As to whether the good exceeds the evil, there is a wide difference of opinion.

CITIZENSHIP AND NATIONALITY

THE people who constitute the state may be divided into two general classes, namely, citizens and aliens. The former class may be again divided into those who possess full civil and political rights and those who do not. Aristotle's definition of a citizen as one who has a share in the government of the state and is entitled to enjoy its honors, does not therefore accord with modern theory or practice, which hardly anywhere identifies the rights of citizenship with political privilege. According to Vattel, "citizens are the members of the civil society, bound to this society by certain duties, subject to its authority, and equal participators in its advantages. ""Citizens, "said the Supreme Court of the United States in a noted case, "are members of the political community to which they belong.

They are the people who compose the state and who in their associated capacity have established or subjected themselves to the dominion of a government for the promotion of their general welfare and for the protection of their individual as well as their collective rights. "

These definitions, however, as well as most of those found in the books, represent the popular, rather than the strictly legal, conception of citizenship. In the United States, as has been said, "citizen "and "elector "are by no means convertible terms. In all of the states there are citizens who are not electors, and in some there are electors who are not citizens. The possession of the electoral privilege is not essential to citizenship and there is no necessary connection between them.

A frequent source of confusion and misconception would be removed if the term "citizen "were restricted to those who enjoy full civil and political rights and a different term employed to describe all others. Both the French and German languages contain suitable terms by which this distinction may be expressed. Thus in France those who enjoy full civil and political privileges are described by the term citoyen, while all Frenchmen who owe allegiance and are entitled to pro. tection regardless of their civil or political status are designated as nationaux.

In like manner the terms Staatsbürger and Staatsangehorige are employed in Germany. In the United States the word "subject "has been suggested as a suitable term which might be employed to describe the unenfranchised class, but it is open to several objections.

In the first place, it is a part of the modern theory of

sovereignty that all persons within the jurisdiction of the state, regardless of their civil or political status, are, legally speaking, subjects, and hence it would be erroneous to restrict the application of the term to a portion only of the population.

In the second place, the fact that the term "subject "has been associated historically with the theories of feudalism and absolutism, and that it has been and still is employed to describe the relation between a hereditary monarch and those over whom he rules, has caused the term to be looked upon with disfavor in states having the popular form of government, as descriptive of a status which is inconsistent with republican institutions.

As descriptive of a strict legal status, however, the term "subject "is as applicable in republics as in monarchies, and but for its historical associations no valid objection could be urged against it.

The employment of this term to describe the status of the inhabitants of the insular possessions of the United States certainly ought not to be objectionable. It also suitably describes the members of Indian tribes; and formerly it might have appropriately been employed to describe the slave class and to a less extent the class of free negroes.

Chapter 8

The Distribution of the Powers of Government

THE THEORY OF THE SEPARATION OF POWERS

THE functions or activities of government are customarily divided into three classes: those which are legislative in character, those which are executive, and those which are judicial. The legislative function consists mainly in laying down rules of conduct for those subject to the jurisdiction of the state; the executive function consists mainly, though not wholly, in enforcing such of these rules as are in the nature of commands; and the judicial function consists in interpreting their meaning in order that they may be applied in particular cases.

Some writers, however, especially among the French, recognize only two classes or groups of governmental powers, namely, those which are concerned with the formulation and expression of the will of the state, and those which have to do with the execution of that will. Thus, says Du Crocq, an eminent writer on administrative law, "the mind can conceive of but two powers: that which makes the law and that which executes; there is no place for a third power by the side of the other two.

Those who adopt this view maintain that the judicial function does not in reality constitute a separate and distinct power, but is rather a part of the executive power, or a particular phase or incident of it, since it is primarily concerned with the application and enforcement of the legislative will.

Thus writes Duguit, another French opponent of the trinity theory, "It necessarily follows that the judicial order is not a distinct power, but simply a dependency of the executive power, under whose surveillance it ought to be placed;... it is a mere agent of execution, subordinate to the executive power. "Consequently, what are popularly treated as three clearly differentiated sets of governmental functions are in fact but two, namely, those which are legislative and those which are executive.

Generally the advocates of the "duality "theory subdivide the activities which have to do with the execution of the state will into three classes: those which are purely executive in character, or which are limited to the supervision and direction of the task of execution; those which are administrative in character, or which are concerned rather with the actual scientific or technical work involved in carrying on the executive functions of government; and those which are judicial, or which have to do with the interpretation and application of the law to concrete cases.

Finally, it should be noted that while most French writers conceive the judicial power to be a particular phase or manifestation of the executive power, they nevertheless separate rigidly the function of administration, in the executive sense of the term, from judicial administration, or the administration of justice, by taking away from the judiciary practically all power of control over the administrative authorities.

In other words, the doctrine of the separation of powers, as Dicey remarks, has in the mind of a French statesman a meaning very different from that attributed to it by a statesman in England or the United States. In France it means not merely that the judges should be independent as understood in the United States, but that the government and its agents ought to be independent of, and to a great extent free from, the jurisdiction of the ordinary courts.

While the "duality "theory is accepted by most French writers, there are a few of high standing who reject it as unsound. Esmein, for example, asserts that the function of the judges in the application of the law is not simply an incident of execution and hence is not subordinate to the executive power. It is true, he admits, that the function of interpretation by the judiciary is preliminary to that of execution; that is, the judges determine in the first place whether the law is applicable, and, therefore, whether it ought or ought not to be enforced in a particular case; but that does not make it a part of the act of execution.

If the judicial power is only an incident of the executive power, then the judges are nothing more than the agents of the executive and render justice in its name. Moreover, since the exercise of judicial power in many cases has no bearing whatever on the execution of the law, how can it be a part or phase of the executive power in such cases ? In the field of non-contentious jurisdiction, where no controversies are involved, there is no question of the execution of the law, and it would manifestly be incorrect to speak of the judicial power as having any agency in the function of execution.

But although much may be said in favor of the duality theory, popular usage and actual practice sanction the doctrine of the trinity of powers. In every modern state, whatever the form of its constitution, the governmental system is in fact organized and administered on the principle that the judicial power is not a part of the executive power, that it is fundamentally different in character, and that its exercise should be in trusted to separate and distinct organs. Even in absolute monarchies where, constitutionally, the whole legislative and judicial power is in the hands of a single individual, it is in practice separated and exercised through agencies largely distinct and independent of each other.

The idea of a threefold division of governmental powers was recognized by Aristotle, Cicero, Polybius, and other ancient political writers. Aristotle, for example, classified the powers of government as: first, the *deliberative,* or those concerned with great questions of practical policy, including decisions regarding war and peace, the negotiation of treaties, the making of laws, etc; second, the *magisterial,* or those corresponding roughly to the executive functions of a modern state; and, third, the judicial power Although the ancient writers distinguished between three classes of governmental powers, corresponding roughly to the modern classification, yet in practice the distinction was not always observed. Thus the Ecclesia of Athens passed the laws, executed many of them, and exercised judicial functions.

The Archons, although primarily administrative officials, possessed judicial powers. The Roman Senate was both a legislative and an administrative assembly, while the magistrates combined both administrative and judicial functions. Throughout the Middle Ages no clear distinction between legislative, executive, and judicial functions was recognized, though in a rough way the functions, especially of legislation and administration, were separated as a matter of convenience.

Generally, the same magistrates exercised both executive and judicial functions. Indeed, the separation of the judicial power from the executive is a comparatively recent innovation, and when it came it undoubtedly marked an important political advance. The purity of justice and the liberty of the citizens, observes Bluntschli, gained by the change, and government did not lose its security.

The distinction is so familiar to us, says Maine, that it is hard for us to believe that even the different nature of the executive and legislative powers was not recognized until the fourteenth century, when it appeared in the "Defensor Pacis "of Marsiglio of Padua. Bodin, in the sixteenth century, was the first political writer to call attention to the danger of allowing the prince to administer justice in person and to point out the advantage of intrusting the judicial power to independent magistrates.

"To be at once legislator and judge, "he declared, "is to mingle together justice and the prerogative of mercy, adherence to the law and departure from it. Writers on the law of nature and of nations had analyzed the nature of the various powers of government, but had generally held that in order that the state might be strong and powerful it was necessary that all powers should be united in the same hands rather than distributed among coordinate and coequal authorities. In England, at the time of the Puritan Revolution, in the middle of the seventeenth century, the division of governmental powers and their exercise by separate and distinct organs became for the first time a political doctrine.

Cromwell, in the constitution of the Protectorate, went to the length of separating the executive and legislative functions, but he did not fully recognize the independence of the judiciary. John Locke, the political philosopher of the English Revolution, in his famous "Two Treatises of Government, "declared that the powers of government naturally divided themselves into those which were legislative in character, those which were executive, and those which were federative. By the latter functions he seems to have meant what is now understood as the diplomatic power.

The first modern political writer to dwell at length upon the separation of the powers of government and to treat it as a fundamental principle of political science was Montesquieu, in his famous work entitled *"L'Esprit des Lois,* "published in 1748. "In every government, "he said, "there are three sorts of power ": the legislative, the executive, and the judiciary. When the legislative and executive powers are united in the same person, or in some body of magistrates, there can be no liberty. Again, there is no liberty if the judiciary power is not separated from the legislative and executive powers.

Were it joined with the legislative power, the life and liberty of the subject would be exposed to arbitrary control; for the judge would then be the legislator. Were it joined with the executive power, the judge might behave with voilence and oppression. There would be an end of everything were the same man or the same body, whether of the nobles or of the people, to exercise these three powers, that of enacting the laws, that of executing the public resolutions, and that of trying the causes of individuals.

Montesquieu was the first writer, therefore, to make the theory of the separation of powers a doctrine of liberty. His views became a part of the political philosophy of the French Revolution and were fully enunciated in the constitutions which were framed in France before the close of the eighteenth century. In England essentially the same doctrine as that announced in France by Montesquieu was laid down by Blackstone in his *"Commentaries on the Laws of England.* ""Whenever, "said Blackstone, "the right of making and enforcing the law is vested in the same man or the same body of men, there can be no public liberty.

The magistrate may enact tyrannical laws and enact them in a tyrannical manner, since he is possessed, in his quality of dispenser of justice, with all the power which he as legislator thinks proper to give himself. ""Were the judicial power joined with the legislative, "he concluded, "the life, liberty, and property of the subject would be in the hands of arbitrary judges whose decisions would be regulated by their opinions and not by any fundamental principles of law; which, though legislators may depart from, yet judges are bound to observe. Were it joined with the executive, this union might soon be an overbalance of the legislative. "

In America, at the time of the framing of the national constitution, the influence of both Blackstone and Montesquieu was powerful and decisive, and their doctrines concerning the separation of powers became a part of the political creed of the early statesmen.

Madison, in almost the very language of Montesquieu, whom he pronounced "the oracle who is always consulted and cited on this subject, "defended the doctrine as essential to the protection of individual liberty. "The accumulation of all powers, legislative, executive, and judicial, in the same hands, "he said, "whether of one, a few, or many, and whether hereditary, self-appointed, or elective, may justly be pronounced the very definition of tyranny. "George Washington, John Adams, Thomas Jefferson, Alexander Hamilton, and later Kent, Story, and Webster, all expressed similar views.

In the early state constitutions framed before the close of the eighteenth century the idea that legislative, executive, and judicial functions must be kept separate, and intrusted to distinct authorities, was expressed in no uncertain language;

and their governments were organized as nearly in accordance with the theory as considerations of expediency and efficiency permitted. Thus the constitution of Massachusetts declared that "in the government of this commonwealth the legislative department shall never exercise the executive and judicial powers or either of them; the executive shall never exercise the legislative or judicial powers or either of them; the judicial shall never exercise the legislative and executive powers or either of them, to the end that it may be a government of laws and not of men.

"Declarations similar in substance were incorporated in most of the other revolutionary state constitutions and in those which followed the adoption of the federal constitution. Practically all of the state tributing clauses "expressly providing for a tripartite division of governmental powers among separate and distinct departments or organs. The few that contain no formal distributing clauses nevertheless vest the legislative, executive, and judicial functions in separate organs, so that whether the theory is formally expressed or not, the government in every case is in fact organized in accordance with the principle of separation.

The present conception as well as the current practice in America has lately been expressed by the Supreme Court of the United States in the following language: "It is believed to be one of the chief merits of the American system of written constitutional law that all powers intrusted to the government, whether state or national, are divided into three grand departments, the executive, the legislative, and the judicial; that the function appropriated to each of these branches of government shall be vested in a separate body of public servants, and that the perfection of the system requires that the lines which separate and divide these departments shall be broadly and clearly defined.

It is also essential to the successful working of the system that the persons intrusted with power in any one of these branches shall not be permitted to encroach upon the powers confided to the others, but that each shall, by the law of its creation, be limited to the powers appropriated to its own department, and no other. "In various foreign constitutions, particularly those which have been framed under the influence of American ideas, the theory is embodied in similar form. In the states of Europe, where the cabinet system of government prevails, the close connection between the legislative and executive organs constitutes an important exception to the theory; yet, upon careful examination, the violation of the principle will be seen to be really less than it appears, since the functions of legislation and execution are in fact intrusted to separate organs, even though one is controlled by and is responsible to the other for the manner in which it exercises its powers.

In none of them is the legislature really the executor of the law or the judge of the controversies raised in the course of its application; nor does the judiciary legislate or administer. The inconvenience and danger, however, of such a confusion of functions is admitted by European writers as well as by those in America.

LIMITATIONS OF THE THEORY OF THE SEPARATION OF POWERS

When we assert it to be a fundamental principle of political science that the legislative, executive, and judicial functions of government should be intrusted to separate and independent organs or departments, we are to understand the proposition as being true only in a limited sense. Both reason and experience abundantly show that no government can be organized on the principle of the absolute and complete separation of the departments among which the legislative, executive, and judicial functions are distributed.

There is not now and never has been a constitution in which the three departments were not more or less connected and dependent one upon the other, and in which each exercised powers that, under a strict application of the theory, did not belong more property to one of the others. In short, the doctrine of the separation of powers has never been anything more than a theory and an ideal.

John Locke, the first political writer to attach great

importance to the theory, while contending that legislative and executive powers should be vested in separate hands, recognized what is now generally admitted, that in practice the principle is incapable of full realization; "for, "he said, "the legislature not being able to foresee and provide by-laws for all that may be useful to the community, the executor of the laws having the power in his hands, has by the common law nature a right to make use of it, for the good of society, in many cases where the municipal law has given no directions. Nay, many things there are which the law can by no means provide for; these must necessarily be left to the discretion of him that has the executive power in his hands.."

Montesquieu, who, as has been said, made the principle of separation a doctrine of liberty and gave it an importance rarely attained by any political theory, obviously did not understand that it involved the absolute independence of each department of the others. He must have known that the British constitution, of which he was writing when he laid down his famous proposition regarding the doctrine of the separation of powers, did not in fact recognize the doctrine except in a qualified sense.

At that time, as now, the Engfish executive was a committee of the legislature; one chamber of the legislature constituted an important part of the judiciary and at the same time "a great constitutional council of the executive "; and the judiciary was to a considerable extent subordinate to both the executive and the legislature, being appointed by the one and dependent on the other for its subsistence. The laws were often executed by authorities which at the same time administered justice, and some of the minor judicial authorities, notably the justices of the peace, were important administrative authorities.

When Montesquieu declared, therefore, that there could be no liberty where the executive and the judicial powers were united in the same hands, and where the executive was not separated from the legislative, he stated what the experience of England then and now contradicts. There is every reason for believing that Montesquieu did not mean to exclude each department from all control over the acts of the others or from all share or agency in their functions. This was the judgment of James Madison, who wrote at a time when Montesquieu's ideas were still fresh in the minds of political writers and when they were being defended by his American followers. "On the slightest view of the British constitution, "observed Madison, "we must perceive that the legislative, executive, and judiciary departments are by no means totally separate and distinct from each other.

"From these facts, by which Montesquieu was guided, "asserted Madison, "it may clearly be inferred, that in saying 'there can be no liberty where the legislative and executive powers are united in the same person or body of magistrates, ' or, 'if the power of judging be not separated from the legislative and executive powers, ' he did not mean that these departments ought to have no partial agency in, or no control over, the acts of each other.

His meaning, as his own words import, and still more conclusively as illustrated by the example in his eye, can amount to no more than this, where the whole power of one department is exercised by the hands which hold the whole power of another department, the fundamental principles of a free constitution are subverted. This would have been the case in the constitution examined by him, if the king, who is the sole executive magistrate, had possessed also the complete legislative power, or the supreme administration of justice; or if the entire legislative body had possessed the supreme judiciary or the supreme executive authority. "

When the framers of the American constitution came to apply the theory in practice, they recognized the impracticability, not to say the undesirability, of absolute and complete separation. "If we look to the constitutions of the several states, "said Madison, "we find, notwithstanding the emphatical and, in some instances, the unqualified terms in which the axiom has been laid down, there is not a single instance in which the several departments of power have been kept absolutely separate and distinct.

"Some of the distributing clauses, in fact, expressly

recognized limitations upon the theory. Thus the constitution of New Hampshire qualified the principle by declaring that the "legislative, executive, and judiciary powers ought to be kept as separate from and independent of each other as the nature of a free government will admit; or as is consistent with the chain of connection that binds the whole fabric of the constitution in one indissoluble bond of unity and amity. "Madison himself, in defending the doctrine in its qualified form, asserted that "unless the departments were so far connected and blended as to give to each a constitutional control over the others, the degree of separation which the maxim requires as essential to a free government can never in practice be duly maintained.

"He stated the principle in a very general way when he said that "the powers properly belonging to one department ought not to be directly and completely administered by either of the other departments; it is equally evident that neither of them ought to possess, directly or indirectly, an overruling influence over the others in the administration of their respective powers. "This was probably all that Locke, Montesquieu, and Blackstone intended the theory to mean, though it will readily be admitted that the principle as though stated is so broad and elastic that it can have little value as a practical rule.

The strict separation of powers is not only impracticable as a working principle of government, but it is one not to be desired in practice. The experience of the English and other constitutions where the principle is not strictly observed shows that it is not a necessary condition of free institutions, and that there is no necessary danger to liberty in allowing the lawmaking body to execute or even to judge.

John Stuart Mill pointed out that if each department of the government were completely independent in its sphere so that it could thwart the actions of the others, frequent deadlocks would be inevitable, since "each department acting in defense of its own powers would never lend its aid to the others; and the consequent loss in efficiency would outweigh all the possible advantages arising from the independence.

"This danger was recognized by Black stone, who, while defending the principle of the separation of the departments, declared that their "total disjunction "would in the end produce the same tyrannical effects as their complete union in the same hands, "by causing that union against which it seems to provide.

"The different attributes of sovereignty, observes Esmein, cannot be exercised separately any more than the different powers of a human being; they coordinate naturally and necessarily in a common action which presupposes their cooperation. The true way to prevent the encroachment of one department upon the domain of the others is, as Madison has aptly remarked, to permit each to participate in the functions of the others to such an extent as to check them and keep them in their proper places without, however, controlling them.

The framers of the United States constitution, impressed as they were with the value of the principle of separation, did not delude themselves into supposing that any precise or exact delineation of the three spheres could be drawn, or that anything was to be gained by an absolute separation of authorities such as the French Revolutionists undertook to introduce.

They had in mind only a general distribution and aimed merely at a rough classification. They did not trouble themselves to inquire whether a particular power was legislative, executive, or judicial in its nature, but were concerned rather with the question of which department was best fitted to exercise a given power.

It was with them a question of administrative convenience and administrative expediency rather than one of pure political philosophy. Certain powers were vested in the executive, not because they were necessarily executive in character, but because the organization and methods of the executive department were such that those powers could be better exercised by it than by the department to which they strictly belonged. Thus the power of issuing ordinances and of negotiating treaties was conferred upon the executive, since both are a species of legislation which experience and reason have clearly shown can be more efficiently performed by the executive department than by the legislative department, where, under a purely scientific interpretation of their nature, they more properly belong. Likewise it is desirable, if not necessary, that the courts be allowed a share in legislation through their power to interpret the written law and to declare what is the unwritten law. For the same reason many other exceptions to the theory of separation were introduced in the organization of the government.

The legislative department was made a sort of depository for many classes of powers which are neither distinctly legislative, executive, nor judicial in character, but which partake of the characteristics of all three, and which were conferred upon the legislature through considerations of administrative convenience or political expediency. Every act which proceeds from the legislature is therefore classed as legislative; every act performed by the executive department is classed as executive; and so on, regardless of its real nature.

While no department exercises all the power which upon a strict interpretation belongs to it, it nevertheless exercises the essential part of it. Each department exercises incidental rights of a nature intrinsically different from the mass of powers logically belonging to it, but they are such only as are necessary to enable it to perform efficiently its functions as an independent branch of the government and are in reality part of the principal power itself.

In practice, therefore, the theory has never been construed to mean that all the legislative power shall be exercised by the legislative department, or all the executive power by the executive department, or all the judicial power by the judicial department. The theory otherwise understood would be impossible of practical application in any governmental system.

It is impossible to draw a strict line of demarcation between the several departments. There is a common borderland between them, within which each department must tolerate the others if government is to be efficient. No legislature can discharge entirely all those functions which under a strict interpretation of the theory are legislative. Details must be filled up and rules issued by the executive, governing the application of the law, if the government is to be conducted on practical lines. In short, functions may be separated, but not the departments themselves.

While the departments are, theoretically, equal and coordinate, they "constitute one brotherhood whose constant trust requires a mutual toleration of what seems to be a 'common because of vicinage' bordering on the domains of each. "In reality, however, the departments are not equal. In all governments the legislative department is in fact the most powerful of the three and the judiciary the weakest. The powers of the legislative department in most governments are not specifically enumerated, but are general or residuary in character; in short, it is a sort of repository, as has been said, of all powers not conferred on the other departments.

It possesses everywhere a large control over the organization and activities of the other departments, through its power of supply and its power to create public offices and to provide for their support. It not only makes the laws that are to be interpreted by the judiciary and enforced by the executive, but lays down the rules and conditions in accordance with which the executive acts. The legislature is thus, in a sense, the regulator of the administration. The very nature of government is such that the will of the lawmaking power must, to a certain extent, be superior to the executive and the judiciary. This is necessarily so because the will of the state must be expressed before it can be interpreted and enforced, and in formulating that will the legislature may, as has been said, prescribe the conditions and circumstances under which execution shall take place.

The judiciary, on the contrary, possesses no control over the source of supply or over the army or the governmental organization of the state. It cannot, as has been remarked by a distinguished commentator, lay taxes, nor appropriate money, nor command armies nor appoint officers. It has no means of influence through the power of patronage, no powers, in short, that can be wielded for itself.

Chapter 9

The Legislative Department

ORGANIZATION: THE UNICAMERAL VERSUS THE BICAMERAL PRINCIPLE

IT has become almost an axiom in political science that legislative bodies should consist of two chambers. At the present time those constructed on the unicameral principle are found only in Greece, Luxembourg, Servia, the Canadian provinces of British Columbia, Manitoba, and Ontario, a few of the smaller German states, and some of the Swiss cantons. Formerly, however, the unicameral idea found more favor than now. In America, in the eighteenth century, it had an influential advocate in Benjamin Franklin, who is said to have compared a double-chambered legislative assembly to a cart with a horse hitched to each end, both pulling in opposite directions.

Largely through his influence the legislature of Pennsylvania under its first constitution was constructed on the unicameral principle, and we have the testimony of John Adams that the question of whether the early American legislatures generally should consist of one or two chambers was one of transcendent importance at the time of the adoption of the first state constitutions.

In France, at the time of the Revolution, the unicameral idea had many supporters, and the principle was incorporated in the constitution of 1791 by an almost unanimous vote of the National Assembly, and was continued in the constitution of 1793. The constitution of the year III, however, established the bicameral system; and it was continued until 1848, when the single chamber was again reverted to, though only for a brief interval. Among the powerful advocates of the unicameral principle in 1848 was Lamartine, as Turgot had been its ablest defender at the time of the Revolution. The experience of France with single-chambered legislative assemblies, however, was not satisfactory; and their proceedings, it is said, "were marked by violence, instability, and excesses of the worst kind. "

With remarkably few exceptions the states which have experimented with the single chamber system have abandoned it for the bicameral system. In England, during the Commonwealth, it was tried for a brief period, but without success; and the House of Lords, which had been abolished, was soon restored.

The lack of a second chamber in the national congress was one of the causes of dissatisfaction with the Articles of Confederation in the United States, and, with the exception of Benjamin Franklin, none of the framers of the constitution favored retaining the unicameral system. In Pennsylvania, where it existed for a time, we are told that it was marked by a "want of stability "and resulted in "extremely impulsive and variable legislation.

"It was soon abandoned in Pennsylvania and in the few other states where it had been introduced. Other countries, notably Spain, Portugal, Naples, Mexico, Bolivia, Ecuador, and Peru, have all abandoned it, after a fair trial, for the double-chambered system.

The chief argument advanced in favor of the unicameral system by the French statesmen and political writers in 1789 and again in 1848 was that it secured "unity "instead of "duality "in the organization of the legislative branch of the government. Two or three chambers, it was argued, meant two or three sovereignties. "The law, "said Sieyès, "is the will of the people; the people cannot at the same time have two different wills on the same subject; therefore, the legislative body which represents the people ought to be essentially one. Where there are two chambers, discord and division will be inevitable and the will of the people will be paralyzed by inaction.

"The same view was expressed by Lamartine, who maintained that the double chamber sacrificed the great principle of unity by dividing the sovereignty of the state. A similar line of reasoning was pursued by Condorcet, Robespierre, and other leaders in

France at the time of the Revolution. In America, likewise, the same kind of argument was advanced by Franklin and others against the bicameral theory. Legislation being merely the expression of the common will, the necessity of committing it to two separate assemblies, each having a veto upon the action of the other, was not apparent. "All the arguments, "says Judge Story, "derived from the analogy between the movements of political bodies and the operations of physical nature, all the impulses of political parsimony, all the prejudices against a second coordinate legislative assembly stimulated by the exemplification of it in the British Parliament, were against a division of the legislative power. "In short, a double-chambered legislature was an assembly divided against itself.

In America, John Adams combated the doctrines of Franklin, Turgot, and the other French critics of the bicameral system, in a rather remarkable essay entitled "A Defense of the Constitutions of Government of the United States, "in which, among other things, he defended with ability and learning the principle of the division of the legislative power between two coordinate assemblies.

He reviewed the history of free governments and undertook to show that government by single assemblies had "generally been visionary if not corrupt and violent and had usually ended in despotism.

"Of all possible forms of government, a sovereignty in a single assembly, successively chosen by the people, is, "he said, "perhaps the best calculated to facilitate the gratification of self-love, and the pursuit of the private interests of a few individuals — in one word, the whole system of affairs and every conceivable motive of hope or fear will be employed to promote the private interests of a few of their obsequious majority; and there is no remedy but in arms.

Notwithstanding all the objections raised against the bicameral system, experience has apparently established its advantages over the single chamber scheme. "It accompanies the Anglican race, "observes Francis Lieber, "like the common law, and everywhere it succeeds.

"Of all the forms of government that are possible among mankind, "says Lecky, "I do not know any which is likely to be worse than the government of a single omnipotent democratic chamber. It is at least as susceptible as an individual despot of the temptations that grow out of the possession of an uncontrolled power, and it is likely to act with much less sense of responsibility and much less real deliberation. "

The advantages of a second chamber may be summarized as follows: First, it serves as a check upon hasty, rash, and ill-considered legislation. Legislative assemblies are often subject to strong passions and excitements and are sometimes impatient, impetuous, and careless. The function of a second chamber is to restrain such tendencies and to compel careful consideration of legislative projects.

It interposes delay between the introduction and final adoption of a measure and thus permits time for reflection and deliberation. "One great object of the separation of the legislature into two houses acting separately and with coordinate powers, "said Chancellor Kent, "is to destroy the evil effects of sudden and strong excitement and of precipitate measures springing from passion, caprice, prejudice, personal influence, and party intrigue, which have been found by sad experience to exercise a potent and dangerous sway in single assemblies. It is clear, says Bluntschli, in explaining the advantages of the bicameral system, that four eyes see more and better than two, especially when a given subject may be considered from different standpoints.

In the second place, the bicameral principle not only serves to protect the legislature against its own errors of haste and impulse, but it also affords a protection to the individual against the despotism of a single chamber. The existence of a second chamber is thus a guarantee of liberty as well as to some extent a safeguard against tyranny. Where the whole legislative power is intrusted to a single omnipotent assembly, the restraining element of a second chamber is lacking. There is a natural propensity on the part of legislative bodies to accumulate power into their hands, to absorb the powers of the executive and the judiciary, in short, to draw into their grasp the whole government of the state. They have a constant tendency, observes Judge Story, to overstep their proper boundaries, from passion, from ambition, from inadvertence, from the prevalence of faction, or from the overwhelming influence of private interests.

Under such circumstances, he adds, the only effective barrier against oppression, whether accidental or intentional, is to "separate its operations, to balance interest against interest, ambition against ambition, the combinations and spirit of dominion of one body against the like combinations and spirit of another. "The existence of a second chamber, continues Story, doubles the security of the people by requiring the concurrence of two distinct bodies in any scheme of usurpation or perfidy where otherwise the ambition of a single body would be sufficient.

"The necessity of two chambers, "says Bryce, "is based on the belief that the innate tendency of an assembly to become hateful, tyrannical, and corrupt, needs to be checked by the coexistence of another house of equal authority. The Americans restrain their legislatures by dividing them, just as the Romans restrained their executives by substituting two consuls for one king.

A third advantage of the bicameral system is that it affords a convenient means of giving representation to special interests or classes in the state and particularly to the aristocratic portion of society, in order to counterbalance the undue preponderance of the popular element in one of the chambers, thus introducing into the legislature a conservative force to curb the radicalism of the popular chamber.

We cannot, says Bluntschli, ignore the distinction between the aristocratic and democratic elements in the population of the state and allow one of these elements alone representation in the legislature without doing the other an injustice. Montesquieu asserted, not without some truth, that there are always persons in every state, distinguished by their birth, wealth, or honors, to whom, if they are confounded with the common people and are given only an equal share in the government with the rest, the common liberty would be slavery and who would have to interest in supporting the government, as most of the popular resolutions would be against them.

"The share they should have in the legislature, "he declared, "ought to be proportioned to their other advantages in the state, which can happen only when they form a body that has a right to check the licentiousness of the people, as the people have a right to oppose any encroachment of theirs.

John Stuart Mill advocated a second chamber constructed on the principle of political experience and training without reference to considerations of birth or wealth. If one chamber, said Mill, represents popular feeling, the other should represent personal merit, tested and guaranteed by actual public service and fortified by practical experience. If one is the people's chamber, the other should be a chamber of statesmen, a council composed of all living public men who have passed through important political offices or employments.

Such a chamber, Mill argued, would be not merely a moderating body, or a simple check, but also an impelling force. It would be a body of natural leaders and would guide the people forward in the path of progress. The best constitution of the second chamber, he declared, is that which embodies the greatest number of elements exempt from the class interests and prejudices of the majority, but having in themselves nothing offensive to democratic feeling.

The bicameral system also affords a means of giving separate representation to the somewhat dissimilar interests of capital and labour. An actual illustration of the value of this principle is found, we are told by a well-known writer, in the Australian state of Victoria, where the upper chamber of the legislature is made up mainly of the representatives of capital, while the other chamber is composed principally of the representatives of labour. This is the result chiefly of a restricted suffrage for the upper house, higher property qualifications for membership in it, and the nonpayment of its members for their services.

Finally, the bicameral system affords an opportunity, in states having the federal form of government, of giving representation to the political units composing the federation. In order to maintain the proper equilibrium between the component members and the federation as a whole, the former ought to be represented in one chamber of the legislature without regard to population, that is, represented as distinct political organizations. This, in fact, is the principle upon which the legislatures of most states having the federal form of government are at present constructed.

The eighteenth century French doctrine that the bicameral system is incompatible with the principle of the unity of sovereignty will, upon examination, be seen to be untenable. Division of the legislative body into two chambers does not involve a division of the sovereignty of the state any more than the distribution of governmental power between legislative, executive, and judicial organs means a division of sovereignty. So long as the concurrence of both chambers is necessary to legislate, that is, so long as legislation. emanates from the assembly as a whole, there is not duality, but unity. Law is the will of the people, observes Laboulaye, whatever may be the mode employed for enacting it.

Where, however, the structural principle of both chambers of the legislature is the same, much of the value of the bicameral system is lost. If the two chambers are identical in constitution, then the second is a mere duplication of the first; and the advantages of the additional chamber are questionable. "If the two houses were elected for the same period and by the same electors, "observes Lieber, "they would amount in practice to little more than two committees of the same house; but we want two bona fide different houses representing the impulse as well as the continuity, the progress and the conservatism, the onward zeal and the retentive element, innovation, and adhesion, which must ever form integral elements of all civilization. One house, therefore, ought to be large; the other comparatively small, and elected or appointed for a longer time. "Some writers maintain that no advantage whatever is to be gained by the bicameral system if the two chambers are identical in constitution. In such a case it is, says Bluntschli, like employing duplicate organs to do the same thing.

Bluntschli argues, with good reason we believe, that the upper chamber ought to rest on a different basis from the lower chamber, that it ought, to some extent at least, to represent special classes or interests or political units as such without full regard to population; while the lower chamber ought to represent the opinion and interests of the mass of population, and to this end the representative ought to be chosen by the whole body of the citizens.

Judge Story was of the same opinion. The division of the legislature into two branches, he declared, would be of little or no intrinsic value unless the organization was such that each house could operate as a real check upon undue and rash legislation.

But it is not necessary to the success of the bicameral system that every class and interest in the community should be given distinct and separate representation. What is required in order to realize the full value of the bicameral principle is that the two chambers should be differently composed and should rest on dissimilar bases.

The members of one chamber ought to enjoy longer tenures, they ought to represent a larger constituency, higher membership qualifications ought to be required of them, and they might well be chosen in a different manner and by a differently constituted electorate. Where these requirements exist there will always be one chamber smaller in size than the other, possessing a higher degree of experience and perhaps of ability, more conservatism of spirit, and representing more fully the higher property and intellectual interests of the state.

Thus the high age qualifications (the attainment of the

fortieth year) required of senators in Belgium, France, and Italy has had the effect of securing more experienced statesmen in the legislatures of those countries. The longer tenure, the larger constituency, and the method of indirect election for members of the United States Senate tend to secure a more experienced, more conservative, and, on the whole, an abler body of legislators than is found in the House of Representatives. The same is true of the upper chambers of the Australian Commonwealth, and the republics of Brazil, Mexico, and Switzerland.

The hereditary principle which prevails almost wholly in the structure of the upper chamber in Great Britain and to a less degree in Austria, Hungary, and Spain diminishes rather than increases the efficiency of the legislature; yet under restrictions which it has been proposed to introduce into the English system the principle would not be without its advantages, since it would provide a means of introducing into the legislature a class of educated and leisured men who have had exceptional opportunities for acquiring political information and for imbibing the result of political experience, without at the same time bringing into the legislature large numbers of men who add little or no strength.

The appointive principle which prevails in Italy for the constitution of the upper chamber, and to a less degree In several other European states, is out of harmony with modern notions of representation, yet it has the advantage of insuring a place in the legislature for distinguished men who have held public office and also for men who have attained eminence in science, art, and the learned professions.

Perhaps the ideal mode of determining the membership of the upper chamber lies in a combination of some or all of the above systems, if we eliminate the Norwegian method of cooptation and the British hereditary principle, neither of which commends itself to us.

A certain number of members of whom high qualifications are required might very properly be elected upon the basis of a restricted suffrage from the larger administrative subdivisions into which the state is divided; a certain number might be elected by the local governments, such as the provincial legislatures or municipal councils; a limited number might be appointed by the excutive from those who have achieved eminence in the state or who have held certain high offices, etc.

With regard to the constitution of the lower house, there is a substantial unanimity of opinion and of practice that it should rest upon a popular basis, that is, its members should be chosen by direct election, upon the basis of a wide suffrage and for short terms. Finally, the experience of the past demonstrates the wisdom of the principle of inequality of powers as between the two chambers.

Nearly everywhere the upper chamber is intrusted with a share, negative or positive, in the administration of the government, often a certain participation in the control of the foreign policy of the state, and sometimes is vested with important judicial functions. This has a tendency to increase the dignity and prestige of membership therein and thus secure legislators of higher ability and added conservatism. The scheme of partial renewal common in the organization of the upper chambers is likewise a valuable principle, in that it tends to secure the element of experience and preserve continuity of membership.

METHODS OF APPORTIONMENT

Several methods of apportioning or distributing legislative representatives have been followed. One is to distribute them among the political divisions of the state without regard to their population, or at least without exclusive regard to it. In all the important federal unions except the German Empire and the Dominion of Canada the principle of equality of representation among the component members prevails in the construction of the upper chambers.

In the German *Bundesrath* the number of votes to which each state of the empire is entitled varies from one to seventeen; and in the Canadian House of Lords the number varies from four to twenty-four, the latter being the number allowed the province of Quebec. In the French Republic the number of senators from each department varies from one to ten. Another method of distribution is to apportion the representatives among the political divisions of the state with some regard to the amount or value of property in each. The chief merit of such a method is that it takes into consideration one of the important elements which enter into the physical make-up of the state.

The doctrine that taxation should go hand in hand with representation has long been a cherished political theory of the people of America and England, and perhaps no better system could be devised for protecting the rights of property than by giving it a share of representation in the legislative branch. For other reasons, however, it has not commended itself to the people of democratic states; and outside of a few European monarchies where property is taken into consideration to some extent in organizing representation in the upper chambers, the system no longer prevails. In no state is property to-day the sole basis of representation in either chamber, and the few remaining traces of the principle that have survived the nineteenth century will doubtless disappear in the course of time.

Another principle is that which bases representation on the total population, citizens and aliens, male and female, enfranchised and unenfranchised alike, and not on the number of voters merely. This is now the almost universal rule governing the apportionment of representation in lower chambers, and in some states it is also the basis of representation in the upper chambers.

It possesses the element of simplicity and uniformity and is regarded as being more in harmony with present day notions of representative government. The ratio of representation varies widely among different states. For the national House of Representatives in the United States it is now one representative for every 193, 000 of the population. In the

with some regard to the amount or value of property in each. The chief merit of such a method is that it takes into consideration one of the important elements which enter into the physical make-up of the state. The doctrine that taxation should go hand in hand with representation has long been a cherished political theory of the people of America and England, and perhaps no better system could be devised for protecting the rights of property than by giving it a share of representation in the legislative branch.

For other reasons, however, it has not commended itself to the people of democratic states; and outside of a few European monarchies where property is taken into consideration to some extent in organizing representation in the upper chambers, the system no longer prevails. In no state is property to-day the sole basis of representation in either chamber, and the few remaining traces of the principle that have survived the nineteenth century will doubtless disappear in the course of time.

Another principle is that which bases representation on the total population, citizens and aliens, male and female, enfranchised and unenfranchised alike, and not on the number of voters merely. This is now the almost universal rule governing the apportionment of representation in lower chambers, and in some states it is also the basis of representation in the upper chambers. It possesses the element of simplicity and uniformity and is regarded as being more in harmony with present day notions of representative government.

The ratio of representation varies widely among different states. For the national House of Representatives in the United States it is now one representative for every 193, 000 of the population. In the United Kingdom of Great Britain and Ireland it is one member for every 62, 700 of the population; in Belgium, one member for every 40, 000; in Brazil, one member for every 70, 000; in Mexico, one for every 40, 000; in Switzerland, one for every 20, 000; in France, one for every 100, 000; in the German Empire, one for every 100, 000; in Canada, one for every 22, 600 of the population.

The same variety prevails among the individual states composing the federal republic of the United States, where the principle of apportionment on the basis of population is generally the rule for the constitution of both the upper and lower chambers. Perhaps an ideal system would be one which would take into consideration the elements of population, geographical area, and property combined, if there were any criteria for determining the relative weight which should be given to each of these elements. As yet no satisfactory scheme of this kind has been devised.

METHOD OF CHOICE

For convenience in choosing representatives it is customary to divide the state into electoral circumscriptions or districts. The entire body of representatives might be chosen from the state at large on a general ticket, each elector being allowed to cast a vote for the entire number; but in states of considerable geographical area, where several hundred members are to be elected, such a method would obviously be impracticable.

The time and effort involved in voting such a ticket would be very great; and, what is of more importance, the ignorance of the elector concerning the candidates from distant parts of the state would be so great that an election under such circumstances would be largely a farce. The practice of all states, therefore, is to divide their territory into electoral districts or to utilize for this purpose the political subdivisions already in existence.

In constituting electoral districts two methods are employed: one is to parcel the state into as many districts as them are representatives to be chosen and allow a single member to be chosen from each; the other is to create a smaller number of districts, from each of which a number of representatives is chosen on the same ticket. The former is known as the single member district plan, the latter, as the general ticket method.

Each has been employed by most states at different times in their history, though nearly all have come at last to the single member district method. In the United States, for a long time, representatives in Congress were chosen from the state at large, each elector being allowed to cast a vote for the entire ticket; but the objections to the method were so serious that Congress, in 1842, enacted that thereafter they should be chosen by districts containing as nearly as possible equal populations, and this rule still prevails.

In Great Britain the single member district method has long prevailed, though from 1867 to 1885 a few of the more populous boroughs were permitted to choose their members by general ticket. These were the so-called "three-cornered "constituencies, thirteen in number, in which the system of proportional representation was applied.

The method first employed in the French Republic for choosing members of the Chamber of Deputies was the single district system; but in 1885 the general ticket method was adopted, under which all the deputies apportioned to each department were elected from the department at large by general ticket. In 1889, however, the single member district method was reverted to, and it is still in force. Italian practice has varied in a manner very similar to that of France, but since 1891 the general ticket method has prevailed.

The general ticket method is employed in the states composing the Commonwealth of Australia, for choosing the six senators to which each is entitled in the Commonwealth Parliament, as well as in those countries where schemes of proportional representation exist, notably in Belgium, Denmark, Cuba, Norway, Portugal, Sweden, certain districts in Brazil, in Italy for provincial and municipal elections, in certain parts of Spain, in Japan, in some of the Swiss cantons, in Iceland, Tasmania, and in other states.

In the states of the American Union the district method of choosing representatives is the rule, though there are a few exceptions. Likewise in the choice of members of municipal councils the single district or ward method generally prevails, especially where the single-chambered council exists, though there are some notable exceptions. In some municipalities a mixed system is employed, according to which a certain number of members, in addition to the ward representatives, are chosen from the city at large on general ticket.

The chief advantage of the single member district method is its simplicity and convenience. Where the country is divided into as many electoral circumscriptions as there are representatives to be chosen, the task of the voter in each district is restricted to the simple duty of casting a ballot for one representative. Owing to the necessarily restricted area of the electoral district under this system, the chances are considerable that the candidate will be better known to the voters than would be possible under the general ticket system, which requires larger districts, and that he will in turn be more familiar with the needs and conditions of the district which he is chosen to represent.

Another advantage of the district method is that it tends to secure representation to the minority party in the state, city, or province, as a whole. Obviously, if all the representatives are chosen from the state at large on a general ticket, the party having a bare majority will elect all and the minority none.

Thus in the United States, as long as representatives in Congress were chosen from the state at large, the majority party in each usually elected the entire congressional delegation; whereas if the district ticket method had prevailed, some districts in states not predominantly in control of one party or the other would have chosen representatives belonging to the minority party. The injustice of such a scheme led to the substitution of the district method, as has been said, by an act of Congress in 1842.

The same inequality is complained of with regard to the general ticket method of choosing presidential electors in the United States to-day, a system which usually gives the predominant party in each state all the presidential electors to which the state is entitled, though the numerical preponderance of the party in the majority may be quite insignificant.

The objections to the single member district method are: first, that it narrows the range of choice and often leads to the election of inferior men. This is notably the case in the large cities where the ward system of choosing aldermen is almost universal. Experience abundantly proves that in cities where such a system prevails not only inferior, but often corrupt, representatives are chosen. In the second place, the district system leads to the choice of men who are apt to represent local interests rather than men who represent the interests of the country as a whole, and who therefore are likely to take a narrow and particularistic view of public questions instead of a broad national view.

The experience of both France and Italy with the *scrutin d' arrondissement* system of choosing deputies clearly established the truth of this statement. In the case of Italy it was finally abandoned for the general ticket method, coupled with provision for a system of proportional representation.

The district system encourages the view that the representative is the *mandataire* of his constituency rather than of the country; that, in short, he is commissioned to represent a part rather than the whole of the state. Moreover, the custom which regards the legislator as the representative of a particular locality is responsible for the election of men whose energies are likely to be engrossed with the pressure of petty local influences, and therefore often deprives the state of the services of able statesmen who would be willing to serve in the legislature could they be freed from such influences and be regarded strictly as representatives of the country at large. In the third place, the district system increases powerfully the temptation of legislative majorities to "gerrymander "the state, that is, to construct the electoral districts in such a way as to give the majority party more representatives than its voting strength entities it to.

It would seem that a combination of the general ticket and district methods by which a certain number of representatives would be chosen according to each method possesses decided advantages over either by itself. It would secure all the principal advantages of both and at the same time diminish the manifest disadvantages of the district method.

Chapter 10

The Electorate

THEORIES OF SUFFRAGE

It was a part of the French political philosophy of the eighteenth century that every citizen has a natural and inherent right to participate in the choice of his representatives. This was a logical consequence of the French conception that sovereignty is the general will and that this will cannot be accurately ascertained and expressed unless all the citizens are allowed to participate in its expression through the choice of representatives.

"All the inhabitants, "said Montesquieu, "...ought to have a right of voting at the election of representatives, except such as are in so mean a situation as to be deemed to have no will of their own. "Rousseau held a similar view. This doctrine was powerfully supported by Robespierre, Condorcet, Petion, Boissy d'Anglas, and other Frenchmen at the time of the Revolution. Sovereignty, said Robespierre, resides in all the people, and every citizen, whoever he may be, should have a share in the representation and the right to participate in the formation of the law by which he is bound.

Notwithstanding the general prevalence of this notion in France in the eighteenth century, the French constitutions of the time did not, as a matter of fact, establish the principle of direct and unrestricted suffrage. The national assembly established instead a system of indirect election based on a restricted suffrage, and it made a distinction between active and passive citizens, the latter of whom were allowed no part in choosing the intermediate electors. In 1792, however, the distinction between ciloyens actifs and citoyens passifs was abolished, as was also the tax qualification for voting; the age requirement was reduced to twentyone years, and a system approaching universal manhood suffrage was substituted, though the system of indirect election was retained.

The constitution of the year III reestablished a tax qualification for voting without specifying the amount; in 1800 this was abolished and the principle of a wide suffrage reestablished. Under the restoration, in 1814, however, France went to the extreme of requiring the payment of a tax amounting to 300 francs and the attainment of the thirtieth year of age as a condition to the exercise of the suffrage. The Revolution of 1830 brought about a reduction from 300 to 200 francs in the amount of the tax contribution required of electors and the lowering of the age requirement to twenty-five years for members of the lower chamber.

Both during the period of the Restoration and the July monarchy, the number of electors in proportion to the population was exceedingly small, and this became the cause of widespread popular discontent.

A movement for direct universal manhood suffrage became active about 1840, and it triumphed in 1848 with the establishment of the second republic, the constitution of which declared that suffrage should be direct and universal and that all Frenchmen twenty-one years of age and in the enjoyment of their civil rights should be electors, regardless of the amount of their property. This system was continued under the second empire and under the third republic, and is still in existence.

The French political dogma of the eighteenth century, that the right of suffrage is a gift of nature, belonging to all citizens alike, has generally been rejected as a false and pernicious principle; and no states, not even France, as we have shown, have in practice acted wholly on such a principle.

The better view is that suffrage is not a natural right of all men, but a privilege granted by the state to such persons or classes as are most likely to exercise it for the public good. Nearly all electoral systems have been framed on this principle, that is, they have conditioned the privilege upon a variety of considerations to be explained later. In the early stages of the evolution of the representative system the restrictions were much more general and stringent than they are to-day, and consequently the body of electors was much smaller in comparison with the whole number of inhabitants.

In the eighteenth century, and indeed far into the nineteenth, the exclusion of the non-property-owning classes was not considered inconsistent with the prevailing notions of popular government; and nowhere outside of France was there any considerable number of statesmen or political writers who believed that government by the masses of the people was practicable.

In England, until 1832, the parliamentary franchise was limited in the counties to freeholders whose landed property was of the annual value of forty shillings; and in the eighteenth century the value of forty shillings was many times what it is to-day. In the English colonies of America freehold qualifications for voting were common in the seventeenth and eighteenth centuries, and in a number of them religious qualifications also existed.

The Massachusetts charter of 1691, for example, limited the suffrage to possessors of freeholds of the annual value of forty shillings or of other estates to the value of forty pounds. Likewise the early state constitutions generally restricted the right of voting to the property-owning classes. In some, like New Hampshire, Delaware, Georgia, and Pennsylvania, the payment simply of a tax was required, but in others the suffrage was restricted to owners of land of an annual value ranging in amount from three pounds in Massachusetts to fifty pounds in New Jersey.

With the rapid spread of democratic ideas after 1820, however, restrictions upon the suffrage began to disappear, and before the middle of the century practically the entire adult white male population was in the enjoyment of the franchise. Only one or two of the older states restricted the right to vote to those who could read and write, though here and there a small property qualification was required. In recent years some of the Southern states, owing to the presence of a large ignorant negro population, have restricted the suffrage to those who can read or "understand "the state constitution. In other Southern states the privilege of voting is limited to those who own a small amount of property, or pay a poll tax, or have served in the Union or Confederate armies or are descended from those who so served, or were voters in the year 1867 or are descendants of such voters. Ability to read and write is a condition to the exercise of the suffrage in several of the Northern and Western states also.

In all the states citizenship of the United States or a declaration of intention to become a citizen is required as well as residence for a specified period in the state and election district in which the voter offers to vote. The attainment of the twenty-first year of age is a universal requirement, and with the exceptions to be noted later the right of suffrage is generally restricted to persons of the male sex. A common requirement also is that the voter's name shall be inscribed on an electoral list, or, in popular language, he shall be "registered. "

In England, as a result of successive extensions beginning in 1832, the franchise has come to embrace the mass of the adult male population, the ratio of the voters to the total population being about one to six. Practically the only classes of adult males now excluded from the franchise are domestic servants, bachelors living with their parents and occupying no premises on their own account, and persons whose change of abode deprives them of a vote.

In the latter class are included vagrants, artisans who move about in obedience to the demands of trade, and many professional persons like teachers whose calling is such that the 'rule requiring twelve months' occupation often excludes them. Among the specifically excluded classes are peers, aliens, idiots, paupers, convicts, persons employed by candidates, and a few public officers, such as those directly concerned with the conduct of elections.

In order to exercise his privilege the name of the voter must be on a registration list, made up in the first instance by the overseers of the poor in each parish and revised and corrected by an official known as the revising barrister. In France, as has been said, practical universal manhood suffrage now prevails except that certain individuals are excluded, such as persons convicted of crime, bankrupts, persons under guardianship, and persons in the active military or naval service.

The suffrage for the election of members of the *Reichstag* of the German Empire also approaches the universal manhood level, though the attainment of a more advanced age is required than in America or England, namely, twenty-five years. The franchise is restricted wholly to Germans of the male sex, while various persons are excluded, notably those under guardianship, bankrupts, paupers, persons who have lost their civil rights, and persons who are in the active military service. The names of all voters must be inscribed on an electoral list for a certain period before the election.

The suffrage in the several German states varies widely, but usually it is more restricted than the imperial franchise. Such, for example, is the three-class system of voting in Prussia, according to which the voters are divided into three categories on the basis of the amount of taxes they pay, each class voting separately and choosing one third of the intermediate electors by whom the members of the *Landtag* are elected. Under this arrangement a few large taxpayers in an election district possess the same electoral power as a large number of voters who own a small amount of property.

The same system is applied in choosing municipal councils in the cities and villages of Prussia. Italy almost alone of the European states requires an educational qualification for the exercise of the suffrage. For the election of members of the Chamber of Deputies the elector must have passed an examination on the subjects embraced in the course of compulsory education, though the examination is not required of certain classes who could obviously pass it, such as the members of learned societies, college graduates, professional men, etc.; nor of those who pay a direct tax of nineteen lire to the state or who pay rents of a certain amount.

In Austria, until 1907, a complicated five-class system

prevailed, according to which the voters were grouped somewhat as in Prussia on the basis of the amount of taxes they paid. By a constitutional amendment adopted in 1907, however, the five-class system was abolished and virtual manhood suffrage was established for the election of all representatives to the popular chamber.

In Hungary, by an amendment of 1907, what amounts to virtual manhood suffrage was also established, though there are some disqualifications, notably in the case of certain public officers. In Switzerland, both in the confederation and in the cantons, the suffrage is enjoyed by all males twenty years of age except the clergy, and a few other classes who are unfit. Likewise in Greece and in Spain (since 1890) virtual manhood suffrage prevails.

Belgium in 1893 introduced a system of plural voting. Every male citizen twenty-five years of age and a resident at least one year in the commune is allowed one vote; a supplementary vote is allowed to every man who has reached the age of thirty-five years and has legitimate offspring and pays a tax of 5 francs to the state; also to every landed proprietor twenty-five years of age the value of whose land aggregates at least 2000 francs.

Two supplementary votes are allowed to every citizen twenty-five years of age who possesses a diploma from an institution of higher learning or a certificate showing the completion of a course of secondary education; or who holds or has held a public office or who practices or has practiced a private profession which presupposes that the holder possesses at least a secondary education. No one, however, may have more than three votes in the aggregate.

The Belgian system represents an effort to combine the advantages of universal suffrage with a scheme of what Sidgwick calls "weighted voting, "with a view to mitigating the evils inherent in a system of universal suffrage by preventing the ignorant and uninstructed mass of the community from overriding the intelligent and capable few. It rests on the assumption that there are some individuals in the state whose votes ought to be given a greater weight in the choice of public officials than those of the rest, that while every one ought to have a vote, some ought to have more than one. It recognizes, in short, that some men are wiser and better fitted to choose, and that some men's opinions should count for more than others' in ascertaining the general will. While admitting that every honest and capable citizen should be allowed a share in choosing those who are to govern him, it denies that every one should be given an equal share, in short, that the judgment of the illiterate and incapable should count for less than that of the capable and educated voter.

The Belgian system takes into consideration the elements of property, education, family relation, and occupation or profession in determining the weight of a man's voice in the government. It assumes that the vote of the owner of property upon which taxes are paid to the state should count for more than the vote of one who contributes nothing to its support; that the vote of the man who has added to the population and power of the community by establishing a family should be given greater weight than the vote of him who has not; and that the share of the citizen who contributes to the advancement of civilization by practicing a profession should be larger than that of a common laborer, etc.

The chief objection to such a system of suffrage lies in the difficulty of finding a just and practical standard or criterion by which the weight of different votes may be graduated. Any scheme for assigning different values to the votes of the property owner, the man of education, the head of a family, the professional man, etc., must be largely arbitrary. The possession of property, for example, is often the result of accident rather than of thrift, economy, or capacity, and even if it were otherwise, popular opinion is so averse to the basing of political rights upon wealth that the scheme would be hard to defend in a democracy.

It is sometimes said in support of the argument that the wealthy have more interests to be protected than the poor and should therefore be given a proportionately larger share in the choice of those who govern. But to this it may be replied that the power of self-help among the rich is correspondingly greater, and hence the need of state protection is less than in the case of the poor. Weighted voting for the wealthy, moreover, tends toward the establishment of class government and government by the wealthy few at that — the most obnoxious of all forms of government.

The nature of one's profession or occupation is regarded by some as a fairly just and practical test for determining the weight of a vote. Thus it is said, an employer is likely to possess more ability and intelligence than an employee; a banker, a merchant, or a manufacturer, more than an artisan; one engaged in a learned profession, more than one engaged in an unskilled trade; and so on.

Thus John Stuart Mill, who was an advocate of the scheme of "weighted voting, "expressed the opinion that two or more votes might properly be allowed to every person who "exercises any of these superior functions. "A system of plural voting in which a superior weight was assigned to the vote of the educated man was strongly recommended by Mill as a "counterpoise to the numerical weight of the least educated. "It would be a means, he argued, of offsetting the "more than equivalent evils "of a "completely universal suffrage.

"In any system providing a widely extended suffrage it might be wise, he said, "to allow all graduates of universities, all persons who have passed creditably through the higher schools, all members of the liberal professions, and perhaps some others who registered specifically in those characters, to give their votes as such in any constituency in which they choose to register; retaining in addition their votes as simple citizens in the localities in which they reside.

All these suggestions are open to discussion as to details; but it is evident to me that in this direction lies the true ideal of representative government, and that to work toward it by the best practical contrivances which can be found is the path of real political improvement.

"But intellectual superiority or academic training is not always a mark of political capacity. A skillful but uneducated artisan may easily possess more political insight and judgment than a schoolmaster, a physician, or other professional man of high academic training. Political privileges based on distinctions of superior intelligence are, moreover, likely to be arbitrary and invidious.

The question has been much discussed whether one who possesses the right to vote ought not legally to be required to exercise it, just as the citizen is compelled to serve on juries and at times to hold certain offices. It is sometimes asserted that voting is a public service, a civic duty, for the neglect of which a penalty ought to be imposed; and that, especially in a democracy, the participation of all citizens in elections ought to be obligatory, otherwise the election returns cannot be said to represent the real will of the electorate.

At the present time, however, Belgium and Spain are the only countries of importance in which the principle of compulsory suffrage has been introduced in practice. In Belgium it has been in operation for a number of years, and in Spain it was introduced in 1908. The Spanish law on the subject requires all males of legal age, except judges, notaries, priests, and men over seventy years of age to vote unless absent or sick.

Failure to do so is punishable by publication of the name of the delinquent as a mark of censure, by a two per cent increase of his taxes, by the loss of one per cent of his salary if he is in the employ of the state, and in case of repetition of the offense, by the loss of the right to hold public office in the future. But the principle of obligatory voting has not generally commended itself to political writers or statesmen.

It assumes that voting is a public legal duty instead of a privilege or a moral duty. However reprehensible may be the conduct of the citizen who neglects his civic obligations and his public duties as a member of society, it is hardly the province of the state to punish by legal means the nonperformance of such duties. The value of universal suffrage depends on its being regarded at once as a privilege and a moral duty.

If it were required by law, the privilege would be exercised as a mere form and without regard to the public good, very much as it was by the *sans-culottes* of Paris, who were paid for their attendance during the French Revolution. The effect would be a marked lowering of the character of the privilege. Moreover, compulsory votes would be much more open to bribery and would soon come to be estimated by their market value.

It is sometimes claimed, as was said in an earlier part of this chapter, that the right of the individual to participate in the choice of representatives is a right inherent in the quality of citizenship; that it is one of the natural rights of man, indispensable to his liberty, and a logical necessity if the doctrine that governments derive their just powers from the consent of the governed has any meaning.

This doctrine, as we have already explained, was one of the cardinal dogmas of the French political philosophy of the eighteenth century and still has many advocates throughout the world. According to this view, the enjoyment of the franchise contributes to the dignity and selfrespect of the individual, and is an agency of political education, as well as a powerful instrument for interesting the masses in public affairs and attaching them to the loyal support of the government.

The doctrine that governments derive their powers from the consent of the governed has, however, always been construed in practice as having important limitations. No one, as Judge Story has well remarked, not even the most strenuous advocate of universal suffrage, has ever yet contended that the privilege should be absolutely universal; and no one has ever been sufficiently visionary to maintain that all persons of every age, degree, and character should be entitled to vote in all elections for all public officers.

As a matter of fact, all states, even the most democratic, restrict the suffrage to a part only of their population. Most of them deny the privilege, wholly or in part, to females, minors, insane persons, and idiots; practically all of them debar those who have been convicted of grave crimes, including corrupt practices at elections; most of them exclude those who have to be supported by the state; some withhold the right from bankrupts; others deny the privilege to vagrants and even to worthy persons who do not have a fixed residence within the electoral district; some exclude the holders of certain offices, particularly those whose duties are connected with the management of election; others, like France, Germany, and Italy (and England indirectly), exclude soldiers in actual military service; some debar persons who do not own property or pay direct taxes to the state; a few exclude illiterate persons on the ground that such persons are presumed not to possess the requisite intelligence for the wise exercise of the privilege, etc.

The truth seems to be, says Judge Story, that the right of voting, like many other rights, is one which, whether it has a fixed foundation in natural law or not, has always been treated in the practice of nations as a strictly civil right derived from and regulated by each society according to its own circumstances.

The extent to which the privilege may be wisely allowed depends upon the general intelligence of the population, the character of the offices to be filled at the election, the political training of the people, and a variety of other circumstances. The best democratic thought of modern times favors as wide an extension of the elective franchise as is consistent with good government, and certainly the trend of recent development has been in the direction of universal manhood suffrage. Educational and property restrictions have almost entirely disappeared both in Europe and in America.

Here and there, however, they still prevail in moderate form, and many able writers defend them not only as consistent with popular government but as legitimate safeguards against inefficient and corrupt government. Among such writers we may mention the names of John Stuart Mill, W. E. H. Lecky, Sir Henry Maine, Professor Sidgwick, Emile Laveleye, and Johann Kaspar Bluntschli.

Mill says, "I regard it as wholly inadmissible that any person should participate in the suffrage without being able to read and write, and, I will add, perform the common operations of arithmetic....

No one but those in whom *a priori* theory has silenced

common sense will maintain that power over others, and over the whole community, should be imparted to people who have not acquired the commonest and most essential requisites for taking care of themselves.... It would be eminently desirable, that other things besides reading, writing, and arithmetic should be made necessary to the suffrage; that some knowledge of the conformation of the earth, its natural and political divisions, the elements of general history and of the history and institutions of their own country, could be required of all electors.

"Mill, however, properly maintains that where the suffrage is made to depend upon ability to read and write, the state should provide as a matter of justice the means of attaining these accomplishments without cost to the poor, otherwise the requirement becomes a hardship. Mill also defends taxpaying qualifications as legitimate even in a democratic state.

"It is important, "he asserts, "that the assembly which votes the taxes, either general or local, should be elected exclusively by those who pay something towards the taxes imposed. Those who pay no taxes, disposing by their votes of other people's money, have every motive to be lavish and none to economize.... The voting of taxes by those who do not themselves contribute is a violation of the fundamental principle of free government; representation should be coextensive with taxation. "

Lecky in his "Democracy and Liberty "dwells upon the dangers of government by the ignorant masses and, like Mill, advocates a system of suffrage which will give some consideration to education and property. The legislature, he points out, is essentially a machine for taxing, and it should be chosen by an electorate restricted mainly to those who contribute the taxes.

"One of the great questions of politics in our day, "he says, "is coming to be, whether, at the last resort, the world should be governed by its ignorance or by its intelligence. "The idea that the "ultimate source of power should belong to the poorest, the most ignorant, the most incapable, who are necessarily the most numerous, is a theory which assuredly reverses all the past experiences of mankind. "The election returns, Lecky goes on to say, very rarely represent real public opinion because under a system of universal suffrage there are multitudes who never contribute anything to public opinion, but cast their votes as directed by other individuals or organizations, or at haphazard, when they are ignorant of the candidates and issues.

One man "will vote blue or yellow "because his father voted that way, without reference to the principles involved; others are governed by prejudices, and so on. "A bad harvest or some other disaster over which the government can have no more influence than over the march of the planets, "he observes, "will produce a discontent that will often govern dubious votes and may perhaps turn the scale in a nearly balanced election.

"Lecky predicts that the day will come when it will appear to be "one of the strangest facts in the history of human folly "that the theory that the best way to improve the world and secure national progress by placing the government under the control of the least enlightened classes should have once been regarded as liberal and progressive.

In considering the attitude of the ignorant masses toward scientific progress, Sir Henry Maine, one of the most powerful critics of popular government, affirms somewhat extravagantly that "universal suffrage, which to-day excludes free trade from the United States, would certainly have prohibited the spinning jenny and the power loom.

It would certainly have prohibited the threshing machine. It would have prevented the adoption of the Gregorian calendar, and it would have restored the Stuarts. It would have proscribed the Roman Catholics with the mob which burned Lord Mansfield's house and library in 1780, and it would have proscribed the Dissenters with the mob which burned Dr. Priestley's house and library in 1791. "

The Belgian publicist Emile Laveleye, another critic of universal suffrage, while admitting its advantages in dignifying the individual and affording a means for the political education of the masses, yet asserts that under a parliamentary system of government it would lead to the "loss of liberty, of order, and of civilization. "He compares the government of a modern state to a delicate machine prodigiously complex and extremely difficult to operate. "How can such a machine, "he asks, "be operated by the ignorant and uninterested?

"If I have to choose between two absurdities, "he says, "I prefer the infallibility of the pope to that of the people. The partisans of the new Catholic dogma do not invoke reason; they believe in the supernatural.

But the partisans of the sovereignty of the masses do not invoke mystery; they affirm a visible, palpable nonsense, namely, that the people, half of whom can neither read nor write, are capable of rendering an intelligent judgment upon grave questions of legislation. "

But notwithstanding the unfavorable opinion of such writers as those quoted above, the movement in the direction of a complete enfranchisement of the masses continues without abatement, and hardly anywhere has it made greater progress in recent years than on the continent of Europe. Nothing has occurred in Europe or America since the beginning of this movement to warrant the belief that the extravagant prophecies of Lecky and Maine regarding the future of democratic government under an extended suffrage are ever likely to come to pass.

In consequence of the extraordinary interest now being manifested in public education throughout the world and the rapid multiplication by governments, monarchical and republican alike, of the facilities for educating the masses, there is every reason for believing that the democracy of the future will not necessarily be government by those whom Lecky characterized as the "most ignorant and the most incapable. "Nevertheless, their warnings concerning the dangers of an extended suffrage are not to be taken lightly.

The truth of much of what they have said regarding the incapacity of the ignorant masses for self-government is abundantly established by reason and the experience of the past. If government by the whole people is to be a success, they must be fitted and made capable for self-government. To vest the power of choosing those who are to rule the state in the hands of the incapable and unworthy classes, as Bluntschli justly remarks, would mean state suicide.

Give the suffrage to the ignorant, says Laveleye, and they will fall into anarchy to-day and into despotism tomorrow. Whatever the truth in either proposition we should do well to heed the saying of John Stuart Mill that universal teaching must precede universal enfranchisement.

Chapter 11

The Executive Department

PRINCIPLE OF ORGANIZATION; PLURAL VERSUS SINGLE EXECUTIVES

IN a broad sense we mean by the executive the aggregate or totality of all those governmental agencies which are concerned with the execution of the will of the state. In this sense the term embraces not only the chief magistrate, but also his principal advisers and ministers, as well as the whole body of subordinate officials through whom the laws are administered. As thus understood, the executive embraces the whole governmental organization, with the exception of the legislative and judicial organs.

In this wider signification cabinet heads, chiefs of bureaus, diplomatic agents, tax collectors, inspectors, commissioners, postmasters and policemen, and even army and navy officers, are a part of the executive and collectively constitute the executive department.

In a still wider sense it includes even the judges of the courts, since they are concerned with the interpretation and application of the law, —functions which in reality have to do with the general act of execution. In the narrowest sense the term is applied to that supreme authority, whether an individual or body, which is intrusted with the appointment, supervision, and control of the various subordinate agencies through which the state will is carried out.

In considering the nature of the executive we must further distinguish between the real or actual executive on the one hand, and the nominal or titular executive in whose name the government is administered, but who in fact has little to do with the actual work of administration. Thus in countries like Great Britain, having the fully developed cabinet system of government, the real executive is the ministry, the crown being the executive only in a nominal sense.

On account of its peculiar nature the executive power must be organized upon principles fundamentally different from those upon which the legislative power is organized. Necessarily, the legislative authority must be a more or less numerous body, that is, it must be an assembly composed of representatives elected at frequent intervals from the body of the people.

Its peculiar function is to deliberate, consult upon the general needs of society and lay down rules of conduct for the guidance of private individuals and public officials. For the wise discharge of such functions a body of persons is manifestly better fitted than a single individual, for it is an old and true maxim that "in a multitude of councilors there is wisdom.

The function of the executive, however, is not primarily to deliberate, nor to formulate and express the will of the state, but to execute, enforce, and carry out the state will as expressed by the legislature. The prime requisites for efficiency in the discharge of such functions are, therefore, promptness of decision, singleness of purpose, energy of action, and sometimes secrecy of procedure. It may be stated in general terms, says Judge Story, that that organization is best which will at once secure energy in the executive and safety to the people. Obviously, therefore, a single person or a very small body of persons is better fitted for the discharge of such duties than a numerous assembly composed of many minds and entertaining a variety of views.

"The advantages of a single chief, "says Woolsey, "are obvious; he is able to bring unity and efficiency into the government, and being alone, he or his ministry is responsible; whereas two presidents would be apt to checkmate one another, if they were of different parties, and would be jealous and rivals if they were of the same party. "To organize the executive power by dividing it among a number of coordinate and equal authorities would necessarily lead to its enfeeblement, if not its utter dissipation, especially in times of crises when promptness of decision and energy of action may be essential to the preservation of the life of the state. In military administration the plural form of executive is wholly out of place and full of peril.

The saying attributed to Napoleon, that "one bad general is better than two good ones, "represents an exaggerated, though not wholly erroneous, estimate of the weakness of a dual executive in military matters. An executive organized on the collegial principle is incompatible with force, energy, unity of purpose, and independence. Unity in organization is essential to strength, while division is a source of weakness. The executive, first of all, must possess strength and power, because it is charged with the great task of enforcing the will of the state.

History furnishes some examples of the plural form of executive, but they were all short-lived. In ancient Athens the executive power was split up into fragments and divided between generals, archons, etc., each being independent of the other. The Roman constitution for a long time provided for two consuls, each of whom was invested, not with a part of the executive power, but the whole of it, and each could in effect veto the action of his colleagues.

Sparta, in early times, had two kings, and the principle of "plurality "was extended to the organization of subordinate offices such as pretors and consuls. France after the Revolution experimented with the plural form of executive under several different constitutions. That of 1795 vested the executive power in a Directory of five persons, but the results were anything but satisfactory. Nevertheless, the principle of plurality was retained in the constitution of 1799, which, in theory, vested the supreme executive power in three consuls appointed for ten years, but in reality the second and third consuls were little more than figureheads. The institution was continued under the senatus consultum of 1802.

At the present time, the executive in every state, with one

exception, is organized on the single-headed principle. The exception is found in the constitution of the Swiss republic, which vests the executive power in a council of seven persons. One of the seven bears the title and dignity of President of the Confederation and performs the ceremonial duties of the executive office, but, in reality, he is merely chairman of the council and shares the executive power equally with his colleagues.

He is in no sense the supreme head of the administration and carries no greater responsibility than his fellow councilors. The practical working of the institution in Switzerland has been attended with less difficulty than the plural form elsewhere, mainly on account of certain habits and traditions of the Swiss people, and because the ground had already been prepared through local experience. For a long time the collegial form of executive had existed in the separate cantons, and hence when it was introduced into the constitution of the confederation, in 1848, the institution had passed the experimental stage.

The testimony of political writers and statesmen has been practically unanimous in favor of the principle of unity in the construction of the executive office. No one has more powerfully defended it than Alexander Hamilton. ""Energy in the executive, "he said, "is a leading characteristic in the definition of good government. It is essential to the protection of the community against foreign attacks.

It is not less essential to the steady administration of the laws; to the protection of property against those irregular and high-handed combinations which sometimes interrupt the ordinary course of justice; to the security of liberty against the enterprises and assaults of ambition, of faction, and of anarchy.

Every man the least familiar with Roman history knows how often Rome was obliged to take refuge in the absolute power of a single man, under the formidable title of dictator, as well as against the intrigues of ambitious individuals who aspired to the tyranny, and the seditions of whole classes of the community whose conduct threatened the existence of all government, as against the invasion of external enemies who menaced the conquest and destruction of Rome. "A feeble executive, he justly observed, implies a feeble government and is but another name for bad government.

"The most distinguished statesmen, "says Judge Story, "have uniformly maintained the doctrine that there ought to be a single executive and a numerous legislature. They have considered energy as the most necessary qualification of the executive power, and this is best attained by reposing it in a single hand Plurality in the organization of the executive also tends to conceal faults and destroy responsibility.

Responsibility under such an arrangement, observes Mill, is a mere name. What the "board "does, he goes on to say, is the act of nobody, and nobody can be made to answer for it. Where a number are responsible, the responsibility is easily shifted from one shoulder to another, and hence both the incentive in the executive and the advantage of the restraint of public opinion are lost.

For convenience of administration a large part of the executive power in a complex, modern state, however, must necessarily be delegated and distributed among subordinate authorities. No single person is physically capable of exercising the whole of that power. But that does not necessarily involve a division of the power in the final analysis; the supreme responsibility is still in the hands of a single magistrate and hence is a unit.

Sometimes, however, the unity of the executive power is in effect destroyed or impaired by vesting it ostensibly in one person, but really dividing it between him and a council to whose advice and control he is made subject. Thus in the early constitutions of the American states the executive in nearly every instance was subjected to the control, in a large degree, of such a council; and indeed in two states, namely, Pennsylvania and Vermont, the executive power was virtually vested in a board.

A strong effort was made in the convention which framed the constitution of the United States to associate an executive council with the President, but the project was finally defeated by a vote of eight states to three. In the German Empire the Federal Council (*Bundesrath*) shares with the chief executive an important part of the executive power, so much so, indeed, that some of the German writers treat the Federal Council as the real executive and the emperor as merely its agent. It participates in the appointment of certain imperial officers, sanctions important ordinances issued by the emperor, frames the arrangements necessary for the administration of the laws when no provision has been made by imperial law, exercises a sort of supervision over the execution of the laws; and its consent is necessary to declarations of war and to the ratification of treaties.

In England, likewise, various acts of the executive, particularly those known as orders in council, require for their validity the approval of the Privy Council. The President of the French Republic is required to consult the Council of State in many cases, especially in regard to issuing ordinances; but the French idea is so averse to the diffusion of responsibility that the executive is not compelled to act upon the advice which the council may give him. There is a saying of the French that "to act is the function of one; to deliberate, that of several; "and while the value of advice is fully recognized, they are unwilling to sacrifice the advantages of responsibility in order to establish a control over the executive.

"The President of the United States, "says De Tocqueville, "was made the sole representative of the executive powers of the Union, and care was taken not to render his decisions subordinate to the vote of a council — a dangerous measure which tends at the same time to clog the action of the government and to diminish its responsibility. The Senate has the right of annulling certain acts of the President; but it cannot compel him to take any steps, nor does it participate in the exercise of the executive power.... The Americans have not been able to counteract the tendency which legislative assemblies have to get possession of the government, but they have rendered this propensity less irresistible. "

No possible objection, it would seem, can be urged against the scheme of associating a merely advisory council with the executive. Such an arrangement ought to bring strength and wisdom to the executive department. Mill has justly observed that a man seldom judges right when he makes habitual use of no knowledge but his own or that of a single adviser. The work of administration is often complex and difficult and requires for its efficient performance highly technical and special knowledge, not only on the part of those who actually perform the service, but often on the part of the chief magistrate who directs the administration.

Such knowledge he rarely possesses, hence the advantage of an advisory council composed in part of men who do possess it is clearly evident. But the ultimate decision in most cases ought to be with the executive, and the responsibility ought to rest upon him. It is easy, as Mill has remarked, to give the effective power and the full responsibility to one, providing him when necessary with advisers, each of whom is responsible only for the opinion he gives.

The principal argument which has been advanced in support of the plural form of executive is that it furnishes greater guarantees against the dangers of executive abuse and oppression and renders more difficult executive encroachments upon the sphere of the legislature and upon the liberties of the people in general. It is mainly for this reason that the executive is often subjected to the control of a council in those branches of administration which afford the largest temptations and opportunities for abuse of power.

An executive constituted on such a principle manifestly could not plan and execute a *coup d'Eat,* nor invade the spheres properly belonging to the other departments, with the same ease and readiness with which a single ambitious individual could, unrestrained by a council or opposed by colleagues who share with him responsibility.

It is sometimes claimed that the vesting of the supreme executive power in the hands of a single person is a relic of absolutism and hence is inconsistent with the genius of a republican government. It is difficult, says Story, to find a sufficient ground on which to rest this notion; and those which are usually stated "belong principally to that class of minds which readily indulge in the belief of the general perfection, as well as perfectibility of human nature, and deem the least possible quantity of power with which government can subsist to be the best. "Finally, it is contended by some that an executive organized on the plural principle, while perhaps lacking the advantages of unity and energy, yet is likely to possess a higher degree of ability and wisdom than can be found in any single person.

The executive power, it is pointed out, involves much more than the mere ministerial function of executing the commands of the legislature; it often involves the formulation of constructive policies, as well as important powers of direction requiring the exercise of wide discretion and judgment, duties that can be more wisely discharged by a body of persons than by a single individual.

But the merits are more than offset by the disadvantages; and when all is said that can be said in favor of the plural executive, the fact remains that experience has demonstrated its inherent weakness and has justified the single form.

MODE OF CHOICE OF THE EXECUTIVE

Four different methods of choosing the executive have been followed in practice: first, the hereditary principle; second, direct election by the people; third, indirect election by a body of intermediate electors, either themselves popularly elected or chosen by some branch of the government; and, fourth, election by the legislature.

In all the monarchical states of Europe to-day the executive (that is, the nominal or titular executive) is hereditary in a particular family or dynasty. Before the rise of popular government this principle of selection was practically universal and it still survives in a large part of the world to-day, but is tolerated perhaps rather than preferred, being more the result of historical conditions than of deliberate creation. It is doubtful whether the principle is destined to be extended in the future either through the reorganization of existing states or the establishment of new ones.

Hereditary tenure of public office no longer seems to be in keeping with the spirit of popular government, and as a practical rational system of appointment it has few merits, as we have explained in the chapter on forms of government. But it must be borne in mind that hereditary executives are not, as has been said, ordinarily the actual chiefs of the administration, but only the titular heads.

Their office is mainly to lend dignity, majesty, and ornament to the government, somewhat as a cupola is intended to add grace and proportion to a building. The institution tends to introduce into the administration of the government elements of stability, permanence, continuity, and experience, and in the relations of the state with foreign powers it tends to add a certain prestige which is not without weight in diplomatic intercourse.

The value of a hereditary executive in the government of the state has been well set forth by the English writers Bagehot and Todd. Bagehot, in his defense of monarchy, declares that the masses have little respect or reverence for an executive which they assist every half-dozen years to create. A hereditary monarch, he argues, is a powerful means of attaching the masses to the government and of securing their loyalty and obedience.

Among the advantages of the hereditary principle, says Burgess, that are manifest even to one surrounded by the prejudices of the New World are: first of all, a respect for government and a readiness to obey the law which can in no other way be attained until the political society shall have reached a degree of perfection far beyond anything which at present exists anywhere in the world.

But when all is said that can be said in favor of the hereditary principle as a mode of selecting the executive, the weight of evidence and the testimony of experience are against it. It can only be looked upon as a survival of a past age, and its ultimate disappearance will doubtless follow in the course of the political evolution of the future.

The choice of the executive by the direct vote of the people represents the opposite principle to that of the hereditary method. It is confined mainly to republics, though there have been, as we have shown in a previous chapter, occasional examples of elective monarchies. At the present time the national executives of a number of the South American republics, notably those of Bolivia, Brazil, and Peru, are chosen by direct popular vote; and this is true, of course, of the local state executives in the United States.

In form, the method of electing the President of the United States is indirect, though, owing to a metamorphosis of the electoral system, the method has to a large degree come to be direct. The advantages of the method of popular election are, that it is more distinctly in accord with modern notions of popular government, stimulates interest in public affairs, affords a means of political education for the masses, and secures the choice of a chief magistrate in whose ability and integrity the people have confidence and to whom he is more or less directly responsible for his official conduct.

The principal objections to direct popular election are: the incompetency of the masses in a country of vast area to judge intelligently of the qualifications of a candidate for so important an office, their liability to be influenced by demagogues, and the general demoralization and the political excitement which are almost inseparable from a contest of such magnitude. "The election of a supreme magistrate for a whole nation, "wrote Chancellor Kent, "affects so many interests and addresses itself so strongly to popular passions and holds out such powerful temptations to ambition that it necessarily becomes a strong trial to public virtue and even hazardous to the public tranquility".

"It has been found impossible, "continues the same distinguished author, "to guard the elections from the mischiefs of foreign intrigue and domestic turbulence, from violence or corruption; and mankind have generally taken refuge from the evils of popular elections in hereditary executives as being the least evil of the two. The most recent and remarkable change of this kind occurred in France, in 1804, when the legislative body changed their elective into an hereditary monarchy on the avowed ground that the competition of popular elections led to corruption and violence. "

Among the framers of the constitution of the United States

only three or four favored direct popular election of the chief magistrate. Nearly all the delegates who expressed an opinion on the subject were full of profound distrust of such a method. Roger Sherman declared "that the people would never be sufficiently informed of the character of men to vote intellectually for the candidates that might be presented ":

Charles C. Pinckney thought "the people would be incited by designing demagogues "; Gerry stigmatized the proposition as "radically vicious "; and Mason went so far as to say that "it would be as unnatural to refer the choice of a proper person for President to the people, as to refer a trial of colors to a blind man; "Hamilton feared that it would "convulse the community with extraordinary and violent movements "and lead to "heats and ferments "that would disturb the public tranquillity.

Experience has shown, however, that the evils which the framers of the constitution predicted were greatly exaggerated, and, happily, their worst fears have not been realized. Nevertheless, it cannot be denied that some of these evils have not been entirely absent.

The long period of business depression, the intense strain upon the public virtue, the heated political excitement and passion, and the general demoralization which have come to be regular features of our quadrennial contests over the choice of the chief magistrate in the United States have abundantly shown that the method of popular election is not in all respects ideal. One of its worst features is what Mill called "the mischief of intermitted electioneering. "When the highest dignity in the state, he declared, is to be conferred by popular election once in every few years, the whole intervening time is spent in what is virtually a canvass.

President, ministers, chiefs of parties, and their followers are all electioneers. The whole community is kept intent on the mere personality of politics, and every public question is discussed and decided with less reference to its merits than to its expected bearing on the presidential election. If a system had been devised, Mill goes on to say, to make party spirit the ruling principle of action in all public affairs and create an inducement not only to make every question a party question, it would have been difficult to contrive any means better adapted to the purpose. "A most important principle of good government in a popular constitution, "to quote Mill further, "is that no executive functionaries should be appointed by popular election; neither by the votes of the people themselves, nor by those of their representatives. "The business of government, he points out, requires skill, special information, and technical knowledge, and only those who possess in some degree those qualifications are capable of choosing such functionaries. The task of finding and choosing them, he asserts, "is very laborious and requires a delicate as well as a highly conscientious discernment. "

So far as the selection of subordinate executive officials is concerned, we believe this to be a sound proposition; and one of the chief weaknesses in the constitutions of the local governments in the United States to-day arises from the wide extension of the elective principle to the appointment of officials whose duties are administrative in character, and the performance of which requires qualifications which are difficult to obtain by popular election.

This evil has lately come to be a source of general complaint in connection with state and municipal government where such officials as railroad and insurance commissioners, clerks of various kinds, law officers, and even engineers and other administrative experts are often chosen by popular election. But does this objection necessarily apply to the choice of the chief executive? Mill, who condemns the system of popular election for all subordinate executive functionaries, has himself raised the question as to whether the chief executive, especially in a republic, might not be made an exception.

"There is, "he admits, "unquestionably some advantage in a country like America where no apprehension need be entertained of a *coup d'Etat,* in making the chief executive constitutionally independent of the legislative body and rendering the two great branches of the government, while equally popular both in their origin and in their responsibility, an effective check on one another. "

The method of indirect election is the system employed in choosing the national executives of the United States, the Argentine Republic, Chile, Mexico, and a few other Latin American republics, although the elective scheme for choosing the President of the United States has, as has been said, come to be largely direct in fact. The advantages claimed for the indirect system are that it affords a means of avoiding the "heats, ""tumults, "and "convulsions "of direct election, and at the same time leads to a more intelligent choice, by restricting the immediate selection to a small body of capable and well-informed representatives.

"The choice of several to form an intermediate body of electors, "said Hamilton, in defense of the scheme adopted for the election of the President of the United States, and the metamorphosis of which was not then foreseen, "will be much less apt to convulse the community with any extraordinary and violent movements than the choice of one who was himself to be the final object of the public wishes. ""It was desirable, "he continued, "that the immediate election should be made by men most capable of analyzing the qualities adapted to the station. A small number of persons selected by their fellow-citizens from the general mass will be most likely to possess the information and discernment requisite to so complicated an investigation. "

In theory, the method of indirect election possesses conspicuous merits; but the difficulty lies in the fact that the electors are apt to be chosen under party pledges to vote for a particular candidate, and thus become mere agents for registering the will of the voters. This is almost inevitable in states where political parties are highly developed and well organized. This is exactly what happened in the United States as soon as party lines came to be fully drawn and party discipline became effective.

In the early presidential elections the best results expected of the electoral scheme were fully realized, the electors exercising their full judgment in choosing the President; but in the course of time they became mere "party puppets, "with no discretion or freedom in the discharge of what were originally intended to be solemn and important functions. Their duties are now restricted to registering the choice of the party voters — a function which an automaton without intelligence or volition could as fittingly discharge.

Thus what was intended to be a scheme of indirect election, in which the immediate choice of the chief executive was to be made by a select body of highly capable men, has in the course of a remarkable development become in reality a system of direct election by the millions, who still go through the form of voting for electors whose real office has long since disappeared. Such was the scheme of which Hamilton did not hesitate to affirm "that if the manner of it be not perfect, it is at least excellent, "and which was the only part of the constitution "that escaped without severe censure or which received the slightest mark of approbation from its opponents.

Finally, the chief executive may be chosen by the legislative branch of the government. This method is followed in Switzerland and in France (where the two chambers organized in national assembly at Versailles constitute the electoral body for choosing the president of the republic.) This was a system employed in a number of the American states for a time after the Revolution, and is still the method prescribed in several of them in case no candidate receives a majority of the popular vote.

It was the method first decided upon by the Philadelphia convention of 1787 for the election of the President of the United States, but was finally abandoned upon reconsideration for the scheme described above.

The main objection to choice by the legislature is that it violates the principle of the separation of governmental powers by imposing upon the legislative branch a duty alien to its primary function, and making the executive to some extent an agent or instrument of the legislature. If the executive owed his office to the legislature, "bargains, ""intrigues, "and "cabals "between him and Congress would not be wanting. "It would be in the power of an ambitious candidate, "observed Judge Story, "by holding out the rewards of office, or other sources of patronage and honor, silently but irresistibly to influence a majority of votes; and thus by his own bold and unprincipled conduct to secure choice, to the exclusion of the highest and purest and most enlightened men in the country.

"A similar opinion was entertained by Chancellor Kent, who remarked that "all elections by the representative body are peculiarly liable to produce combinations for sinister purposes. "Both reason and experience teach that election by the legislature not only impairs the independence of the executive and tends to make him subservient to its will, but creates a powerful temptation to an ambitious candidate to gain the support of the legislature by promises of official reward or influence.

Once elected, he is under the same temptation to secure reelection. To be fully independent of legislative control and free of such temptations, the executive must owe his office to a different source.

Finally, it should be observed that the imposition of so important a political duty upon the legislature is likely to interfere with its normal function of lawmaking, by introducing into its procedure a distracting element which on occasions of great and exciting contests must necessarily consume its time, lead to conflicts and deadlocks, and give a party coloring to the consideration of many measures which are in reality nonpartisan in character.

If proof of this were needed, one has only to consider the effect upon the procedure of the American state legislatures in choosing United States senators, when there are close and exciting contests. In most such contests, if of long duration, the legislative output is generally inferior in quality.

The chief argument in favor of choice by the legislature is that the selection is likely to be more wisely made than when done by the masses of voters, or by any body of intermediate electors especially chosen for the purpose.

Being actively concerned with public affairs and acquainted with the leading statesmen, the members of the legislative branch are of all persons most qualified to choose a fit man for so high a station. John Stuart Mill was an advocate of this method for the election of executives of republics although he questioned whether it was the best for all times and places. "It seems better, "he said, "that the chief magistrate in a republic should be appointed avowedly, as the chief minister in a constitutional monarchy is virtually, by the representative body.

The party which has the majority in parliament would then as a rule appoint its own leader; who is always one of the foremost, and often the very foremost, person in political life. "But this is by no means always true, as experience with the convention method of nominating candidates in the United States and the election of United States senators by the state legislatures have clearly shown.

Chapter 12

The Judiciary

INDEPENDENCE OF THE JUDICIARY

It has been well observed by a noted jurist and commentator that "in every well-organized government -with reference to the security both of public rights and private rights — it is indispensable that there should be a judicial department to ascertain and decide rights, to punish crimes, to administer justice, and to protect the innocent from injury and usurpation. "Where there is no judicial department to interpret and execute the law, to de. cide controversies, and to enforce rights, "the government must either perish, "said Chancellor Kent, "by its own imbecility, or the other departments of government must usurp powers, for the purpose of commanding obedience, to the destruction of liberty. "

It has been contended by some doctrinaires that, while in monarchical states the independence of the judiciary may be essential to protect the people from the arbitrary interference and oppression of the crown and also to prevent the judges from being reduced to a position of cringing subserviency to the executive, the same reasons do not apply in a republic.

But experience has abundantly shown that the independence of the judiciary is just as essential to protect the constitution and laws against the encroachments of party spirit and the tyranny of faction in a republic, as it is in a monarchy to protect the rights of the subject against the injustice of the crown.

Upon no other branch of the government are the people so dependent for the enjoyment of personal security and the rights of property, and it is hardly nécessary to add that the degree of protection thus afforded is conditioned in turn upon the wisdom, stability, and integrity of the courts. To fulfill its high purpose the judiciary ought, therefore, to possess learning, faithfulness to the constitution, independence, and firmness of character. The existence of such qualities must depend largely upon the mode of appointment of the judges, the permanency of their tenure, the adequacy of the provision made for their support, and the extent and nature of the jurisdiction conferred upon them.

First, as to the mode of appointment. The judiciary may be chosen by the legislature, by popular election, or by appointment of the executive, either with or without the concurrence of a council or one of the chambers of the legislature. Choice by the legislature has not commended itself generally to statesmen in the past because it renders the judiciary to a certain extent dependent upon a coordinate department of the government, in violation of the principle of the separation of powers.

Furthermore, the system of legislative choice usually means nomination by a party caucus and often a parceling out of judicial positions among the political divisions of the state with reference to geographical considerations rather than fitness for the judicial office. In short, as a great jurist has pointed out, it presents "too many occasions and too many temptations for intrigue, party prejudice, and local interest to secure a judiciary best calculated to promote the ends of justice.

"Choice by the legislature was a favorite method of selection in the American states for a time after the Revolution, a circumstance due to the prevailing jealousy of the executive on the one hand and the distrust of popular election on the other. This system, however, has been abandoned in all the American states but four, and is not followed in any Euro pean country except Switzerland, where the judges of the federal tribunal are chosen by the legislative assembly of the Confederation.

The method of popular election is now the rule in the great majority of the states of the American federal union, though outside of the United States it has made almost no headway. In Europe and in the English self-governing colonies it is unknown, except occasionally for the election of inferior magistrates, and even in the republics of Latin America, where democratic government has made great advance, popular election of the judges has found little acceptance.

The chief disadvantage of popular election is that it is apt to secure a judiciary at once weak and lacking in independence. Where such a method prevails the election is usually made from candidates who have been nominated by party conventions or by primary elections following campaigns through the filth and mire of which the judicial ermine must often be dragged. The qualities which distinguish an able and fearless judge are not usually those of the successful politician; and hence judges frequently make poor candidates, and are sometimes defeated by men of less fitness, who are better gifted with the arts of winning public favor.

Moreover, the masses of voters do not always possess the discrimination and understanding necessary to appreciate the soundness of judicial opinions, and hence the judge who renders a decision that does not meet the approval of public opinion, however sound it may be in law, can be reelected only with difficulty if at all. The judicial history of the American states, where popularly elected judiciaries are most common, abounds in instances of the defeat of able and distinguished jurists because of unpopular judicial opinions rendered by them. Altogether it constitutes a chapter of history which is not creditable to American democracy and forms a strong indictment against the system of popular election.

Moreover, the necessity of submitting themselves and their legal opinions at frequent intervals to the judgment of the masses creates in the judges a strong temptation to shape their decisions and indeed their whole judicial conduct in such a way as to meet the approval of those to whom they must look for reelection. No judge should be exposed to the necessity of having to curry popular favor in order to retain his office. As Chancellor Kent has well observed, the fittest men are likely to have "too much reservedness of manners and severity of morals to secure an election resting on universal suffrage. "It lowers the character of the judiciary, tends to make a politician of the judge, and subjects the judicial mind to a strain which it is not always able to resist.

The experience of the past and the testimony of the majority of political writers concur in holding the method of executive appointment to be the best system yet devised for selecting the judiciary. The peculiar qualities adapted to the judicial station can be better discerned by a wise executive than by the masses of uninstructed voters, who, as has been said, are likely to be influenced by per sonal qualities which are often lacking in great judges.

Besides, the method of executive appointment removes the office, to a large extent, from the low level of party politics, destroys the temptation of the judges to popular subserviency, and thus adds to the independence and dignity of the judiciary. This method of selection has commended itself to the vast majority of countries outside of the United States, and even here it is the method in force for the appointment of all federal judges and of the higher judges of a number of the states.

In regard to the tenure of the judges we find the same variety of opinion and practice. Most of the original thirteen states of America, in their first constitutions, established a good behaviour tenure for their higher judges, and this rule was adopted by the national constitution for the federal judges. The substitution of short tenures, however, became a part of the democratic movement in the early nineteenth century, and in the course of time all the American states except three abandoned the good behaviour principle for limited terms.

These terms range from two years, which is the rule in Vermont, to twenty-one years, which is the limit in Pennsylvania, the average being from six to nine years. In Europe, Switzerland is the only country in which the tenure of the higher justices is limited to a definite term, the period being six years for the members of the federal tribunal.

In Latin America, Mexico is the only important republic in which the good behaviour tenure is lacking, the term of the supreme judicature in that country being six years. Outside of the United States, therefore, the good behaviour principle is practically universal. "The standard of good behaviour for the continuance in office of the judicial magistracy, "said Hamilton, "is certainly one of the most valuable of the modern improvements in the practice of government. In a monarchy, it is an excellent barrier to the despotism of the prince; in a republic, it is a no less excellent barrier to the encroachments and oppressions of the representative body.

And it is the best expedient which can be devised in any government, to secure a steady, upright, and impartial administration of the laws. "It requires but little reflection to see, as Hamilton pointed out, that the judiciary from the very nature of its functions must necessarily be the least dangerous to the rights of the other departments, because it possesses the least capacity to annoy or injure them. "The executive, "he remarked, "not only dispenses the honors, but holds the sword of the community.

The legislature not only commands the purse, but prescribes the rules by which the duties and rights of every citizen are to be regulated. The judiciary, on the contrary, has no influence over either the sword or the purse; no direction either of the strength or of the wealth of the society; and can take no active resolution whatever. It may truly be said to have neither force nor will, but merely judgment; and must ultimately depend upon the aid of the executive arm even for the efficacy of its judgments.

"Finally, as Hamilton showed, a good behaviour tenure is necessary to secure the experience and knowledge of judicial precedent which constitutes one of the most important sources of strength in the judicial office. In the course of a long judicial career marked by laborious study and constant application, the judge acquires a familiarity with the precedents which obviously cannot be gained by one whose tenure is limited to a brief period.

Hence it is that "there can be but few men in the society who will have sufficient skill in the laws to qualify them for the station of judges; and, making the proper deductions for the ordinary depravity of human nature, the number must be still smaller of those who unite the requisite integrity with the requisite knowledge. In all states, however, provision must be made for the removal of corrupt and inefficient magistrates; for the continuance in office, and especially for life, of an incapable or corrupt judge would be intolerable. The English judges in earlier times held their offices at the royal pleasure, but this proved to be a dangerous power to vest in the executive, because it made the judiciary subservient to the crown, especially in state trials, and gave the king a control over the administration of justice at once dangerous to private rights and subversive of the liberties of the people.

In the time of Lord Coke the barons of the exchequer were given a good behaviour tenure; and during the reign of Charles II the same tenure was created for the common law judges, though the crown retained until after the revolution of 1688 the right to prescribe what tenure it might allow. Finally, by an act of Parliament passed in the thirteenth year of the reign of William III, the commissions of the judges were made to run during good behaviour, and they were forbidden to be removed by the crown except upon an address of both houses of Parliament. In the course of time the same principle was adopted in many of the continental states of Europe.

Removal of Judges

In the United States the customary mode of removal is by impeachment, that is, through the preferment of charges by one chamber of the legislature, usually the lower, and trial by the other. The chief objection to this procedure is the danger that the legislature may employ its power of removal for party purposes, but this danger is largely eliminated by the provision that an extraordinary majority of the trial chamber shall be required to remove.

In the German Empire and certain other European states the possibility of this danger is eliminated by vesting the power of removal or suspension in the court of which the judge is a member, sitting as a disciplinary tribunal, and then only after a regular trial for reasons expressly provided in the laws. In Italy the independence of the judiciary is weakened by the power of the executive to assign the judges to their stations. Thus a magistrate who refuses to show the desired subserviency to the executive may be "reassigned in the interest of the service "and sent to a less desirable judicial station in another part of the country.

Frequent complaints have been made of the arbitrary exercise of this power. Such a practice is prohibited in Germany by a constitutional provision to the effect that no judge may be transferred without his consent to another district except as a punishment inflicted by a disciplinary court, or in consequence of the reorganization of the judicial system, in which case the judge so transferred must be assigned to another station of equal rank and pay, and with an allowance sufficient to cover the cost of changing his residence.

Next to permanency of tenure nothing contributes more to the independence of the judiciary than a fixed and adequate provision for the support of the judges. In considering the necessity for such provision, Hamilton aptly remarked that "in the general course of human nature a power over a man's subsistence amounts to a power over his will. ""To give the judges the courage and the firmness to do their duty fearlessly, "said Chancellor Kent, "they ought to be confident of the security of their salaries and station.

"This is the opinion of practically all political writers of note, and it has become the practice of the great majority of states. In England, by a statute passed in the reign of George III, the full salaries of the judges were guaranteed during the continuance of their commissions; and this principle was introduced into the constitutions of a number of the American states. The constitution of the United States, in providing that the salaries of the federal judges should not be diminished during their time of office (without, however, forbidding their increase) was an improvement over all existing constitutional arrangements in this respect.

JUDICIAL ORGANIZATION

The organization of the judiciary differs essentially from either that of the executive or the legislative departments.

The supreme executive power practically everywhere is vested in the hands of a single person, while the legislative power is intrusted to a more or less numerous assembly. The judicial power, on the other hand, is neither vested in a single person nor in an assembly, but in a number of magistrates, sometimes sitting singly and sometimes in bodies, constituting tribunals or benches, usually arranged in a hierarchical series one above the other.

In some countries, of which the German Empire is a notable example, all the courts from the lowest to the highest are collegial in organization, that is, each is held by a bench of judges rather than by a single magistrate. In other countries only the highest courts, usually those having appellate jurisdiction, are organized on the collegial principle. Thus in the judicial organization of the United States the district courts are held by a single judge, and the circuit courts may be, and frequently are, held by one judge. Among the individual states, generally, all the inferior courts are held by single judges, leaving only the highest courts to be constituted on the collegial principle.

Usually standing at the top of the hierarchy is a supreme court which has jurisdiction over cases brought up from the lower courts by way of appeal or upon writs of error, and whose decision is final and conclusive. This court may be a tribunal of review, that is, with power to revise the decisions of the lower courts; or it may be simply a court of cassation, with power only to "break "or quash the judgments of the lower courts; or it may be both. Sometimes instead of a single court of final authority there are several with equal and coordinate jurisdiction.

This is the case, for example, in Italy, where there are five independ ent supreme courts of cassation, each having final and supreme authority within its own territorial jurisdiction. Between these courts the ordinary higher civil jurisdiction of the kingdom is divided; no appeal lies from one to another, and none of the five feels bound to accept the decisions of the others or follow them as precedents. This decentralization of the judicial system has proved to be a source of great weakness in the governmental system of Italy. On the continent of Europe the division of the judicial tribunals into chambers or senates for convenience of administration is a common practice. Thus in the German Empire all the courts except the lowest (the *Amtsgericht*) are divided into civil and criminal chambers; and the imperial court (the *Reichsgericht*) is similarly divided into criminal and civil "senates, "there being four of the former and six of the latter.

Likewise, the highest court of France, the tribunal of cassation, is divided into sections, three in number. In order to avoid conflicting decisions where the court with final authority is divided into chambers or sections, sessions in plenum are sometimes necessary. In the United States the practice of dividing the courts into sections or chambers has rarely been followed.

In states having the federal system of government there are usually two separate and distinct series of judicial bodies, one to exercise the national or general jurisdiction of the whole union, the other the local jurisdiction of the component states.

This is not necessarily so, however, as the organization of the German judicial system clearly shows. Instead of two separate and distinct systems, one to exercise the judicial power of the empire and the other that of each individual state, there is a single uniform system for the empire and the states alike, all being organized under imperial law and exercising their functions in accordance with an imperial code of procedure.

Thus the entire judicial system of the country, from the bottom to the top, rests upon the same basis; the competency and procedure of all the courts are determined by imperial law, and they are held by judges whose qualifications and tenure are prescribed by the same authority. There is no division of jurisdiction between the empire and the states; in short, the federal principle has no place in the judicial organization of that country.

Nevertheless, with the exception of the *Reichsgericht*, the courts are all regarded as state tribunals rather than as imperial courts, the judges being appointed by the state governments and their compensation being determined and provided by the same authorities. Moreover, they exercise their jurisdiction in the name of the local governments and are subject to the oversight of the states in which they are situated. As there is one uniform judicial organization for all the German states, so there are common imperial codes of civil and criminal law and of procedure. Thus neither diversity in judicial organization nor of law exists in Germany, though the state is federal in its organization.

In the United States, on the contrary, there are as many systems of judicial organization and of law and procedure as there are states. Each individual commonwealth organizes its own judiciary and frames its own codes of law and procedure, according to its own notions and its own conception of its local needs and conditions. Nevertheless, there is in reality far more of resemblance than of diversity, owing to the common basis which is afforded by the common law, upon which the legal system of each of the states rests.

There are, of course, variations, but in essentials there is remarkable similarity and uniformity. Only in a limited sense are the courts of one state regarded by those of another as foreign. The constitution of the United States requires that the courts of each state shall give full faith and credit to the records and judicial proceedings of the other states; and the spirit of judicial comity — the deference paid by the courts of one state to the decisions of the others — which characterizes interstate judicial relations constitutes a powerful unifying force. This rule of comity, together with the full faith and credit provision, makes possible the enforcement in one state of rights acquired in others and likewise contributes to the prevention by one of acts which would infringe on prohibitions created by others.

Moreover, there are many points of connection between the national and state judiciaries. Thus every judicial officer of a state is required by the constitution of the United States to bind himself by oath to support its provisions and this obligation makes it incumbent upon him in his judicial capacity to respect the laws and treaties of the United States and in case of conflict between them and the laws of the state which he is commissioned to enforce, to uphold and give precedence to the former. Both the national and state courts are in a sense complementary parts of the same governmental system. Rights arising under the national constitution and laws may ordinarily be enforced by the state courts, though the federal government cannot compel them against their will to exercise the jurisdiction and discharge the duties which properly belong to the national courts. There are many cases which can be brought at the option of the plaintiff in either a federal or a state court, but in most instances if brought in the latter the defendant has the right of removing it to a federal court if he chooses.

Furthermore, in any case tried in a state court, if the decision turns on a claim of right arising under the constitution or laws of the United States and if the decision is adverse to the claim, the losing party may appeal therefrom and have the decision of the state court reviewed by the highest federal court in the land. This is necessary, otherwise the constitution and laws of the United States would not be what they are declared to be, namely, the supreme law of the land.

ADMINISTRATIVE COURTS AND ADMINISTRATIVE JURISDICTION

On the continent of Europe, particularly in France and Prussia, a special class of tribunals, separate and distinct from the ordinary courts of justice and constituted on different principles, has been provided, for the determination of administrative controversies, that is, disputes between private individuals and the public authorities as well as disputes among administrative officials themselves.

In general, where such a system prevails, so called administrative controversies are not allowed to be determined by the regular judicial courts. The idea originated in France at the time of the Revolution, and may be said to have resulted from the extreme conception of the doctrine of the separation of powers, then held by the French. Montesquieu's famous theory concerning the necessity of intrusting the legislative, executive, and judicial powers to separate and distinct organs was embodied in extreme form in the "declaration of rights of man and the citizen "of 1791 by the Constituent Assembly, which asserted that if the judiciary were permitted to meddle with administrative officials in the discharge of their duties the constitution would be violated and the operations of the government hindered.

The administrative authorities were therefore made completely independent of judicial control, and the judges were interdicted under pain of forfeiting their offices from interfering in any manner with the acts of the administration. This principle was in turn introduced into other continental states, particularly into Prussia and Italy, and has been retained by them to the present day.

The chief advantage claimed for the system is that the subjection of the public authorities to the continual control and interference of the judicial courts is detrimental to prompt and efficient administration.

Administrative controversies are somewhat peculiar in their nature and involve questions which for proper consideration require a special and technical knowledge not ordinarily possessed by judges whose training and experience have been confined to the field of private law, and whose education has been academic rather than practical.

Such judges are likely to have exaggerated notions of the rights of private individuals, as against those of the public; they are inclined to a natural timidity in deciding issues between individuals and the government adversely to the claims of the individual; and with their disposition to adhere strictly to legal rules and traditions they sometimes unnecessarily hamper and obstruct the legitimate operations of the government.

The history of administration in the United States and England abounds in illustrations of the truth of these observations. Only men who have been trained in the study of administrative law and who have had practical experience in the actual work of public administration, it is said, are capable of deciding wisely controversies involving a technical knowledge of administrative questions. Judges without such special knowledge or experience are apt to apply to the interpretation of controversies between private individuals and the public authorities the pure principles of private law, rather than those of the public law.

This sometimes leads to results that are wholly inconsistent with sound public policy and efficient administration, for the rules of law governing the organization and functions of the administration are quite different from those governing the relations of private individuals, since the purpose of the former is the public welfare rather than private interests.

When the government is a party to a dispute it cannot be treated like a private litigant without seriously injuring at times its efficiency and impeding its operations. The law of contract and tort, for example, which plays so important a part in the regulation of the conduct of private individuals occupies a very unimportant place in the law governing the relations of the public authorities.

The administration of two such widely different bodies of rules requires, therefore, different habits of mind, traditions, and training. It is also to be remarked that the individual under the continental system can often obtain redress where he could not do so in America or England, as, for example, in a case of neglect or abuse of power by an official who would not in America or England be liable in damages.

The chief objection that has been urged against the European method of relieving the public authorities from the control of the regular courts of justice and intrusting the determination of so-called administrative controversies to special tribunals, is that it destroys to a large extent the legal protection of the individual against the acts of the administrative authorities.

The legal remedies which are allowed by these courts for the infringement of individual rights by the authorities are quite different from, and, it is asserted, less effective than, those afforded by the regular judicial courts in other cases. Moreover, their responsibility is to a class of tribunals made up largely of administrative officials who, being a part of the government themselves, are apt to be less favorable to individual rights than are judges of the regular judicial courts.

This may be due partly to their natural zeal for the rights of the administration, or the result of pressure on the part of the government itself. The possibility of this danger is especially great in France, where the administrative judges do not enjoy the same independence as the other judges, but hold their commissions at the pleasure of the administration and hence are subject to its control and dictation.

They are so much a part of the administration, observes an American writer, that they fall into the department of the interior rather than that of justice and may be "controlled absolutely in case of necessity. "In France, therefore, continues the same writer, there is one law for the citizen and another for the public official, and thus the executive is really independent of the judiciary, for the government has always a free hand, and can violate the law if it wants to do so without having anything to fear from the ordinary courts.

Theoretically this rather harsh judgment has some justification, but in practice the French administrative courts have not shown any such extraordinary subservience to the government and but little disposition to trample upon individual rights in the alleged interest of public expediency. Indeed, it is the opinion of a careful student of French public law that the administrative courts have in fact shown themselves more favorable to private rights than have the regular courts of justice.

Whatever may be the facts as to the adequacy of the remedies which are afforded by the administrative courts for the protection of private rights, there can be no doubt that, from the point of view of administrative efficiency, administrative control has decided advantages over judicial control. This is admitted by the severest critics of the system.

Where there are two sets of tribunals and two separate bodies of law, disputes must sometimes arise as to which domain a particular controversy belongs to and which tribunal should have jurisdiction of it. For the determination of such disputes of jurisdiction the French law provides for a tribunal of conflicts, while in Germany there is usually a similar tribunal known as a competence-conflict court. In both countries these courts are composed of a certain number of regular judges and of persons in the administrative service. In the German imperial system, however, all conflicts of jurisdiction between the imperial administrative courts and the judicial courts are settled by the latter, there being no special conflict courts.

In both countries the power of raising the question of a conflict of jurisdiction belongs to the administration only, the theory being that it alone can be interested. When the administration notifies the judicial court that in taking jurisdiction over a particular controversy, it is encroaching upon the sphere of the administration, the court suspends further proceedings, and the question of competence is referred to the tribunal of conflicts for determination. If the decision is in favor of the claim set up by the administration, the case is removed to the administrative courts for final decision, otherwise it is decided by the judicial court.

In England and America, and in countries generally where English legal institutions have been introduced, the doctrine of administrative jurisdiction, as it is known and practiced on the continent of Europe, is little known. There administrative law is not a separate branch of jurisprudence, and specially constituted administrative courts with jurisdiction over controversies between private individuals and public officials do not exist, at least not in the form in which they are found on the continent.

Disputes between the public authorities and private citizens, like differences between private individuals themselves, are decided by the regular judicial courts and according to the ordinary law of the land. The private citizen who is injured by the action of the public authorities has exactly the same remedies that he would have if the injury had been committed by another private individual, and his recourse is in the same courts.

In short, there is one law and one court for the citizen and the public functionary alike. Public officials enjoy no special privileges or immunities and are not exempt from responsibility for their wrongful acts, but must answer equally with private individuals to the regular courts of justice. "In England, "observes Dicey, "the idea of legal equality, or of the universal subjection of all classes to one law administered by the ordinary courts, has been pushed to its utmost limit. With us every official, from the prime minister down to a constable or a collector of taxes, is under the same responsibility as any other citizen for every act done without legal justification.

The reports abound with cases in which officials have been brought before the courts and made in their personal capacity liable to punishment or to the payment of damages for acts done in their official capacity. ""Every act of public authority, no matter by whom or against whom it is directed, is liable to be called in question before an ordinary tribunal, and there is no other means by which its legality can be questioned or established. "

Nevertheless, both in England and America, there are numerous boards, commissions, and authorities which possess what may not improperly be described as administrative jurisdiction. They are, in fact, often referred to as administrative tribunals; they possess the power of adjudication and determination in many cases, and not infrequently their decisions are conclusive, and hence not subject to review by the courts. Although they are not a part of the judicial system, their procedure when hearing and determining controversies is often characterized by the formalism of the courts of justice.

A regular system of appeal is often allowed from one to another, and in some cases their decisions are published and cited as precedents. In England examples of authorities which exercise a limited administrative jurisdiction are the Railway Commission, the Local Government Board, the Board of Trade, the Board of Education, and the Board of Agriculture. In the United States similar bodies are the Interstate Commerce Commission, whose powers have been described as "quasi administrative, quasi judicial "; the Pension Office, the Patent Office, the Land Office, the Bureau of Immigration, the office of Comptroller of the Treasury, the General Board of Customs Appraisers, the United States Customs Court, and the Court of Claims.

In the state governments there are almost countless boards and commissions which possess similar powers. Among these may be mentioned railroad commissions, boards of health, departments of education, pure food commissions, etc. There is, in fact, scarcely any department of the administrative service in which controversies involving both public and private rights do not frequently arise, which can be more wisely determined by the administration itself than by a court of justice.

This fact has been recently recognized by the Congress of the United States in the act creating a customs court vested with power to determine controversies between the government and importers, regarding the value and classification of imported articles upon which a customs tariff is imposed.

Whatever, therefore, may be said against the European system of administrative justice and of administrative law, with its somewhat exaggerated emphasis upon the rights of the government in contradistinction to those of private individuals, the fact remains that it exists in England and America, though in less developed form; and the role which it is destined to play in the future is bound to increase with the multiplication of governmental functions and the increasing complexity of the governmental organization.

Index